# RESEARCH IN
# THE HISTORY OF
# ECONOMIC THOUGHT
# AND METHODOLOGY

*Volume 9* • 1992

# RESEARCH IN THE HISTORY OF ECONOMIC THOUGHT AND METHODOLOGY

*A Research Annual*

*Editor:*  WARREN J. SAMUELS
*Department of Economics*
*Michigan State University*

VOLUME 9 • 1992

 JAI PRESS INC.

*Greenwich, Connecticut*                    *London, England*

*Copyright © 1992 JAI PRESS INC.*
*55 Old Post Road, No. 2*
*Greenwich, Connecticut 06836*

*JAI PRESS LTD.*
*118 Pentonville Road*
*London N1 9JN*
*England*

*ISBN: 1-55938-428-X*

# CONTENTS

## REVIEW ESSAYS

# LIST OF CONTRIBUTORS

*Sohrab Behdad*

Department of Economics
Denison University
Granville, Ohio

*R.D. Collison Black*

Department of Economics
Queen's University
Belfast, Northern Ireland

*Lawrence A. Boland*

Department of Economics
Simon Fraser University
Burnaby, Canada

*John E. Elliott*

Department of Economics
University of Southern California
Los Angeles, California

*Ross B. Emmett*

Department of Economics
Camrose Lutheran College
Camrose, Alberta, Canada

*Mary K. Farmer*

School of Social Sciences
University of Sussex
Brighton, England

*Christopher L. Gilbert*

Department of Economics
Queen Mary and Westfield College
University of London
London, England

*Peter Groenewegen*

Department of Economics
University of Sydney
Sydney, Australia

*James P. Henderson*

Department of Economics
Valparaiso University
Valparaiso, Indiana

*Rajani Kanth*

Department of Economics
University of Utah
Salt Lake City, Utah

*S. Todd Lowry*

Department of Economics
Washington and Lee University
Lexington, Virginia

*Susan Pozo*

Department of Economics
Western Michigan University
Kalamazoo, Michigan

*Edward Puro*

Department of Economics
Michigan State University
East Lansing, Michigan

*Salim Rashid*

Department of Economics
University of Illinois
Champaign, Illinois

*Keith Tribe*

Department of Economics and
  Management Science
University of Keele
Keele, Newcastle, England

# EDITORIAL BOARD

# ACKNOWLEDGMENTS

The editor wishes to express his gratitude for assistance in the review process and other consultation to the members of the editorial board and to the following persons;

*Jeff Biddle*

*Michael Bleaney*

*Peter Boettke*

*Sheila Dow*

*Elizabeth Durbin*

*W.E. Mason*

*Philip Mirowski*

*D.E. Moggridge*

# ASTRONOMY, ASTROLOGY, AND BUSINESS CYCLES:

## HYDE CLARKE'S CONTRIBUTION

James P. Henderson

By accepting both Say's law of markets and the quantity theory of money, the classical school relegated macroeconomics to a lower order of concern. Faulty government policy was viewed as the most likely cause of short-run problems arising at this level. Such short-run problems were of little urgency as they would solve themselves or could be resolved with minimal effort. The recurring business crises were treated as isolated, anomalous events by the classical economists. Therefore, it was left to writers outside the mainstream of economic thought, writers unencumbered by classical school laws and theories, to discover these cyclical phenomena. In Britain, the earliest efforts to measure and analyze business cycles were carried out by members of the statistical societies, both the Royal and the Manchester. One of the most interesting and perceptive of these was

**Research in the History of Economic Thought and Methodology, Volume 9, pages 1-34.**
**Copyright © 1992 by JAI Press Inc.**
**All rights of reproduction in any form reserved.**
**ISBN: 1-55938-428-X**

Hyde Clarke (1815-1895). He was an active member of the Royal Statistical Society and the British Association for the Advancement of Science, as well as a frequent contributor to various railway journals.

Clarke's analysis of business cycles influenced William Stanley Jevons' work in this field. In his "Commercial Crises and Sun-spots," Jevons recommended Clarke's pamphlet as "well worth reading" (Jevons, 1878/79). Schumpeter refers to Clarke's work as "a striking anticipation of the major cycles or spans of later days" (1954, p. 743). Yet Clarke and his writings are not well known to modern economists. His major contribution to economics was his 1847 pamphlet, *Physical Economy, A Preliminary Inquiry into the Physical Laws Governing the Periods of Famines and Panics*, which appeared originally as an article in the *Railway Register* that same year.

After reviewing Clarke's methods, his measurement and dating of business cycles in England is considered. Clarke's "attention was [next] directed to the general elementary laws which govern periodical or cyclar action." Clarke's influence on Jevons, as well as their differences, shall be examined. Finally, his later contributions to business cycle analysis will be reviewed.

## I.  CLARKE'S METHODS

Clarke made a distinction between political economy and what he proposed to call "physical economy." In his view:

> While political economy restricts itself principally to the moral laws which influence society, it seems advisable that the influence of physical laws and operations upon mankind, should, for their better study, be formed also into a distinct science. This would include the laws of life (vital statistics), those which regulate famines and pestilences, and the operations of physical phenomena as affecting mankind and society. Such a science might usefully be called physical economy (1847, p. 1).[1]

Clarke drew important policy considerations from this distinction between political economy and physical economy. Since physical economy is based upon "the operation of physical phenomena affecting mankind and society," it is useless, in Clarke's view, to legislate against such phenomena. Thus he concluded that a policy of laissez-faire must be followed in such cases:

> The chief question to be solved is whether times of speculation, of famine, and of panic are periodical, as the result of organic laws, or whether they are merely isolated and accidental events. The determination of this question is of the greatest importance, as thereon depends the propriety of measures of legislation, and of the business operations of individuals. If the mania for speculations be a periodical consequence of a regular series of events, it must be utterly futile to pass laws for its suppression, and interference inconsistent with such a fact can only have the effect of doing mischief (1847, p. 2).

It seems not to have occurred to Clarke that it might be possible to reduce the adverse impact of these periodic crises through "measures of legislation." While it might well "be utterly futile to pass laws for [the] suppression" of such "times of speculation, of famine, and of panic," it does not necessarily follow that legislative "interference" with the consequences of these crises "can only have the effect of doing mischief." Moreover, as Professor R. D. Collison Black makes clear, because of Clarke's parallel interest in railways, he was anxious to make the case that the periodic economic crises were "regularly generated by some exogenous cause" and that "far from the railways being major contributors to an investment cycle they appear as being passively involved in a process which would have occurred even had they never existed" (1987, pp. 18-19).

In analyzing these periodic crises, Clarke adopted an inductive approach to his subject, rather than the deductive approach preferred by the classical economists. This was in keeping with the traditions of both Section F (Economic Science and Statistics) of the British Association for the Advancement of Science and the Royal Statistical Society, both of which were founded by economists who opposed the deductive methods of the Ricardians and who sought to make economics an inductive science. (For a history of these two organizations, see Goldman, 1985, and Henderson, 1990). Clarke was an active member of the Royal Statistical Society, contributing six papers to its journal and rising to the position of Vice-President of the Society. Between 1864 and 1889, he presented 18 papers to Section F and 47 papers to various other sections of the British Association. In his 1847 pamphlet, Clarke revealed his methods and his data sources:

> In conducting such an investigation as is necessary to enable us to decide on this subject, it seems needless to resort to any theory *a priori*, and much better to begin with the consideration of such facts as we have immediately before

us. With this view the yearly prices of wheat will be sufficient for all general
purposes, leaving all partial causes of error and disturbance for subsequent
determination and correction, if required (1847, p. 2).

The "yearly prices of wheat" which Clarke examined came from
several sources. He rejected two such price data collection—that
gathered by Bishop Fleetwood covering the period 1202 to 1597
which was "exceedingly deficient" and Sir F. M. Eden's data from
1200 to the 1800s, "which I have not seen" (1847, pp. 2-3). Instead,
Clarke employed data from two other sources: "From 1595
downwards we have the prices of wheat at Windsor market, kept for
Eton College, and from 1771 we have the averages returned by the
government Comptroller of Corn Returns" (1847, p. 3).[2] Clarke,
employing the notion of periodicity, combed these wheat-price data
trying to discover regular patterns in the ebb and flow of economic
activity. This search led Clarke to important discoveries which mark
his contribution to the measurement and dating of British business
cycles. The specifics of this inductive search for periodicities in the
British wheat-price data will become clearer as we examine his
measurement and dating of both his 54-year long wave and his 10-
or 11-year cycles.

In a letter to Jevons, written August 31, 1878, Clarke recounted
his own earlier efforts to date the cyclical activity in Britain. Here
Clarke pointed out that "many of us were struck by the ten yearly
occurrence of these panics" (Clarke, 1878a). As a result of his initial
studies, Clarke concluded that economic crises occurred in the years
1796, 1806, 1817, 1827, 1837, and 1847 (1847, p. 1).[3] But further study
led Clarke to revise his dating:

> Still thinking the interval was an interval of about ten years, I was during
> the present famine [1847] led to look for a larger period, which would contain
> the smaller periods, and as the present famine and distress seemed particularly
> severe, my attention was directed to the famine so strongly felt during the
> French revolution. This gave a period of about fifty-four years, with five
> intervals of about ten or eleven years, which I took thus:
> 1793   1804   1815   1826   1837   1847
> This seemed a much better approximation than I had got before, and I
> proceeded to examine it closely (1847, p. 3).

It is this combination of a series of 10 or 11-year cycles within a 54-
year long wave that led Schumpeter to credit Clarke with "a striking

anticipation of the major cycles or spans of later days, especially of Kondratieff's long waves" and, we might add, of Juglar's major cycles as well.

## II. CLARKE'S MEASUREMENT AND DATING OF THE 54-YEAR CYCLES

To test the 54-year long wave hypothesis, Clarke developed a table comparing his dates (calculated backward from 1847) with the historical estimates of crises using the information in Smith's *Wealth of Nations* and the Eton College wheat price data (Table 1.). However, concerned that his calculations did not match exactly the dates in his two sources, Clarke:

> ...considered that the investigation was beset with some difficulty, because from the want of attention of historians to the fluctuations of the harvests, there was a great deficiency of materials and some uncertainty as to the data. A bad harvest might occur in one year, but the effect on prices might be felt only in the next year, as we now find it in 1847, and I therefore felt justified, and indeed called upon, to try every empirical mode of obtaining a solution. Thus I tried periods of 53 years, of 54 years, of 56, 55, 54, and 53 years, of 54, 54, 54, and 53 years, and several other forms, but without obtaining an exact result, though the approximations to the recorded facts were so close as to give every promise to the possibility of obtaining some form or other of exact solution (1847, p. 6).

This concern led Clarke to compare his calculated estimates of the 54-year cycle with the observations drawn from Smith and the Eton College wheat price data to see if some pattern emerged (see Table 2). Clarke concluded that:

> The result of the whole of these inquiries was to satisfy me that the harvests and the phenomena which produced them were regulated by a period of fifty-four years, but that the critical time or culminating point did not serve as a point of determination of the beginning or end of the period (1847, p. 7.)

It is revealing to compare Clarke's dating of the "fifty-four year cyclar series" with that of the more renowned Kondratieff. In his 1935 article, "The Long Waves of Economic Life," Kondratieff specified the following dates to mark the "beginning of the rise" of the "First Cycle" and the "Second Cycle" in England: for prices, 1789 to 1849

Table 1.   "Approximate Elements of
the Cyclar Series"
(Clarke, 1847, p. 6)

| Calculated | Observed |
|---|---|
| 1199 | 1202 |
| 1253 | 1257 |
| 1307 | 1309 |
| 1361 | 1363 |
| 1415 | 1416 |
| 1469 | —— |
| 1523 | 1521 |
| 1577 | —— |
| 1631 | 1631 |
| 1685 | 1685 |
| 1739 | 1740 |
| 1793 | 1795 |
| 1847 | —— |

Table 2.   "...the observed periods form a curve oscillating
around the calculated or empirical periods"
(Clarke, 1847, p. 8).

| Difference | Calculated | Difference | Observed | Difference |
|---|---|---|---|---|
|  | 1199 |  | 1202 | 3 |
|  | 1253 |  | 1257 | 4 |
|  | 1307 |  | 1309 | 2 |
|  | 1361 |  | 1363 | 2 |
|  | 1415 |  | 1416 | 1 |
|  | 1469 |  | —— |  |
| 2 | 1523 |  | 1521 |  |
|  | 1577 |  | —— |  |
|  | 1631 | 0 | 1631 |  |
|  | 1685 | 0 | 1685 |  |
|  | 1739 |  | 1740 | 1 |
|  | 1793 |  | 1795 | 2 |
|  | 1847 |  | —— |  |

*This may be thus represented:* ——

|  |  | 2, |  | 1, 2, |
|---|---|---|---|---|
|  | 3, 4, 2, 2, 1, |  |  | 0, 0, |

60 years); for the interest rate, 1790 to 1844 (54 years); and for the wages of agricultural workers, 1790 to 1844 (also 54 years) (Kondratieff, 1951, Table 1, p. 31). These three series—prices, interest rate, and wages of agricultural workers—were the only ones cited by Kondratieff for the "First Cycle" in England. Notice that the dating of Kondratieff's three measures closely match Clarke's dates,

and that the length of the last two measures is equal to Clarke's 54-year period. Professor Black's extensive treatment of the similarities and differences in their analysis of these long waves releaves us of the need for further discussion of the relationship between Clarke and Kondratieff's work (see Black, 1987, Section V).

Still not completely satisfied, Clarke pressed on with his investigations into this 54-year period:

> In order to ascertain whether the period of fifty-four years might not be a binary, ternary, or other compound of some simpler period, I instituted the requisite comparisons of the several portions of the cycle, but without obtaining any such results. On the contrary, the cycle was found to consist of two halves distinct in character, as compared with each other, but congruous with the corresponding halves of the other periods. . .
>
> Near the beginning is what I have termed the culminating cyclar, or characteristic period of dearth. This is followed by a point of severe dearth at about nine years after, and so on by successive points of dearth... (1847, p. 7).

Employing the price data available to him, Clarke summarized his empirical investigations into the history of famines in Britain in a large, complex table dating these events and grouping them into similar series (Table 3). The table is a compilation based on his grouping of the wheat price data into "well-defined series" labeled A through L, there being two A series which differ slightly. As an introduction to this empirical study, Clarke identified "many other well-defined series, particularly C, E, H, I, and L... [which] will be found to present much the same characters as B" (1847, p. 9). It is the "observed periods" rather than the "calculated periods" found in his two earlier tables that make up Clarke's B series in this table. This B series of wheat price observations serves as the foundation for this summary of various "empirical periods" or "series" (compare the "observed" figures in Tables 1 and 2 with the B series in Table 3).

Within the crucial B series, Clarke was most confident in the data after 1631. In characterizing these later periods, Clarke described the "empirical periods" in the B series in these words:

> All of these periods were preceded by a year of very great abundance. Of these periods one thing only appears determinate, that they have a very severe famine attendant on them; but whether the period of distress shall be ten years or two years, there is nothing to indicate (1847, p. 9).[4]

*Table 3.*   "Other Well-defined Series…which Coincide in Sets"
(Clarke, 1847, p. 9).

| A | B | C | D | E | F | G | H | I | J | K | L | A |
|---|---|---|---|---|---|---|---|---|---|---|---|---|
| … | … | … | … | 1004 | … | … | … | … | … | … | … | … |
| … | … | … | … | … | … | … | 1069 | … | … | … | … | … |
| … | … | 1098 | … | … | … | … | 1125 | … | … | … | 1139 | … |
| … | … | … | … | … | … | … | … | … | … | … | … | … |
| … | 1202 | 1205 | … | … | 1223 | … | … | 1237 | … | … | 1247 | … |
| … | … | 1258 | … | 1270 | … | … | 1286 | 1290 | 1294 | … | 1302 | … |
| … | 1309 | 1315 | … | … | … | … | 1339 | … | … | … | … | … |
| … | 1363 | 1369 | … | 1379 | … | … | 1390 | … | … | 1401 | … | … |
| … | 1416 | 1423 | … | 1434 | 1439 | … | 1447 | 1451 | … | 1457 | 1460 | … |
| … | … | … | … | 1486 | … | 1497 | … | … | … | … | … | … |
| … | 1521 | 1527 | … | … | … | … | … | … | … | … | … | … |
| 1574 | … | 1587 | … | 1597 | 1603 | 1605 | 1608 | 1613 | 1617 | * | 1623 | * |
| * | 1631 | 1638 | … | 1648 | … | 1659 | 1662 | 1669 | 1671 | 1674 | 1679 | 1681 |
| 1681 | 1685 | 1693 | 1698 | 1704 | 1709 | 1713 | 1716 | … | 1725 | 1728 | … | 1735 |
| 1735 | 1740 | 1746 | 1753 | 1757 | 1765 | 1767 | 1772 | 1774 | * | 1783 | 1785 | 1789 |
| 1789 | 1795 | 1800 | 1805 | 1810 | 1817 | 1821 | 1825 | 1829 | … | … | 1839 | * |

Another distinguishing characteristic of this series was the political discontent associated with these years. Clarke noted that 1631 launched a long series of bad harvests. This "state of affairs embittered men's minds, and in England paved the way for the great civil war" (1847, p. 10). During the next period, "unfavourable" prices had prevailed from 1668, "and great discontent had prevailed, which in 1685, on the accession of James II, reached its height," culminating in the revolution of 1688 (1847). The period beginning in 1739, "was indeed a severe one throughout Europe, but its political consequences were trifling" (1847). Finally, "the great French revolution was the crowning event" of the 1793 cycle (1847). Though the "political consequences [of 1739] were trifling," Clarke attempted to show that a series of significant political events in European history resulted from economic causes. He tied these events together with his B series, 54-year cycle. That series, then, is significant for its long, severe famines nearly all of which had serious political consequences.

Turning next to the C series of 54-year cycles, Clarke found "this series is very well defined in its early members, and in its lower members, but is deficient in the three periods of the fifteenth and the sixteenth centuries, as to which we have the least data" (1847, p. 11). After reviewing the evidence available, Clarke concluded that the C series:

is one which, for severity, may very well compete with the characteristric period B; but its political consequences were not so important, as at the former period agitation and dissatisfaction had already reached its height.... It follows B in a mean period of six years. In the best recorded periods it has been preceded by years of abundance, and consists of two or three years of greater scarcity (1847).

Turning to the D series which follows the C series by six years on average, Clarke found that its "character is not well defined" (1847). Furthermore, "it is not remarkable for political events, but has not been favourable to active enterprise" (1847).

Next the E series of 54-year cycles "presents a character of some importance, and is tolerably well defined throughout. It is however variable in its extent" (1847, p. 13). This series dated back the furthest, to 1004, and contained years with the highest wheat prices in English history, the record price occurring in 1270. "Two prices are recorded that year £4/16s. per quarter and £6/8s. per quarter. These would be equivalent to £14/8s. and £19/4s., say £20 per quarter of modern money" (1847).

Following the E series by about five years was the F series and four years later the G series. "As the two series F and G are so closely connected, they may be described together" (1847, p. 14). These two series of 54-year cycles, in Clarke's words, formed "a remarkable group. The two seem to run nearly parallel at about four years interval, and to give a character of dearth to the harvests during the period of about five or six years, more or less, in connection with each other" (1847). In summary, Clarke noted:

The series connected with the points F and G is of a milder character than its predecessors, and has been accompanied with good harvests, which have favoured political quiet, and contributed to the national advancement, though during the period of dearth there has been considerable social and political disturbance (1847, p. 15).

The pamphlet breaks off here and Clarke gives no indication of the characteristics of the H, I, J, K, L, or A series. Most curious was his failure to review the H, I, and L series, which he earlier described as being among the "many other well-defined series...[which] will be found to present much the same characters as B" (1847, p. 9).

Though incomplete, Clarke's table and the accompanying descriptions of these various series gives us a clear idea of his methods. The table summarized his conclusions drawn from his careful review

of the historical evidence available to him. Notice that each of the
series approximates his 54-year long wave, yet "were far from
answering determinately to a rigorous period of fifty-four years
throughout..." (1847, p. 6). In commenting on his decennial cycle,
Schumpeter concluded that Clarke's dates "suggest a little
manhandling" of the data. On the contrary, Professor R. D. Collison
Black concludes that "to his credit it must be recorded that he did
not try to force the data to fit" (Black, 1987, p. 16). Clearly, Professor
Black's conclusion more correctly describes Clarke's empirical study.

## III.   CLARKE'S MEASUREMENT AND DATING OF THE DECENNIAL CYCLES

Clarke believed that his 54-year period consisted of "five intervals
of about ten or eleven years." This was not a unique finding, as Clarke
admitted that "many of us were struck by the ten yearly occurrence
of these panics." While any number of classical economists mentioned
economic crises, none of them recognized that these were regularly
recurring phenomena and thus the classicals made no effort either
to date or to measure this cyclical activity. Yet these cycles and their
dates were of interest to a number of other British writers.

Prior to Jevons's publications, four British writers identified dates
for that nation's early business cycles. The first of these was John
Wade in his 1833 *History of the Middle and Working Classes*. Wade
identified three "mercantile revulsions" in the eighteenth century in
1763, 1772, and 1793, and "within the last twenty-two years we have
had no fewer than four mercantile revulsions; namely, those of 1811,
1816, 1818, and 1825-6" (Wade, p. 255). These periods of "commercial
depression and prosperity" showed up in the evidence of both prices
and employment. Clarke's 1847 pamphlet was only the second
published effort to place specific dates on these "times of speculation,
of famine, and of panic" (p. 2). The next writer to mention a decennial
cycle was William Langton, who presented his "Observations on a
Table shewing the Balance of Account between the Mercantile Public
and the Bank of England," to the 1857-58 session of the Manchester
Statistical Society. However, since his table and diagram was limited
to the period from 1844 to 1857, the ten year cycle is only mentioned
in passing, while Langton focused on much shorter periods of activity
(1858, pp. 9-22). Ten years later, John Mills, drawing on Langton's
observations, identified specific dates for six commercial panics in

his paper, "On Credit Cycles, and the Origin of Commercial Crises," which also appeared in the Transactions of the Manchester Statistical Society (1868, pp. 11-40; see also Table 4).

Clarke's dates are compared with those of Wade, Mills, and Jevons, as well as Clement Juglar's dates and the more sophisticated modern measures developed by Willard Thorp and Gayer, Rostow and Schwartz (Table 4). Three of these authors, Wade, Mills and Juglar, analyzed periods which do not coincide with Clarke's particular 54-year time frame.

Among these analysts, there is unanimous agreement with Clarke's 1793 and 1837 dates. The three studies by Juglar; Wade; and Gayer, Rostow and Schwartz side with Clarke's 1826 date, the others picking 1825 instead. Yet this last date appeared as part of the H series in his empirical table (Table 3) and in his descriptive statement, Clarke noted that: "By the failure of the harvest a panic came on in the end of 1825, which was characterized by the failure of a large number of private bankers" (1847, p. 2). It is fair to conclude that none of the other writers actually dispute Clarke's finding in this case. Clarke selected 1804 to mark his second crisis; Jevons chose 1805, while Juglar and Thorp as well as Gayer, Rostow and Schwartz picked 1803, disagreeing with Clarke's finding. Yet Clarke, like Jevons, cited 1805 as part of the D series in his empirical table marking the various series of the 54-year long wave (Table 3). Only Gayer, Rostow, and Schwartz, and Wade, dispute Clarke's 1815 date, believing that this crisis occurred a year later. Finally, only Gayer, Rostow, and Schwartz place the last cycle in 1848 rather than Clarke's 1847 date, their date falling a year after he published his study.

Several of these other writers have identified cycle dates not specifically cited by Clarke on this particular list of the "five intervals of about ten or eleven years." Thus Thorp cites 1807, while Gayer, Rostow and Schwartz choose 1808 to mark a cycle. Gayer, Rostow and Schwartz alone find a crisis in 1842. However, other crises cited by several of these writers can be found in Clarke's empirical table listing the various series of 54-year long waves (Table 3). Thus Juglar and Thorp find 1810 to mark the beginning of a crisis, though Gayer, Rostow and Schwartz mark that year as a peak, the trough occurring the following year, in their view. Clarke included 1810 in his empirical table, as part of his E series. Next, Wade and Juglar find a crisis in 1818, Gayer, Rostow and Schwartz the following year. Clark cited 1817 as belonging to the F series in his empirical table. While Clarke

*Table 4.*   Comparison of Cycle Dates

|        | Clarke | Wade   | Mills  | Juglar | Jevons | Thorp | Gayer, Rostow, and Schwartz |
|--------|--------|--------|--------|--------|--------|-------|-----------------------------|
| **1793** | D    | M.R.   | \|     | \|     | M      | B     | T                           |
| 1797   | ...    | ...    | \|     | \|     | ...    | ...   | T                           |
| 1803   | ...    | ...    | \|     | C      | ...    | B     | T                           |
|        |        |        |        |        |        |       |                             |
| **1804** | D    | ...    | \|     | ...    | ...    | ...   | ...                         |
| 1805   | ...    | ...    | \|     | ...    | M      | ...   | ...                         |
| 1807   | ...    | ...    | \|     | ...    | ...    | B     | ...                         |
| 1808   | ...    | ...    | \|     | ...    | ...    | ...   | T                           |
| 1810   | ...    | ...    | \|     | C      | ∴      | B     | P                           |
| 1811   | ...    | M.R.   | \|     | ...    | ...    | ...   | T                           |
|        |        |        |        |        |        |       |                             |
| **1815** | D    | ...    | C.P.   | C      | M      | B     | ...                         |
| 1816   | ...    | M.R.   | C.P.   | ...    | ...    | ...   | T                           |
| 1818   | ...    | M.R.   | ...    | C      | ...    | ...   | ...                         |
| 1819   | ...    | ...    | ...    | ...    | ...    | ...   | T                           |
| 1825   | ...    | M.R.   | C.P.   | ...    | M      | B     | P                           |
|        |        |        |        |        |        |       |                             |
| **1826** | D    | M.R.   | ...    | C      | ...    | ...   | T                           |
| 1830   | ...    | ...    | ...    | C      | ...    | ...   | ...                         |
| 1831   | ...    | \|     | ...    | ...    | ...    | B     | P                           |
| 1832   | ...    | \|     | ...    | ...    | ...    | ...   | T                           |
| 1836   | ...    | \|     | C.P.   | ...    | ...    | ...   | P                           |
|        |        |        |        |        |        |       |                             |
| **1837** | D    | \|     | C.P.   | C      | M      | B     | T                           |
| 1838   | ...    | \|     | C.P.   | ...    | ...    | ...   | ...                         |
| 1839   | ...    | \|     | C.P.   | C      | ...    | ...   | P                           |
| 1842   | ...    | \|     | ...    | ...    | ...    | ...   | T                           |
|        |        |        |        |        |        |       |                             |
| **1847** | D    | \|     | C.P.   | C      | M      | B     | ...                         |
| 1848   | ...    | \|     | ...    | ...    | ...    | ...   | T                           |

*Sources:*  Hyde Clarke (1848, "Distress," p. 3). John Wade (1833, "Mercentile Revulsions," p. 255). John Mills (1867, "Synopsis of Commercial Panics," p. 9). Juglar (1889, Crises in England, p. 256). Jevons (1878, Aug. 19, "trade reached a Maximum," p. 214). Thorp (1926, Beginning of Business Cycles, p. 50). Gayer, Rostow, and Schwartz (1975, Annual dates, Peak/Trough, p. 348).

included 1829 in his I series, three other studies find a cycle occuring in the early 1830s; Juglar citing 1830, Thorp 1831 (which Gayer, Rostow and Schwartz see instead as a peak), while these last three authors cite 1832 as a crisis year.

Clarke's dating was not a simple listing of years, for he also included short descriptions of the economic activity which occurred during much of this 54-year period (1847). The years 1814 and 1815 were characterized as a period when the harvest was good and speculation rife. The period between 1816 and 1820 was described by Clarke as a time of high food prices, great distress, and Luddite political agitation. From 1822 through 1825, there was a period of speculation associated with "the foreign loan and foreign mine speculation." Furthermore, 1822 had the lowest wheat price since 1792, while a "panic came on in the end of 1825." Next came "a long period of depression" between the years 1828 and 1831, during which time "the pressure was particularly severe." Both 1835 and 1836 were characterized as a period of "very active business," still there were some problems as 1835 had a low wheat price, while 1836 had a railway mania followed by a panic which carried through 1837. Then came a period of bad harvests and depression from 1838 through 1841. Between 1842 and 1844, there were good harvests which brought low averages for the annual wheat prices. Finally, this last "burst of business and speculation [was] nipped off by the panic in October, 1845, arising from the failure of the harvest." The years 1846 and 1847 were characterized by Clarke as a period of bad harvests and high wheat price averages.

When we recognize that his pamphlet broke new ground, there is remarkably little disagreement with the dates Clarke assigned to his decennial cycles. This speaks well of the care he exercised in his examination and use of the available historical data. As was the case with his treatment of the empirical evidence for his 54-year long wave, Clarke clearly "did not try to force the data to fit" his decennial cycle hypothesis either. Having posited the existence of "a period of about fifty-four years, with five intervals of about ten or eleven years," Clarke asked what laws governed these business cycles?

## IV. "LAWS WHICH GOVERN PERIODICAL OR CYCLAR ACTION"

In his introductory remarks in *Physical Economy* (1847), Clarke commented that the "present state of famine and distress" was not unique since "the same things have befallen us often within the knowledge of those now living". Yet these periodic crises had, up to 1847, been neglected by political economists:

> On a corn bill or a navigation act Adam Smith can be quoted either way, but the matter of panics and famines hardly makes a part of political science. Hitherto the unpromising nature of the subject, and the little success attendant on the investigations made, have frightened inquirers from following the matter further (1847, p. 1).

This combination of recurring crises and the absence of any successful investigations into their nature and causes led Clarke to pursue the topic.

Clarke claimed that he was drawn originally to this study by the events of the speculative period which began in 1832 and 1833 and which seemed to him to mirror a similar episode in 1823, 1824, and 1825. While examining these events, his "attention was directed to the general elementary laws which govern periodical or cyclal [sic] action..." (p. 3). He then claimed to have laid out his findings in an 1838 article in Herapath's *The Railway Magazine and Annals of Science*. There is only one article directly credited to Clarke in this magazine during 1838 that meets this discription: "On the Political Economy and Capital of Joint-stock Banks." However, in that article, there was only the most general commentary on periodic or cyclical events. In discussing the large number of public companies, both joint-stock banks and railroads, that sprang up in 1835-36, Clarke asked:

> Why did not Homer and Milton compose a fixed number of lines every day? Why do so many of our geniuses pass whole years in inactivity? Because it is the energy of great excitement which produces great works... Why are there golden ages in literature and the arts? Why are there revolutions in politics? Why sudden periods in the progress of science? And why did steam appear some thousand years after other inventions? The heaven-born genius who can govern these events, can regulate the operations of public enterprise, as Murphy does those of the weather; but in my opinion the essay would prove equally futile as to attempt to manufacture a Raphael, or compose so many "Iliads" per annum (Clarke, 1838, p. 291).

This is hardly an explanation of the "general elementary laws which govern periodical or cyclar action." Professor Black has found another article, "On the Mathematical Law of the Cycle," which appeared in Herapath's *Railway Magazine* in 1838 which may have been written by Clark and which seems to fit Clarke's description in his letter to Jevons. Yet, as Black says, "it is noteworthy that in his letter to Jevons of 31 August 1878 Hyde Clarke did not claim authorship" of this particular article (Black, 1988, see in paricular his review of the article in question on pp. 12-13). In this letter to Jevons, Clarke revealed what motivated his search for periodicity in business activity:

My results were obtained altogether by computations, as although many of us were struck by the ten yearly occurrence of these panics no known astronomical period would fit. I had a good chance of getting at such notions had they been known, being intimate with the late James T. Hackett, a very fair mathematician and astronomical computer, who had been Secretary of the London Astrological Society, and whose inner craze was astrology and consequently periodicity (Clarke, 1878a).

So Clarke's conception that there exists a set of "general elementary laws which govern periodical or cyclar action" derived, at least in part, from the periodicity found in astrology. As strange as that sounds, Jevons, in his 1875 paper, "The Solar Period and the Price of Corn," remarked:

...we get back to something which might be mistaken for the astrology of the middle ages. Professor Balfour Stewart has shown much reason for believing that the sun-spot period is connected with the configuration of the planets.

Now, if the planets govern the sun, and the sun governs the vintages and harvests, and thus the prices of foods and raw materials and the state of the money market, it follows that the configurations of the planets may prove to be the remote causes of the greatest commercial disasters....

It would be...curious if the pseudo-science of astrology should...foreshadow the triumphs which precise and methodological investigations may yet disclose, as to the obscure periodic causes affecting our welfare when we are least aware of it (Jevons, 1884, p. 205).[5]

Jevons's paper was delivered three years before Clarke's 1878 letter which suggested a connection between astrology and business cycles. Clarke admitted that he derived the idea of cyclical business activity from the periodicity of astrology; Jevons, on the other hand, traced the cyclical movement of corn prices to sunspot activity and contending that there was "much reason for believing" that sunspots are connected with the configuration of the planets. But Jevons did not want his hypothesis to "be mistaken for the astrology of the middle ages" which he labelled as "pseudo-science." Further distancing himself from that "pseudo-science," Jevons remarked, in a footnote added after 1875: "I have since re-read some of Professor Stewart's 'Memoirs' on the subject, and am inclined to think that the relation of the planets and solar variations is of a more remote nature than he believes" (Jevons, 1884). Clarke, himself, did not suggest any connection between sunspots and business cycles, for the cyclical nature of the sunspots was unknown in England when his pamphlet appeared in 1847.

Clarke developed two hypotheses to explain his 54-year period. These can be classified as an astronomical hypothesis, based on the Saros eclipse cycle, and a meteorological hypothesis. Clarke's astronomical hypothesis read:

> A period of fifty-four years seemed to agree with the triple of the period of eclipses sometimes called the Saros, and which is mentioned by Ptolemy, Pliny, and others, and of which some account is to be found in the "Companion to the Almanac for 1847"in an article written by Professor De Morgan. The true Saros used by the Caldeans, according to the Professor, is not ascertained to be a period of eighteen years. The period of the eclipses is one of eighteen years and ten or eleven days, which would give a triple period of fifty-four years and thirty-one days (1847, p. 6).[6]

Clarke showed little enthusiasm for this explanation, for he never bothered to divide the 54-cycle into the three 18-year sub-periods suggested by the Saros period of eclipses, at least, no such dates appeared in his pamphlet.

Clarke's other hypothesis was the result of an extensive search for an explanation of the significance of this particular 54-year period. He consulted James Thomas Hackett, whose interest in astrology led him to devote considerable attention to questions of periodicity, because he had a large collection of data on the subject. "Mr. Hackett told me that such a [54-year] period had been suggested by a Mr. [George] Mackenzie, in reference to the weather" (Clarke, 1847, pp. 4-5). Mackenzie had developed a diagram comparing wheat prices and the weather.[7] Clarke quotes Hackett's description of Mackenzie's theory:

> He says that the great law in the weather is founded upon a principle of compensation, and that series or lots of wind which have unfavourable weather at one time, have the contrary at another; thus they continually change their properties. Hence he assumes the supposed inexplicable nature of weather had its origin (1847, p. 4).[8]

This clearly foreshadowed Jevons's later work, positing that the business cycle was essentially based on a meteorological cycle. While Jevons traced the cause of the meteorological cycle to sunspot activity, the most important cause of these weather cycles in Clarke's and Mackenzie's theory was the "continued variation of the magnetic axes" (Clarke, 1847, p. 4). These two explanations are not unrelated.

After a thorough review of his evidence and after testing a variety of alternative periods against the available wheat price data, Clarke concluded that:

> The characteristics already described of this [fifty-four year] period have a resemblance to those observed in the variation of the magnetic needle... Mr. Mackenzie has alluded to the shifting or oscillation of the magnetic poles in connection with the periods of the weather, and my own impressions and observations go far to persuade me that the great causes of the phenomena manifested in the seasons and the harvests at present are referable to fluctuations in the electro-magnetic condition of this globe (1847, p. 9).

To understand the significance of Clarke's hypothesis and its subsequent influence on Jevons, one needs to briefly consider the history of astronomy during the nineteenth century. In 1843, some four years before Clarke's pamphlet appeared, Heinrich Schwabe published the results of his solar studies. Searching for an inter-Mercurian planet, Schwabe had begun his solar observations in 1826 and concluded that sunspot activity was cyclical. "His first announcement of a probable decennial period... met with no general attention" (Clerke, 1887, p. 158). However, in 1851, when Humboldt published a table of sunspot activity collected by Schwabe, the importance of the discovery was clear. Schwabe, an amateur astronomer, pursued his studies as an escape from the drudgery of an apothecary's shop, and his ten year sunspot cycle was widely celebrated. In a paper presented to the Royal Society on March 18 and read on May 6, 1852, Sir Edward Sabine announced that Schwabe's sunspot cycles agreed perfectly with the cyclical activity of the earth's magnetic disturbances (Clerke, 1887, p. 161). Further observation led astronomers to conclude that the sunspot cycle was 11.11 years in length. The discovery of a regular sunspot cycle and its connection with the earth's magnetic disturbances led to renewed interest in William Herschel's efforts to tie sunspot activity to the weather on earth. Thus Clarke's 1847 hypothesis, that "the shifting or oscillation of the magnetic poles" was connected "with the periods of the weather," foreshadowed similar hypotheses pursued by astronomers when they realized, in 1851, that sunspot activity was cyclical. These astronomers' hypotheses, and Clarke's pamphlet, later led Jevons to put forth his sunspot theory of the business cycle.

Given the variations in the 54-year period (which Clarke had laid out with some care in Table 3), how could such oscillations of the magnetic poles explain the cyclical behavior of wheat prices? Clarke's explanation was:

> The cycle can scarcely be an exact period of fifty-four years, and the crisis coming at various periods of the natural year will, according to the time of incidence, variably affect the crops. If it be supposed that the crisis should fall in seed time, its effects would be very different from those consequent on its incidence during harvest. In adjoining countries, differing in the earliness and lateness of their crops, and in the crops cultivated, the effects would be of unequal extent. It is also presumable that a retardation of effect might take place under some circumstances, and an immediate and destructive effect at others. As part of a larger cycle the period would at certain points of its course vary in intensity, and perhaps at some points have no injurious effects at all (1847, p. 9).

Having considered and rejected a theory of cyclical business activity based on astronomical phenomena, the Saros eclipse cycle, Clarke settled on a meteorological explanation. This weather cycle was itself driven by "fluctuations in the electro-magnetic condition of this globe." However, because of variations in its intensity and the timing of its affect on the crops, Clarke concluded that it was nearly impossible to predict, with any precision, what impact that this weather cycle would produce on economic activity. The marked differences between Clarke's "laws which govern periodical or cyclar action" and Kondratieff's explanation of the long wave are examined in Black's piece (Black, 1987, Section V).

## V.   CLARKE'S INFLUENCE ON JEVONS

William Stanley Jevons's first contact with Hyde Clarke's writings came in November and December, 1856, when "Jevons began to study economics seriously" (Konekamp in Black, 1977, Vol. I, p. 27). After reading Adam Smith's *Wealth of Nations* during the first three months of that year, Jevons turned next to "Burton's *Political Economy* and [Hyde Clarke's] volume on *Railway Statistics* in Weale's Series" (Black, 1977).[9] Despite their shared interests in railway matters, it was Clarke's analysis of business cycles that most strongly influenced Jevons's work. In his "Commercial Crises and Sun-spots," Jevons recommended Clarke's pamphlet as "well worth reading," because Clarke argued:

> in a highly scientific spirit that events so regularly recurring cannot be attributed to accidental causes; there must be, he thinks, some physical groundwork, and he proposed to search this out by means of a science to be called Physical Economy (Jevons, 1884, p. 222).

Jevons distinguished Clarke's contributions to business cycle analysis from those of other writers in these words:

> The peculiar interest of Dr. Hyde Clarke's speculations consists in the fact that he not only remarked the cycle of ten or eleven years, but sought to explain it as due to physical causes, although he had not succeeded in discovering any similar astronomical or meteorological variation with which to connect it. Writing as he did in 1838 and 1847, this failure is not to wondered at. His supposed period of fifty-four years is perhaps deserving of further investigation, but it is with his period of ten or eleven years that we are now concerned (Jevons, 1884, p. 224).[10]

This comment is somewhat frustrating because Jevons asserted that Clarke "had not succeeded in discovering any similar astronomical or meteorological variation with which to connect" the economic cycle. This failed to acknowledge either Clarke's astronomical hypothesis, the Saros period of eclipses, or his meteorological hypothesis, his adoption of Mackenzie's theory that variations of the earth's magnetic axes cause weather cycles.

Though he did not give Clarke specific credit, Jevons employed Clarke's measures to analyze the data on wheat prices found in J. E. Thorold Rogers's book. Jevons claimed that "in 1875 I made a laborious reduction of the data contained in Professor Thorold Rogers' admirable 'History of Agriculture and Prices in England from the Year 1259'" (Jevons, 1884, p. 225). In his 1875 and 1878 articles on the sunspot hypothesis, Jevons drew the following conclusion which indicates his reliance on Clarke's earlier work:

> Thus the principle commercial crises have happened in the years 1825, 1836-39, 1847, 1857, 1866, and I was almost adding 1879, so convinced do I feel that there will, within the next few years, be another great crisis. Now if there should be in or about the year 1879 a great collapse comparable with those of the years mentioned, there will have been five such occurrences in fifty-

four years, giving almost exactly eleven years (10.8) as the average interval, which sufficiently approximates to 11.11, the supposed exact length of the sun-spot period, to warrant speculation as to their possible connection (Jevons, 1884, p. 203, 225).

Here Jevons chose a 54-year period, predicting the next crisis in 1879, and then divided this long wave into five shorter periods averaging 10.8 years. Since "the supposed exact length of the sun-spot period" is 11.11 years, selecting either a 55- or 56-year long wave and predicting the next "great crisis" to occur in 1880 or 1881 would have given Jevons an even better fit than the 10.8 average he selected. In his 1878 version, Jevons claimed that

> I was led to assign the then coming (that is, the now present) crisis to the year 1879, because 11.1 years added twice over to 1857, the date of the last perfectly normal crisis, or to 1847, the date of the previous one, brings the calculator to 1879. If I could have employed instead Mr. J. A. Broun's since published estimate of the sun-spot period, to be presently mentioned, namely 10.45 years, I should have come exactly to the present year 1878 (Jevons, 1884, p. 225).

A quick calculation reveals that 11.1 years added to 1866, the previous crisis cited by Jevons, predicts the next crisis in 1877; "added twice over to 1857, the date of the last perfectly normal crisis," gives the 1879 date found in both articles; but added thrice over to 1847, the date of the crisis previous to the 1857 "perfectly normal crisis," yields the next predicted crisis in 1880. Jevons's 1878 commentary explaining these dates elicited these remarks from Wesley C. Mitchell:

> Jevons had an admirably candid mind; yet in 1875, when the sun-spot cycle was supposed to last 11.1 years, he was able to get from Thorold Rogers' *History of Agriculture and Prices in England* a period of 11 years in price fluctuations, and when the sun-spot cycle was revised to 10.45 years he was able to make the average interval between English crises 10.466 years (Mitchell, 1927, p. 384).

However, this ignores Jevons's remark that the prediction rested on the proposition, taken from Clarke, that "if there should be in or about the year 1879 a great collapse...*there will have been five such occurences in fifty-four years*..." (emphasis added). His strong commitment to "five such occurrences in fifty-four years" too closely matched Clarke's dating to be a coincidence. More significantly, given a choice between Clarke's "period of about fifty-four years with five intervals of about ten or eleven years" and the scientific finding that the sunspot cycle averaged 11.11 years, Jevons chose Clarke's hypothesis over the astronomers' conclusion.

Thus Jevons relied on Clarke's dating in both his 1875 paper and the paper which was published in the November 14, 1878 issue of *Nature*. In response to the latter, Clarke indicated at least partial support of Jevons's position in a letter published in the next (November 21) issue of *Nature*. Here Clarke suggested that meteorological phenomena, recurring droughts, can have a "bearing...on our trade and the prospects of its revival" in two different ways:

> They act to prevent the growth of produce, and in many countries, by reducing the water-ways, they impede its shipment. The people cannot consume our imports, the transit of which is in some cases impeded. The whole of these difficulties affects the exchanges and interfers with the money market and remittances... Thus the study of meteorological phenomena and facts acquires a new value for practical men and society at large, as stated by Prof. Jevons in your last number (Clarke, 1878c, p. 53).[11]

Very shortly thereafter, Clarke backed down from his support of Jevons's sunspot theory. At a meeting of the Society of Arts which he chaired, Clarke "drew attention to the fact that it was by a paper of his thirty years ago that public attention was first directed in what he might term a scientific form to this periodicity" in business activity (Clarke, 1879, p. 300).[12] Clarke now took the position that:

> he was no advocate for what was called the sun-spot theory...as far as he could discover from the facts before him, there were, besides the periods of ten years, other periods of about twenty-six years, and likewise a period of about 104 years, and the opinion he formed was that these longer periods interfered with the shorter ones, and prevented any absolute calculation as to the future. At the same time the observation of these phenomena was not by any means an idle matter; there was this practical lesson to be drawn from it, that in periods of prosperity we must look forward to a period of adversity and prepare for it. Therefore the observation of Governments, and of the commercial community and financial institutions should be directed to these phenomena of nature, which after all, did govern the individual operations of man (Clarke, 1879, p. 300).

While Clarke rejected Jevons's sunspot hypothesis, he retained the conviction that business cycles were "phenomena of nature, which after all, did govern the individual operations of man." Thus he continued to believe that while neither government, nor the commercial community, nor the financial institutions could act to prevent the cycles, still "there was this practical lesson to be drawn, [namely that] in periods of prosperity we must look forward to a period of adversity and prepare for it." Clarke had all but given up any hope of ever predicting these cycles with any accuracy because the very multiplicity of cycles, which he had been the first to posit, caused interactions so complex that it "prevented any absolute calculation as to the future."[13]

It is somewhat curious that Clarke rejected Jevons's sunspot theory since one of his own explanations of the physical cause of business cycles in his 1847 pamphlet was that "the shifting or oscillation of the magnetic poles" was the cause of "the periods of the weather." By 1852, astronomers had shown that such "shifting or oscillation of the magnetic poles" was directly related to the cycles of sunspot activity. Thus Clarke could claim that his work clearly anticipated Jevons's cycle theory. There is little question of Clarke's influence on Jevons's work, as we have seen that Jevons was so wedded to Clarke's "period of about fifty-four years, with five intervals of about ten or eleven years," that he ignored the astronomers' calculations that the sunspot period averaged 11.11 years. In two separate articles on his business cycle findings, Jevons took the position that between the commercial crisis of 1825 and "in or about the year 1879...there will have been five such occurrences in fifty-four years, giving almost exactly eleven years (10.8) as the average interval, which sufficiently approximates to 11.11, the supposed exact length of the sun-spot period, to warrant speculation as to their possible connection." Thus we are struck by the curious fact that, in his 1875 and 1878 articles, Jevons was strongly committed to Clarke's findings at a time when Clarke himself was vacilating.

## VI.  THE LATER YEARS

The British economy, which had been plagued by the Great Depression of the 1870s, enjoyed only mild prosperity in the early 1880s. In 1883, recession returned and the economy again declined into depression until a slight revival began in mid-1886. The renewed depression revived Clarke's interest in business cycles and he presented a number of papers on the topic at Section F (Economic Science and Statistics) during the annual meetings of the British Association for the Advancement of Science. In these papers, Clarke developed three themes—the available price statistics were unreliable, "currency variations" were not the cause of the periodic depressions, and the cause of these depressions was to be found in physical phenomena.

The first of the papers, "Prospective Prices in Europe, America and Asia," was presented at the Montreal meeting in 1884. The published summary of the paper reveals the three themes which would dominate Clarke's final contributions to business cycle analysis:

> The author objected to artificial averages of prices as calculated to mislead, and stated that the effect of prices was rather to be gauged by the great and governing commodities, such as corn which supplies the food of labour, and steel (iron), which furnishes its instruments and machines. With regard to vegetable and animal commodities, and even to man, the primary influence was due to the physical phenomena of the universe, and their cycles and fluctuations. He was the first to point out, in 1847, the periodical laws affecting natural production, and thereby, as the consequences, panics and crises. This, now dealt with as the sunspot period, had been worked out by Professor Jevons, but Mr. Clarke still advocated the terms of his original propositions as most practically meeting the requirements of economical science. Steel, reduced by the improvements of Heath, Bessemer, and Seimens, and not by currency variations, from 60£. a ton, and so to 40£., and now to 4£. or 5£. a ton for rails, had become a factor of prices under new conditions. Corn raised on prairie lands of uncropped fertility, and moved by cheap transport on land and sea, must also be regarded as produced under another economical standard (Clarke, 1884b, p. 868).

Clarke, believing that the early efforts to construct price indices were "calculated to mislead," preferred instead to track the prices of "the great and governing commodities." Notice too that he took a position similar to Jevons's regarding the cause of the current depression, yet continued to separate himself from Jevons's sunspot theory. Thus the cause of the depressed prices was to be sought in "the physical phenomena of the universe," rather than in monetary phenomena, "currency variations." Yet there is something new in Clarke's analysis, for the most prominent of these "physical phenomena" were improvements in technology—"the improvements of Heath, Bessemer, and Seimens" in the steel industry, while lower corn prices were largely influenced by improved technology which allowed corn to be "raised on prairie lands of uncropped fertility, and moved by cheap transport on land and sea." Although he failed to make the distinction between cyclical phenomena and secular trends, he did introduce into his analysis the issue of the role of played by technology. Clarke's view that technological innovations in the steel, transportation, and agricultural industries "had become a factor of prices under new conditions," that these innovations had so changed conditions that now goods must "be regarded as produced under another economical standard," foreshadows the key role assigned to innovation in Schumpeter's theory.

The following year, at the Aberdeen meeting, Clarke reviewed the causes of the depression in a paper titled "On Depression of Prices and Results of Economy of Production, and on the Prospect of Recovery."

> Corn, sugar, and coffee are now produced in large quantities, because all the best producing countries are laid open by cheap railways, and freight to the ocean markets is reduced.
>
> The effective cause of the great reduction in production and transport is due to the reduction in the cost of steel and iron, consequent on the inventions of Bessemer, Seimens, Thomas, Gilchrist, and others. Whatever the quantity of gold may be, the former price of steel in relation to other commodities will not be regained. As steel or steel iron rails can be made for one-tenth of the cost of thirty years ago, this is an economical fact to be dealt with. Cheap railways and cheap ocean steamers are now making their influence felt (Clarke, 1885, p. 1168).

It seems likely that Clarke meant to say "the effective cause of the great reduction in [*the cost of*] production and transport," in this comment. In this paper, Clarke came close to treating technological innovations as secular, rather than cyclical phenomena, though he himself did not recognize this distinction.

In opposition to the notion that monetary forces caused the depression, Clarke maintained that "no practical evidence has been adduced that a diminished supply of gold is the cause of lower prices" (Clarke, 1885, p. 1168). There was a fundamental error in the analysis of those who put forth a monetary explanation for the depressed prices, Clarke believed. A diminished supply of gold could not be the source of the problem, because:

> With regard to gold coinage, the effect of any supposed short supply cannot be measured from one year's supply, or five, or ten years, as the effect has to be calculated on the whole mass of gold coinage existing in the world, whatever that may be. Gold is a metal coined over and over again, sometimes for centuries, and the coinage of a year is in reality in a great degree recoinage (Clarke, 1885, p. 1168).

Having shown that "no practical evidence has been adduced that a diminished supply of gold is the cause of lower prices," Clarke turned his attention to some issues concerning silver. At the 1886 meeting of the British Association, held in Birmingham, Clarke read a paper on "The Causes affecting the Reduction in the Cost of Producing Silver." Again a central theme was to show how improved technology lowered the costs of production. Clarke summarized: "The chief causes which have operated on the silver market have been, 1st, reduction of cost of metal; 2nd, over-production of silver; 3rd, over-coinage of silver; 4th, over-stock of coin and other silver" (Clarke, 1885, pp. 767-768).

The next year, at the B.A.A.S. meeting in Manchester, Clarke again questioned the reliablity of the available price statistics. In particular, Clarke wanted to "call attention to the statistical discrepancies between the figures of the importation of commodities derived from the Board of Trade returns and those of actual consumption" (Clarke, 1887, p. 832). At issue was Clarke's charge that retailers were guilty of diluting and adulterating a wide variety of imported commodities:

> Thus the figures of imports would not show the real consumption or the price which affected the consumers. A decrease of the import might not signify a diminished demand for a retail article...The matter to be considered is not strictly adulteration in a sanitary sense, but the substitution of one article for another and the statistical consequences. ...The purchasing power of the community has no immediate dependence on the conditions of importation, but rather on that of the article presented by the retailer....Consequently importation and consumption do not exactly represent each other....[Clarke's] purpose was to invite closer attention to retail consumption and prices as statistical bases (1887, p. 832).

This series of papers, presented at the meetings of Section F of the British Association when Clarke was in his late sixties and early seventies, is revealing. They were partly an attempt to stake his claim as discoverer of the business cycle. While proclaiming his anticipation of and influence on Jevons's business cycle analysis, Clarke separated himself from the sunspot cycle as a cause. That an old man would engage in such tactics is not surprising. What was most interesting was his effort to advance the analysis of business cycles. By pointing out that more and better statistical data was needed, Clarke emphasized his commitment to induction. His attacks on monetary theories of the cycle were based on his understanding of the institutional aspects of gold and silver production and coining. Finally, his committment to physical causes of economic cycles remained strong. Yet we find that this committment did not close the door to further research and exploration. As noted earlier, Jevons was strongly committed to Clarke's findings at a time, during the 1870s, when Clarke himself was vacilating. During the 1880s, Clarke continued to grapple with the topic and came up with a new version of his "physical phenomena" explanation. In the papers presented at the meetings of the British Association, Clarke even began to move away from the position he had taken at the 1879 meeting of the Society of Arts, the view that business cycles were, in the strictest sense, a "phenomena of nature, which after all, did govern the individual operations of man." His lifelong interest in railways is seen clearly in his new "innovation" hypothesis of the cycle. While this new hypothesis is put rather crudely, in particular his failing to make the distinction between cyclical phenomena and secular trends, nonetheless Clarke deserves some credit for anticipating Joseph Schumpeter's theory.

Shortly before Clarke presented this last series of papers, Francis Galton proposed, at the 1877 meeting of the British Association, the abolition of Section F (Economic Science and Statistics). Galton found that: "This Section... occupies a peculiar position of isolation, being neither sufficiently scientific in itself, nor receiving help from other Sections" (Galton, 1877, p. 471). Galton "freely conceded that Section F deals with numerous and important matters of human knowledge," but that did not give it title to existence (p. 471). Galton drew a careful distinction between general knowledge and science. Science was confined "in the strictest sense to precise measurement and definite laws, which lead by such exact processes of reasoning to their results, that all minds are obliged to accept the latter as true" (p. 471). Galton proceeded to examine all of the papers read before Section F in the years 1873-1875. Of the 72 papers presented, he found only four that met his definition of "scientific." It was his contention that one of these four "scientific" papers could have been read before Section A (Mathematics and Physics) and the other three could have been presented before Section D (Biology), in the Anthropological Department of that Section. One of the three papers suitable for presentation to Section D was Hyde Clarke's 1873 piece, "Influence of Large Centres of Population on Intellectual Manifestation," the only paper he read in Section F during the period under consideration. The paper Galton judged fit for Section A was Jevons's 1875, "Influence of the Sun-spot Period upon the Price of Corn" (p. 471).[14] Thus while Galton found grounds for claiming that "the subjects actually discussed in Section F...depart so widely from the scientific ideal as to make them unsuitable for the British Association," he excluded Jevons and Clarke from that charge.

His work judged to be "scientific" by his contemporaries, Clarke's contribution to business cycle theory and analysis is noteworthy for its originality. Clarke was an original discoverer of the cyclical nature of business activity. His efforts to date the cycles, a combination of a series of ten or eleven year cycles within a 54-year long wave, was indeed "a striking anticipation of the major cycles or spans of later days." Finally, his explanations of these cycles, both in his 1847 pamphlet and in the papers presented at the meetings of the British Association for the Advancement of Science during the 1880s, anticipated hypotheses later developed by Jevons and Schumpeter.

## ACKNOWLEDGMENT

The author is Professor of Economics at Valparaiso University. Professor R. D. Collison Black and I have exchanged much information and I have benefited greatly from his insights and research. I would also like to thank Professor Royal Brandis, University of Illinois at Urbana-Champaign, for a number of useful suggestions. A number of improvements in this paper are the direct result of questions raised and comments made at a presentation of this piece at Warren Samuels's History of Economic Thought and Methodology Workshop held at Michigan State University in the fall of 1987. Finally, I benefited from the discussion by Prof. William O. Thweatt, Vanderbilt University, and Hans Jensen, University of Tennessee, when the paper was presented at the annual meeting of the History of Economics Society held in Toronto in June, 1988.

# NOTES

1. There is a very clear parallel between Clarke's proposal and the distinction between the laws governing production and those governing distribution drawn by John Stuart Mill. In the "Preliminary Remarks" to his *Principles of Political Economy*, Mill said:

In so far as the economical condition of nations turns upon the state of physical knowledge, it is a subject for the physical sciences, and the arts founded on them. But in so far as the causes are moral or psychological, dependent on institutions and social relations, or on the principles of human nature, their investigation belongs not to physical, but to moral and social science, and is the object of what is called Political Economy (Mill, 1969, p. 21).

Mill continued in his chapter, "Of Property," in Book II, "Distribution," in these words:

The laws and conditions of the Production of wealth partake of the character of physical truths There is nothing optional or arbitrary in them. What ever mankind produce, must be produced in the modes, and under the conditions, imposed by the constitution of external things, and by the inherent properties of their own bodily and mental structure.... But howsoever we may succeed in making ourselves more space within the limits set by the constitution of things, those limits exist; there are ultimate laws, which we did not make, which we cannot alter, and to which we can only conform (Mill, 1969, pp. 199-200, as it appeared in the first edition, 1909).

The first edition of Mill's *Principles* appeared in 1848, one year after the appearance of Clarke's *Physical Economy*.

2. In 1801, William Herschel, the astronomer, published the results of his study of sunspot activity. Herschel believed that by varying the quantity of light and heat emanating from the sun, these spots were "liable to produce a great variety in the severity or mildness of the seasons of different climates and under different local circumstances" (Herschel, 1801, p. 311). However, the historical records of solar activity were inadequate, both because solar observations had not been done continuously and because the telescopes and other instruments were so crude. "[A] very imperfect account of solar spots may therefore be expected" (p. 313). Furthermore, Herschel explained: "With regard to the contemporary severity and mildness of the seasons, it will hardly be necessary to remark, that nothing decisive can be obtained" (p. 313). These deficiencies in both the weather data and the solar observations forced Herschel to turn "to an indirect source of information" to estimate "the influence of the sun-beams on the vegetation of wheat in this country" (p. 313). That indirect source of information was "the table of the prices of the quarter of nine bushels of the best or highest priced wheat at Windsor, marked in Dr. Adam Smith's valuable Inquiry into the nature and causes of the wealth of nations..."

(p. 314). Herschel recognized that wheat prices were an imperfect source of information by which to track changing weather conditions, since these prices would be affected not only by the weather, but they "will certainly be regulated by the demand" for wheat as well (p. 313). Thus the first suggestion of a connection between sunspots and economic activity was offered by William Herschel, who used Smith's table of wheat prices as a proxy for changing weather conditions in an attempt to answer questions in astronomy, not economics.

Clarke noted that Adam Smith's "investigations into the fluctuations in the money price of wheat and the value of money" were based on Fleetwood's prices and the Eton College prices (Clarke, 1847, p. 3. For Smith's table of wheat prices, see pp. 251-258).

3. Schumpeter noted these dates and concluded that this ten-year cycle "suggests a little manhandling" of the data, but that charge does not apply to Clarke, as we shall see (1954, p. 743.).

4. Beginning with the year 1631, Clarke summarizes the last four periods in the B series in these words:

The state of the harvests at the B periods has, in the cycles recorded, been subjected to such fluctuations that it is impossible to predict their future tendency. In the first period there were *ten* years of bad harvests. In the second period there were *two* years of bad harvests. In the third period there were *two* years of bad harvests. In the fourth period there were *five* years of bad harvests (1847, pp. 10-11).

5. The notion that sunspot activity is influenced by the configuration of the planets has a long history:

The idea that solar maculation depends in some way upon the position of the planets occurred to Galileo in 1612. It has been industriously sifted by a whole bevy of ... solar physicists. [Rudolf] Wolf [then director of the Zurich Observatory] in 1859 found reason to believe that the eleven year curve [of sunspot activity] is determined by the action of Jupiter, modified by that of Saturn, and diversified by the influences proceeding from the earth and Venus... [Richard Christopher] Carrington [an independent astronomer] pointed out in 1863 that while, during *eight successive periods*, from 1770 downwards, there were approximate coincidences between Jupiter's aphelion passages and sun-spot maxima, the relation had been almost exactly reversed in the two periods preceding that date; and the latest conclusion of M. Wolf himself is that the Jovian origin must be abandoned...

That outbreaks of solar activity are *modified* by influences depending upon planetary configuration has been tolerably well ascertained by the Kew observations. This no less significant than surprising result was imparted by Professor Balfour Stewart to the Royal Society of Edinburgh....[He] has shown that inequalities in [the] development [of the spots] exist corresponding severally to the revolution of [an unknown planet] round the sun in twenty-four days, and to its "synodical periods" or successive meetings with Jupiter,

Venus, and Mercury. But the prediction still awaits fulfilment (Clerke, 1887, pp. 204-206).

6.   The Saros cycle of solar eclipses has an interval of 6585.32 days (just 10 or 11 days in excess of 18 years) (Abell, 1964, pp. 184-185). This approximate one-third-day remainder is significant because it "causes successive eclipses in the cycle to occur about one third around the world from each other" (p. 185). Many eclipses occur during this period. Furthermore, these eclipses are of varying duration of totality, the longest lasting less than eight minutes. Given these circumstances, it is difficult to imagine how the Saros series of solar eclipses could have much impact on agriculture, much less be a cause of business cycles in Britain. Clarke himself appears to have had little confidence in this hypothesis.

7.   Here is Clarke's description of Mackenzies' diagram:

This diagram is a circular card or compass. The outer or fourth circle gives the computed average price of wheat for each year; the third circle gives estimates of deficit or excess of the west winds; the second circle is numbered with fifty-four years from 1801 to 1854, so the author carried his prognostications far enough in advance; the inner circle is one of the same kind as the third circle, but the winds are easterly...

    Mr. Hackett...gives me the following as a fair view of [the diagram]:— "The diagram represents the excess and deficiency of west winds, and the excess and deficiency of east winds. The cycle of excess and deficiency of the east and west winds is fifty-four years, being what he [Mackenzie] calls the primary circle of the winds. He terms the excess of east and the deficiency of west winds *Solar* winds, and the deficiency of east and excess of west winds *Lunar* winds. The compound of these he terms Proper winds" (1847, p. 4).

Professor Black treats Mackenzie's contribution in some detail (Black, 1988, pp. 14-16).

8.   In his *Manual of the Weather*, George Mackenzie had this rather curious explanation of the 54-year weather cycle or "circle":

The circle of the revolution of the winds, weather, prices, &c., by the years, is of a compound nature; and therefore arises the continual variation of effect around its periphery. This circle, being a compound, or composed of other figures, still more original, as can be proved by the primary cycle of the weather, which is in a circle, and the only perfect circle in the whole system, is resolvable into still simpler figures; thus a square and a triangle, the value or parts of whose sides respectively are as 6 and 10, upon whose parts being combined in any order in a circular form, completes the figure or sum of both (1829, pp. 29-30).

Mackenzie included in his *Manual*, a complex table covering the 54-year period from 1794 to 1847, which measured: "Physical Year—Increments and Decrements of

Phenomena, and of the Prices of Wheat, by the annual rate." Included among the 19 columns of data, were separate columns of figures for "Prices of Wheat" and "Average Prices of Wheat." Remember, however, that Clarke claimed not to have seen Mackenzie's work, but quoted extensively from and relied upon the description of Mackenzie's analysis provided to him by Mr. Hackett.

9.  Clarke's pamphlet is titled "Contributions to Railway Statistics in 1845" (1846).

10.  Jevons's reference to "Dr. Hyde Clarke" was somewhat upsetting to Clarke as Professor Black makes clear in his introductory quotation (Black, 1987, p. 1).

11.  In the September 27, 1877 issue of *Nature*, Dr. Balfour Stewart posited another effect of sunspot activity. In his view, increased sunspot activity caused a greater number of cyclones, which, in turn, led to increasing numbers of shipwrecks (Stewart, 1877, pp. 461-462).

This near mania with sunspot cycles provoked the short note, printed in the March, 1879 issue of the *Journal of the (Royal) Statistical Society* "from an able correspondent," which analyzed, with a table, "University Boat Races and Sun-Spot Cycles." Black attributes this article to the astronomer Richard Anthony Proctor (1837-1888), who authored "numerous articles on astronomy and related subjects and [who] enjoyed poking fun at ideas to which he was opposed" (Black, 1977, vol. V, pp. 51-52). Proctor showed that for the period from 1829-1878:

> Of *twelve* races rowed in the *minimum* sun-spot group of years Oxford won *two-thirds* of the whole; of *nine* races rowed in the *maximum* sun-spot group of years Cambridge won *two-thirds* of the whole, while of *fourteen* races rowed in the *intermediate* sun-spot group of years each university won *exactly half* (vol. XLII, pp. 328-329).

12.  Professor Black has drawn my attention to the January 15, 1884 meeting of the Statistical Society where Professor J. H. Poynting read a paper, "A Comparison of the Fluctuations in the Price of Wheat and Cotton and Silk Imports into Great Britain." In the discussion following the presentation of that paper, Clarke specified his objections to the sunspot hypothesis. Referring back to his 1847 pamphlet, "Physical Economy," Clarke described how he made a careful study of the available wheat price data, paying particular attention to:

> the long series of Wincester wheat prices which were commonly appended to Adam Smith's "Wealth of Nations". . . Having done that, it was evident on the series that there were indications of periodicity; and he endeavoured to ascertain what general law of periodicity there was by trying various periods, and that resulted in the determination of what had been called the ten-yearly period. They must not understand that there was an exact period of ten years in meteorological influences on crops, or economic results; it was generally a practical, though not an astronomical period of ten years, but not exactly. Generally speaking they had a period of financial crises at this distance of about ten years. Within the last few years the attention of astronomers had been more particularly directed to the sun spots; but instead of assisting the economical investigation or the meteorological discussion, it had rather interfered with our

obtaining clear results. In all these discussions with regard to sun spots, periods had been laid out almost in some cases like minutes and seconds (*Journal of the (Royal) Statistical Society*, vol. xlvii, March, 1884, p. 66).

13.   In the February 13, 1879 issue of *Nature*, Piazzi Smyth challenged Clarke's conclusion regarding such future calculations, saying "I object to the ruling of that sentence" (February 13, 1879, p. 338).
14.   This was brought to my attention by Prof. Royall Brandis, University of Illinois at Urbana-Champaign. He claims, however, that Jevons's paper on sunspots was the only "scientific" paper if one uses Galton's definition in its strictest sense. In Galton's view, Section F:

occupies a peculiar position of isolation, being neither sufficiently scientific itself, nor receiving help from the other Sections. In the first respect it may be alleged that the Anthropological Department and the Geographical Section are open to the same charge; but in the latter respect the case is very different. The leading anthropologists are physiologists, geologists, or geographers, and the proceedings of the department are largely indebted to their special knowledge. Geography is apt to receive light from every department of science, and to give no less than it receives. This is not the case with Section F: it stands detached from all the other Sections, except in regard to a few subjects which might severally be handed over to one or other of them (Galton, 1877, pp. 471-472).

Brandis holds that Jevons's sunspot paper is the only "scientific" paper of the four cited, because Galton suggested that the other three be placed in the slightly suspect Anthropological Department. On the other hand, Galton proposed that Jevons's paper "might properly have been read in. . . Section A [Mathematics and Physics]" (Galton, 1877, p. 471).

In addition to the papers by Clarke and Jevons, Galton declared that two other papers presented at the 1875 meeting were "scientific:" "Legislative Protection to the Birds of Europe" by C. O. Groom Napier and "Need of Systematic Observations on Physical Characteristics of Man in Britain" by Dr. John Beddoe.

# REFERENCES

Abell, George. 1964. *Exploration of the Universe*. New York: Holt, Rinehart and Winston.

Anonymous. 1879. "University Boat Races and Sun-Spot Cycles." *Journal of the (Royal) Statistical Society*. XLII(March): 328-329.

Black, R. D. Collison, ed. 1977. *Papers and Correspondence of William Stanley Jevons*. 7 vols. London: Augustus M. Kelley, Publishers.

————. 1987. Dr. Kondratieff and Mr. Hyde Clarke. Unpublished manuscript.

Clarke, Hyde. 1838. "On the Political Economy and Capital of Joint-stock Banks." *The Railway Magazine and Annals of Science* IV(xxvii):288-293 and IV(xxviii):360-362.

————. 1846. *Contributions to Railway Statistics, in 1845*. London: J. Weale.

_____. 1847. *Physical Economy, A Preliminary Inquiry into the Physical Laws Governing the Periods of Famines and Panics.* London: N.P.

_____. 1878a. (Letter numer 541). In *Papers and Correspondence of William Stanley Jevons*, Vol. IV, (1977), edited by R.D. Collison Black, pp. 274-6. London: Augustus M. Kelley, Publishers.

_____. 1878b. In *Papers and Correspondence of William Stanley Jevons*, Vol. IV, (1977), edited by R.D. Collison Black, pp. 295-6. London: Augustus M. Kelley, Publishers.

_____. 1878c. Untitled letter. *Nature* XIX (November 21): 53.

_____. 1879. *Nature* XIX (January 30): 299-300.

_____. 1884a. "Discussion on Professor Poynting's Paper." *Journal of the (Royal) Statistical Society* XLVII (March): 65-68.

_____. 1884b. "Prospective Prices in Europe, America and Asia." *Report of the 1884 Meeting of the B.A.A.S.* 54(August and September): 868-869.

_____. 1885. "On Depression of Prices and Results of Economy of Production, and on the Prospect of Recovery." *Report of the 1885 Meeting of the B.A.A.S.* 55(September): 1168-1169.

_____. 1886. "The Causes Affecting the Reduction in the Cost of Producing Silver." *Report of the 1886 Meeting of the B.A.A.S.* 56(September, 1886): 767-768.

_____. 1887. "Effective Consumption and Effective Prices in Their Economical and Statistical Relations." *Report of the 1887 Meeting of the B.A.A.S.* 57(August and September): 832.

Clerke, Agnes M. 1887. *A Popular History of Astronomy during the Nineteenth Century.* Edinburgh: Adam & Charles Black.

Galton, Francis. 1877. "Considerations adverse to the Maintenance of Section F (Economic Science and Statistics), submitted by Mr. Francis Galton to the Committee appointed by the Council to consider and report on the possibility of excluding unscientific or otherwise unsuitable papers and discussions from the sectional proceedings of the Association." *Journal of the (Royal) Statistical Society* XL(September): 468-473.

Gayer, Arthur D., W. W. Rostow, and Anna Jacobson Schwartz. 1975. *The Growth and Fluctuation of the British Economy, 1790-1850. An Historical, Statistical, and Theoretical Study of Britain's Economic Development.* New York: Harper & Row.

Goldman, Lawrence. 1983. "The Origins of British 'Social Science': Political Economy, Natural Science and Statistics, 1830-1835." *The Historical Journal* 26(3): 587-616.

Henderson, James P. (1990). "Induction, Deduction and the Role of Mathematics: The Whewell Group vs. The Ricardian Economists." *Research in the History of Economic Thought and Methodology*, Vol. 7: 1-36, edited by Warren J. Samuels. Greenwich, CT: JAI Press.

Herschel, William. 1801. "Observations tending to investigate the Nature of the Sun, in order to find the Causes or Symptoms of its variable Emission of Light and Heat; with Remarks on the Use that may possibly be drawn from Solar Observations." *Philosophical Transactions* 265-318.

Jevons, William Stanley. 1875. "The Solar Period and the Price of Corn." In Jevons, 1884, *Investigations in Currency and Finance*, pp. 194-205, London: Augustus M. Kelley, Publishers.

————. 1878. "The Periodicity of Commercial Crises and Its Physical Explanation." *Journal of the Statistical and Social Inquiry Society of Ireland* VII(August): 334-42. (Reprinted in Jevons, 1884, *Investigations in Currency and Finance*, pp. 206-221, London: Augustus M. Kelley, Publishers.)

————. 1878/1879. "Commercial Crises and Sun-spots." *Nature* XIX (November 14): 33-37, and (April 24): 588-590. (Reprint 1886 in Jevons, *Investigations in Currency and Finance*, pp. 221-243, London: Augustus M. Kelley, Publishers.)

————. 1884. *Investigations in Currency and Finance.* London: Augustus M. Kelley, Publishers.

Juglar, Clement. 1889. *Des Crises Commerciales et de Leur Retour Periodique en France, en Angleterre et aux Etates-Unis.* (Reprint 1967, New York: Augustus M. Kelley, Publishers.)

Kondratieff, Nikolai D. 1951. "The Long Waves in Economic Life." In *Readings in Business Cycle Theory*, pp. 20-42. Homewood, IL: Richard D. Irwin, Inc.

Konekamp, Rosamond. 1977. "Biographical Introduction." In *Papers and Correspondence of William Stanley Jevons*, edited by R. D. Collison Black, pp. 1-52. London: Augustus M. Kelley, Publishers.

Langton, William. 1858. "Observations on a Table shewing the Balance of Account between the Mercantile Public and the Bank of England." *Transactions of The Manchester Statistical Society*, pp. 9-22.

Mackenzie, George. 1829. *Manual of the Weather for the Year MDCCCXXX, including a Brief Account of the Cycles of the Winds and Weather, and the Circle of the Prices of Wheat.* London: W. Blackwood.

Mill, John Stuart. 1969. *Principles of Political Economy.* New York: Augustus M. Kelley, Publishers. (First published 1909).

Mills, John. 1868. "On Credit Cycles, and the Origin of Commercial Crises." *Transactions of The Manchester Statistical Society*, pp. 9-40.

Mitchell, Wesley C. 1927. *Business Cycles, The Problem and Its Setting.* New York: National Bureau of Economic Research.

Schumpeter, Joseph A. 1954. *History of Economic Analysis.* New York: Oxford University Press.

Smith, Adam. 1937. *An Inquiry into the Nature and Causes of the Wealth of Nations.* New York.

Smith, Piazzi. 1879. (Untitled letter). *Nature* XIX (February 13): 338.

"Sun-spots and the Nile." 1879. (Report of the Society of Arts meeting). *Nature* XIX (January 30): 299-300.

Stewart, Balfour. 1877. "Famines and Shipwrecks." *Nature* XVI (September 27): 461-462.

Thorp, Willard Long. 1926. *Business Annals.* New York: National Bureau of Economic Research.

Wade, John. 1833/1966. *History of the Middle and Working Classes; with a Popular Exposition of the Economic and Political Principles which have Influenced the Past and Present Condition of the Industrious Orders.* New York: Augustus M. Kelley, Publishers.

# DR. KONDRATIEFF AND
# MR. HYDE CLARKE

R.D. Collison Black

_If you can avoid calling me Doctor I shall be glad, for I find that people
are indisposed to treat me as a practical man if I am a colonel or a
Doctor._

—Hyde Clarke
(quoted in Jevons, 1977, p. 296).

## I

In the recent years of international economic disturbance and
depression there has been a considerable increase of interest in the
phenomenon of "long waves" in economic activity, just as there was
during the world economic depression of the thirties.[1] The original
suggestion of the existence of such a phenomenon is usually
attributed to the Russian economist N.D. Kondratieff (1892-1931),

**Research in the History of Economic Thought and Methodology, Volume 9, pages 35-58.**
**Copyright © 1992 by JAI Press Inc.**
**All rights of reproduction in any form reserved.**
**ISBN: 1-55938-428-X**

and through the work of Schumpeter the long wave hypothesis has come to be widely known as the "Kondratieff cycle."

In some of the current writing on the subject it has been suggested that Kondratieff may have had anticipators in the two Dutch socialists, S. de Wolff and Jacob van Gelderen, and the Russian Marxist Alexander Helphand who wrote under the pseudonym "Parvus" (Van Duijn, 1983, pp. 60-63). In a postscript to his well-known 1926 article Kondratieff himself acknowledged the work of the first two of these writers, but stated that while he had arrived at the long wave hypothesis in 1919-1921, he had not seen de Wolff's writings until 1926 and had not read van Gelderen's—which appeared only in Dutch—at all.

De Wolff and van Gelderen were fairly close contemporaries of Kondratieff and their writings predated his by only a few years, while Helphand's earliest work on crises and cycles appeared in 1901. Considering that Kondratieff's observations covered only 140 years, or approximately two-and-a-half long cycles, it would seem unlikely that there could have been any earlier anticipations of his hypothesis; yet those with an interest in the history of trade cycle theories could find tucked away in a footnote in Schumpeter's *History of Economic Analysis* a reference to one Hyde Clarke who "had a ten year cycle, and *in addition a longer period of about 54 years*, a striking anticipation of the major cycles or spans of later days, especially of Kondratieff's long waves" (Schumpeter, 1954, p. 743). More recently, J.J. van Duijn in a chapter on "The Discovery of the Long Wave" has credited "Dr. Hyde Clarke" (sic!) with making "the first reference to a possible long wave in economic activity" (van Duijn, 1983, p. 59).

In fact the name of Hyde Clarke has figured in footnotes to various contributions to the history of economic thought for the past half-century or more. It occurs in the review of various theories given by Wesley Mitchell in the first chapters of *Business Cycles* (Mitchell, 1930, pp. 10-11) and also receives mention in Link's *English Theories of Economic Fluctuations* (Link, 1959, p. 205) and Leland H. Jenks' *The Migration of British Capital to 1875* (Jenks, 1963, p. 153). At an earlier period, W.S. Jevons in his article on "Commercial Crises and Sun-Spots," first published in *Nature* in 1878, gave an extended and favourable notice of the views of "Dr. Hyde Clarke" on the periodicity of crises.[2] This was probably the source of another reference to Hyde Clarke by the French economist A.M. de Foville in an article which dealt in some detail with the work of Jevons and Juglar (de Foville, 1879, p. 191). Certainly Schumpeter stated that he knew Hyde Clarke's writings "only from Jevons' report."

With the current revival of interest in the concept of long waves in economic life, it would seem to be worthwhile to rescue one of the people who first articulated it from the obscurity of footnotes and to attempt at least to provide some more details of his life and work. Who then was Hyde Clarke and to what extent did his writings anticipate the work of Kondratieff and others who have taken up the long wave theory?

## II

During his own lifetime Hyde Clarke was sufficiently well know to receive mention in works of reference such as *Men and Women of the Time* (Moon, 1891, pp. 194-5) and *Celebrities of the Century* (Sanders, 1887, pp. 256-7) and on his death there were obituary notices of him in *The Times* (Mar. 7, 1895, p. 10b.) and the *Annual Register* (*The Annual Register*, 1895, p. 164)[3], as well as in journals such as *Nature* (51, 468) and *The Engineer* (79, 217). From these sources a picture can be built up of a long, varied and colourful career, but not all its details can now be filled in or adequately verified.

Hyde Clarke was born in London in 1815[4] and appears to have been a precocious youth. Details of his education are lacking, but he evidently took up engineering at an early age. According to the writer of the obituary in *The Engineer*, Clarke's first engineering work was done in Spain and Portugal during the Wars of Succession, while he was "attached to the Duke of Saldanha." There was a detachment of Royal Engineers among the British troops which went to assist the Spanish constitutionalist forces against the Carlists between 1835 and 1839, but Hyde Clarke's name does not appear in the Royal Engineers Lists for this period.[5]

If Hyde Clarke was with the forces of the Duke of Saldanha, this would place him in Portugal; Saldanha's military campaign there ended in May 1834 but until 1837 he remained an important figure in the government formed after the war by Queen Maria II. So the writer of *The Times* obituary of Hyde Clarke may have been nearer the mark in describing him as "employed in diplomatic missions" in Spain and Portugal at this time. The variant offered by *The Annual*

*Register* (1895, p. 164), which states that Hyde Clarke "fought with the British legion in the Portuguese and Spanish Wars of Succession, 1830-31," seems obviously unreliable if only because of the fact that this legion was not formed until 1834 (Ridley, 1970, pp. 196-8).

Whatever the young Hyde Clarke may or may not have done in the Iberian peninsula there seems to be no doubt that in 1836 he was back in England, where he became involved in plans for the building of a railway from Lancaster via the West Cumberland coast to Carlisle and thence to Glasgow via Nithsdale. Although I have not been able to discover anything precise about how and where Hyde Clarke received his engineering training, he seems to have made the engineering of dams and embankments one of his specialities. Although never actually a Member of the Institution of Civil Engineers, he later took part in discussions on these subjects at several meetings of the Institution (Clarke, 1847a, 1878-79) and among his many publications was one entitled *Engineering of Holland: On the Construction of Dykes* (cf. Henderson, 1992b). Presumably on the basis of his knowledge in this field, Hyde Clarke proposed a bold plan to build an embankment across Morecambe Bay, designed not only to carry the railway but at the same time to provide the capital for it from the proceeds of the sale of land reclaimed from the Bay. Although this scheme gained the support of no less a railway engineer than George Stephenson, it was not carried into effect for a variety of local reasons. While the project fell through as a trunk route, the railway was nevertheless completed by several companies, the Nithsdale section becoming the Glasgow and South Western Railway and subsequently part of the Midland Anglo-Scottish route (Clarke, 1884b).

Through this Morecambe Bay project Hyde Clarke became acquainted with John Rooke, since recognised as one of the neglected economists of this period (Seligman, 1903, pp. 511-14). Of Rooke, Clarke afterwards wrote: "Many of his writings are wild, but contain striking and original thoughts. In 1836 he came in contact with me and some of his writings passed under my hand." On more than one occasion Hyde Clarke asserted that Lonsdale, the author of a six-volume work of reference entitled *The Worthies of Cumberland*, had represented Rooke therein as the originator of the scheme for a west coast railway as being Clarke's employer, "but it was directly the reverse" (Clarke to Jevons, August 31, 1878; Black, 1977, Vol. IV, 275-6). In fact, while Lonsdale did mention both Rooke and Clarke, he did not portray their relationship in this way.[6]

From 1836 until 1849, Hyde Clarke appears to have been engaged not so much in the actual construction of railways as in financial operations and journalism connected with the growth of the English railway system. There are indications that he had significant connections in the London financial community at this period. The author of *The Times* obituary followed the writer of the biography in *Men and Women of the Time* in stating that "in 1836 Hyde Clarke founded the London and County Bank." The claim is a considerable one, for after an initial period of difficulty the London and County had by the end of the nineteenth century become one of the largest branch banking concerns in the south of England. If the twenty-one-year-old Hyde Clarke had indeed founded, or even helped to found, such a bank it would presumably have provided him with ample remuneration and occupation for the rest of his life; but no evidence which supports the claim can now be discovered.[7] Nevertheless, it is clear from his correspondence and other writings that Hyde Clarke was known to the London bankers of the 1830s and 1840s and had contact with such men as James Wilson, J.W. Gilbart, Thomas Tooke and Thomas Joplin (Black, 1977, Vol. IV, p. 275). Like them, his attention was drawn to the fluctuations of the price level and the "commercial panics" of 1839 and 1847 and it is from this period that his most original economic writings date.

The promotion of railways continued to occupy a large place in Hyde Clarke's concerns at this time of his life and in 1844 he founded a periodical called the *Railway Register* which he edited until 1847, writing extensively in it on railway management and finance. His interest extended to the promotion of railways in India which, like many others at the time, he considered could make a major contribution to the economic development of the sub-continent (Clarke, 1847c; Ambirajan, 1978, p. 250).

Hyde Clarke concerned himself with Indian development to a considerable extent in the decade from 1849 to 1859. In 1849 he was associated with Francis Whishaw, another railway engineer who was also Secretary of the Royal Society of Arts from 1843 to 1845, in producing a report for the East India Company on the practicability of a telegraph system for the country; he advocated a chain of telegraphs linking Calcutta with Simla, Darjeeling and other hill settlements (Clarke, 1881, pp. 544-5). It was in the development of these parts of Northern India that he was especially interested: at one time he was honorary agent for Darjeeling in London and in 1857 he was concerned with the flotation of a Northern Bengal Railway Company, pressing for the extension of railways to hill stations such as Simla.[8] Yet these activities did not absorb the whole of Hyde Clarke's energies; in the intervening years he found time to produce *A Grammar of the English Tongue* in 1853, *A New and Comprehensive Dictionary of the English Language* in 1855—which went through many subsequent editions—as well as several pamphlets on *The Statistics of Fire Assurance* between 1853 and 1986 (cf. Henderson, 1992b).

According to his own account, from 1859 to 1866 Hyde Clarke lived and worked in "the East," mainly apparently in Turkey, where he acted as Commissioner of Works for the province of Smyrna and as "Cotton Councillor" during the period when attempts were being made to develop cotton exports to Lancashire from the Ottoman Empire in place of American supplies (Henderson, 1934, pp. 46-7). Typically, again Hyde Clarke found time to add other activities to these official duties. He used his years in the Middle East to extend his knowledge of languages and began to develop the interests in comparative philology and anthropology which occupied him for much of the rest of his life.

For almost thirty years following his return to England in 1866 until his death in 1895, Hyde Clarke seems to have lived a busy life in London not only writing extensively on these subjects but concerning himself with many financial and public activities. In 1868 he founded the Council of Foreign Bondholders and, according to *The Times*, "in the commercial world his services were frequently in requisition as an expert in the ways of States which borrow, but forget to repay their loans" (March 7, 1895, p. 10b). Clarke was also Treasurer of the Newspaper Press Fund, a charitable organisation for journalists which still exists today, and it is on record that one of those who helped him in raising funds for it was Charles Dickens.[9]

In addition, Hyde Clarke played an active part in a number of the learned societies of Victorian London. He had a substantial influence on the organisation of the Royal Society of Arts; already in 1857 he had proposed to its Council that "a special section should be formed for India, another for Australia, one for English America, and so on." He renewed this proposal in 1868 and an Indian Section was then established, followed by an African section in 1874—"again, largely due to the zeal of Hyde Clarke" (Hudson and Luckhurst, 1954, pp. 344-5).

That zeal was also exerted on behalf of the London (later Royal) Statistical Society on the Council of which Hyde Clarke served at various time from 1868 until his death. As with the Royal Society of Arts, he seems to have played an active part in attempts to alter the organisation of the society. In November 1885, Hyde Clarke proposed that the Statistical Society should hold periodical Economic meetings, a development which had the support of the newly appointed Professor of Political Economy at Cambridge, Alfred Marshall. Hyde Clarke's motion was in fact passed but against such opposition from other members that Foxwell pronounced it "rather a Pyrrhic victory." In consequence, Clarke's proposal was not implemented and Foxwell and others turned their attention to the establishment of a separate Economic Society (Coats, 1968, pp. 351-3).[10]

Hyde Clarke also contributed a number of papers to the proceedings of the London Statistical Society. Like many contributions of the period, they could only be described as statistical in the sense that they contained statistical material to illustrate the social or political problems with which the author was concerned. Papers such as "On the Debts of Sovereign and Quasi-Sovereign States, owing to Foreign Countries" (Clarke, 1878) or "On a Form of Savings Banks among the Christians of Asia Minor" (Clarke, 1865), reflect the range and character of Hyde Clarke's later interests, although his contributions to the discussions on other papers sometimes reveal a continuing interest in the economic problems on which he had written in earlier years.

His membership of the Ethnological Society of London and the Anthropological Institute provide further indications of the direction of Hyde Clarke's intellectual concerns in later life. For these and for the Royal Historical Society he wrote numerous papers on philology and the origins of languages and races—interests which led him into the related fields of archaeology and ancient history. The period after 1870 witnessed the rediscovery of the monuments and inscriptions of the Hittites, the ancient inhabitants of Turkey and northern Syria. Hyde Clarke is said by some contemporary sources to have been the first to identify the Hittite inscriptions of Khita and Hamah, but his theories as to their possible origin did not find favour with other experts on the archaeology of the Middle East (Wright, 1884, pp. 129-31). Indeed in this area of study the comment of *The Times* obituarist seems to accord with the judgement of history—"while his views on many subjects were undoubtedly original, most of his generalisations failed to commend themselves as sound to really scientific philologists."

# III

Hyde Clarke's long life of varied activity makes him difficult to characterise: an engineer who filled a variety of administrative posts at home and abroad, he seems like many Victorians to have combined enormous energy with wide intellectual curiosity. It was in the period from 1838 to 1848 that Hyde Clarke did most of his writing on economic problems and in these years produced his most original ideas. Not surprisingly, the starting point for his thinking on economic matters was his involvement as an engineer and journalist in the rapid growth of the English railway system. In that respect, it could be argued, he was evolving in a way which was not uncommon, and certainly not unfruitful, at this period. The development of railways and public works in the nineteenth century led a number of engineers—and some scientists with engineering training—in Britain, France, Germany and the United States to look at the economic problems involved. The works of Lardner, Dupuit, Minard, Launhardt and Ellet broke important new ground and their significance is now well recognised in the history of economic thought (Ekelund and Hébert, 1975 part IV). Most of this work belonged to the area of what would now be called pricing and allocation theory or the related field of welfare economics. Hyde Clarke's writings, on the other hand, fall into the area now called macroeconomics. He was conerned essentially with two problems—understanding in real as well as in financial terms the process of investment in railways, then taking place in Britain on an unprecedented scale, and tracing and explaining the cyclical phenomena which he detected in economic life.

Concerns such as these, as Professor Henderson (1992a) has noted lay outside the mainstream of classical political economy. Indeed, in the mid-nineteenth century most economists had little if any grasp of the concept of economic cycles. Perhaps the most striking feature of Hyde Clarke's thought is not merely that he at this time recognised the existence of such cycles, but that, as Schumpeter noted, he "recognised a muliplicity of cycles that run their course simultaneously" (Schumpeter, 1954, p. 743). Hyde Clarke himself explained how this recognition came about, in a passage which shows him already much involved in observing the workings of the economy at the age of 17 or 18:

> I begun in 1832 and 1833, when I saw the dawn of a period of these speculations, which from a close acquaintance with the history of the mania of 1823, 1824 and 1825, I was induced to look upon as a recurrence of the same phenomena. I therefore gave a particular attention to the events of the railway mania of 1835, and [formed] a conviction that the true nature of that epoch was connected with periodical laws. While entertaining these views my attention was directed to the general elementary laws which govern periodical or cyclal [sic] action, and I wrote a paper on the subject in Herapath's *Railway Magazine* in 1838. At this time it was my impression that the period of speculation was a period of ten years, but I was led also to look for a period of thirteen or fourteen years as half a period of twenty-seven or twenty-eight years, and for a period of seven or eight years as the quarter revolution, and I vainly endeavoured to obtain information on these points from scientific friends, or to collect corroborative facts. In the course of these inquiries I looked at the astronomical periods and the meterological theories, without finding anything at all available for my purposes" (Clarke, 1847b, p. 3).

Hyde Clarke did not give an exact reference for the article which he here claims to have written and its identification presents something of a problem. There is an article in two parts by Hyde Clarke in Vol IV of Herapath's *Railway Magazine*, entitled "On the Political Economy and Capital of Joint-Stock Banks" but as Professor Henderson says, "in that article, there is only the most general commentary on periodic or cyclical events" and its content "is hardly an explanation of the "general elementary laws which govern periodical or cyclar action" (Henderson, 1992a). However, in his letter of August 31, 1878 to Jevons, Hyde Clarke wrote: "There was a paper on Cycles in Herapath's Journal about 1837 or 1838, which contains an hypothesis for a selfworking variable cycle, but it has no reference to the cycle of crises." Now this description exactly fits an anomymous article which appeared in Volume V of Herapath's *Railway Magazine* in October 1838, entitled "On the Mathematical Law of the Cycle." This curious article runs to no more than two-and-a-half quarto pages and contains no actual mathematics. Its starting point is "Babbage's discovery, that after a certain extent the formulae of equations ceased to operate, but that new formulae were required"; the author's claim is that this "instead of being a mere exception in one particular branch of science...is a universal law of nature" (Clarke, 1838, p. 378).

After the fashion of his day, the writer does not give any specific reference to indicate the part of Babbage's work to which he was referring—it may well have been *Examples of the Solutions of Functional Equations*, published in 1820 (cf. Dubbey, 1978). In any event, it is clear from the context that what the author had in mind was certain properties of abstract periodic functions which may be duplicated in natural phenomena. As instances he quotes irregularities in the procession of the equinoxes, and eccentricities in the variation of the magnetic needle, while "in mechanics there is every presumption that after a certain number of revolutions of a machine the ratio of those movements is changed, and something of this may certainly be perceived in watches. It is perceptible in a watch going very irregularly, that the ratio of its movement will change as if by starts.... In statistics this cyclar action decidedly prevails, and although we cannot point out any more prominent instances, yet there is sufficient of these examples to authorize the presumption that in other instances it equally exists" (Clarke, 1838, p. 379).

Essentially all that the article was saying was that certain types of equation might define series which would display damped cyclical movements, that similar cycles could be traced in a variety of natural phenomena and that further reseach might lead to the establishment of a general law explaining their form (Kendall, 1948, p. 402; Dubbey, 1978, pp. 51, 87). Interest in such "cyclar action" was in fact quite widespread at this period; astronomers, for example, were interested in how it might affect the accuracy of chronometers used for navigational purposes (Bennett, 1980). To modern specialists it may appear strange that a contribution of this kind should appear in a railway journal, but the explanation of this may lie in the fact that its full title was *The Railway Magazine and Annals of Science* and its editor John Herapath was, according to Hyde Clarke himself, "a zealous physical mathematician." Forty years later he recounted to Jevons how Herapath "more than once talked with me of cosmical cycles, down to 1844, but he had no idea of any period affecting production, and exhibiting itself in economical results" (Black, 1977, Vol. IV, p. 276).

It is noteworthy that in his letter to Jevons of August 31, 1878, Hyde Clarke did not claim the authorship of the 1838 *Railway*

*Magazine* article, but as many of the articles in that periodical were anonymous it seems reasonable to suggest that this was the same piece as the one to which he laid claim in *Physical Economy* in 1847.

From that pamphlet, which bore the subtitle "a Preliminary Inquiry into the Physical Laws governing the Periods of Famines and Panics," it is evident that Hyde Clarke, like Jevons a generation later, had become fascinated with the idea of periodicity in nature and its possible influence on the affairs of men. In it he not only developed the idea of cyclical fluctuations in natural phenomena with a considerable volume of supporting evidence but sought to emphasise the relation of such fluctuations to economic activity:

> While political economy restricts itself principally to the moral laws which influence society, it seems advisable that the influence of physical laws and operations upon mankind should for their better study, be formed also into a distinct science. This would include the laws of life (vital statistics) those which regulate famines and pestilence, and the operations of physical phenomena as affecting mankind and society. Such a science might usefully be called physical economy" (Clarke, 1847b, p. 1).

From an initial and somewhat sketchy outline of the course of prices and economic activity since 1815, Hyde Clarke argued that "this outline is enough to show the close connection of abundant food, active enterprise and speculation, and of scarce food, panic and political disturbance. It is sufficient also to suggest that there is some definite period which governs the occurrence of these phenomena." Recalling his earlier preoccupation with the ten-year period, Hyde Clarke explained that "the present famine" (in Ireland) had led him "to look for a larger period" and directed his thoughts "to the famine so strongly felt during the French Revolution," fifty-four years earlier.

One of Hyde Clarke's closest friends at this time, as he later explained to Jevons, was James Thomas Hackett, "a very fair mathematician and astronomical computer, who had been Secretary of the London Astrological Society and whose inner craze was astrology and consequently periodicity" (Black, 1977, Vol. IV, p. 275). It was Hackett who pointed out to Hyde Clarke that the idea of a 54-year cycle was central to the work of George Mackenzie, a Scottish climatologist who in 1818 had published *The System of the Weather of the British Isles*—a system in which he placed so much confidence that in 1829 he was prepared to publish a *Manual of the Weather for the year MDCCCXXX* giving forecasts for each month a year in advance.

Mackenzie's system was based on a weather register which he had kept since 1802; his records led him to the idea that the wind was "the foremost element" in the weather and that its movements followed a regular pattern. Over a period of 14 years he believed that he had established that there were (in the part of Scotland where he made his observations) on average 135 days of east wind and 216 days of west wind annually. When the number of days of east wind in a year was greater than 135 he termed this an "excess" or a year of "Solar east winds" and similarly if the number fell below 135 this would be in his terminology a "deficiency" of easterly winds or a year of "Lunar east winds." "Having in this manner found the excesses and deficiencies of the east and west winds for 14 years, he began to compare them together, and was surprised to find that they followed one another in a regular progression, the excesses and deficiences of both winds arranging themselves in groups.... Now it is a very remarkable fact that by following out these progressions the series returns into itself in 54 years, forming a perfect cycle" (Brewster, 1818, p. 86).

It may well be asked how Mackenzie arrived at this result on the basis of only 14 years of observations; he seems simply to have observed that the terms in the "regular progression" of the winds noted in his journal formed part of a series which would "return into itself" in 54 years, but in 1829 he claimed that "the observations of subsequent years which have been kept by the Register have exactly corresponded with the series of alternations of the Solar and Lunar winds made out at that time by induction—and it could not be otherwise" (Mackenzie, 1829, p. 27).

"From this time of discovering the primary cycle of the winds in 1817" Mackenzie went on to search for a relation between his weather cycle and movements in the price of wheat, using the Eton College records and Fleetwood's *Chronicon Preciosum* as quoted by Adam Smith. He claimed to have discovered in 1826 "the regular rotation of the cheap and dear prices of wheat in every 54 year period." His contention was that the 54-year cycle could be divided into two periods of 27 years each—"one of these is generally wet, windy and cloudy with generally high prices of corn; the other dry, less windy, and clear with generally low prices of corn" (Mackenzie, 1829, pp. 45, 49).

Although Hyde Clarkes's conclusion was that "the general prognostications of Mr Mackenzie as to prices have...certainly been borne out hitherto," he did not adopt either Mackenzie's figures or his theories. However, they do seem to have encouraged him to search through the available data—again primarily Fleetwood and the Eton College returns—for evidence supporting or contradicting his hypothesis of a 54 year periodicity. To his credit, it must be recorded that he did not try to force the data to fit, but frankly stated his conclusion that "the elements thus obtained, although in some points corresponding to 54 years, were far from answering determinately to a rigorous period of 54 years throughout, though there was sufficient conformity to justify the assumption that some general period regulated the critical years" (Clarke, 1847b, pp. 5, 6).

Hyde Clarke's measurement and dating of both decennial and longer cycles are examined in detail by James P. Henderson (1992a) and therefore need not be further discussed here, but we may particularly note that Professor Henderson finds that the dating of Kondratieff's main measures—prices, agricultural wages and interest rates—for his "First Cycle" closely matches Hyde Clarke's dates.

## IV

Between 1838 and 1847 then, Hyde Clarke had moved from formulating a very broad hypothesis about cycles in natural phenomena to empirical investigations which had convinced him of the existence, among others, of a 54 year cycle in economic activity resulting from physical causes. But in 1846 Hyde Clarke had published another pamphlet, reprinting material which first appeared in Volume IV of the *Railway Register*, under the title *Theory of Investment in Railway Companies*. Now to modern economists who remember Schumpeter's words—"railroad developments in the forties, particularly in England, are a chief reason for dating the beginning of the second Kondratieff as we do" (i.e., in 1843) (Schumpeter, 1939, Vol. I, p. 304)—this title naturally suggest the interesting possibility that Hyde Clarke's intention was to present a theory of the influence of investment in railways on fluctuations in economic activity, but such was not the case.

In fact, Hyde Clarke's purpose in expounding a theory of railway investment was strictly practical and by no means disinterested. He was concerned to argue a case against those "panic mongers," as he called them, who were urging a restriction on the number of railway bills sanctioned by Parliament annually (Simmons, 1978, Vol. I, pp. 40-42), and therefore to show that the very large volume of railway investment then being pushed forward could be financed without damage to the national economy. In endeavouring to do so, Hyde Clarke did present a sound and interesting account of the real transfers of resources which lay behind the then unfamiliar facade of finance throught joint-stock company promotion. His main argument was that it could not "be said, with any degree of truth or seeming, that capital has been diverted from any of the great staples by the extensive progress of railway enterprise in the present year. Till this pressure takes place, till it makes itself felt, interference is surely needless" (Clarke, 1846, p. 9).

In real terms, Hyde Clarke suggested, the labor required for railway building need not be drawn from that employed in other industries, but could come partly from those unemployed in workhouses and partly from reductions in the labor force required in agriculture, where improvements had generated increases in productivity. "To extract this *dormant* labour, a small additional stimulus only would be required, which is to be obtained from the increasing surplus of agricultural produce yearly provided." Here an echo of Gibbon Wakefield's views can be detected, for Hyde Clarke suggested that to employ labor released from agriculture in manufactures "is dangerous, because it is only increasing production at a time when the foreign markets are overstocked." On the other hand, "employment in public works does not interfere with the markets, while it increases the fixed capital or working plant of the community and at the same time, enlarges the permanent resources of subsistence." And for this, "railways fulfil, in the most eminent degree, all the conditions required" (Clarke, 1846, p. 14).

Turning to the capital which would employ the labor, Hyde Clarke contended that much of the capital required for railways was merely a transfer and not a net new investment—as most notably in the case of land acquired against payment in railway shares. Where actual new investment was required Hyde Clarke, as might be expected, stressed the extent to which it came from the small savings of farmers and tradespeople, mobilised through the joint stock mechanism, and minimised or ignored the possibilities of speculative share purchases financed by short-term credit.

In all this, there was no mention of the cyclical theory which he must by then have largely formulated and was to publish a year later in *Physical Economy*. Yet the two were connected, though not by the mechanism which a twentieth-century economist would expect. Most economists nowadays would consider that if fluctuations in economic activity can be shown to be regularly generated by some exogenous cause, then it would be desirable to arrange, through government policy or otherwise, that other factors influencing the level of activity should do so in a counter-cyclical fashion. Writing in 1847, Hyde Clarke did not see the matter in that light; to him the only policy conclusion which seemed clear was that "if the mania for speculation be a periodical consequence of a regular series of events, it must be utterly futile to pass laws for its suppression and interference inconsistent with such fact can only have the effect of doing mischief" (Clarke, 1847b, p. 2; cf. Henderson, 1992a). So, far from the railways being major contributors to an investment cycle, they appear as being passively involved in a process which would have occurred even had they never existed.

This may give rise to the suspicion that Hyde Clarke was no more than a spokesman for the railway interests, inventing arguments to justify unlimited scope for their activities. That there is some substance in this is undeniable: Hyde Clarke was writing *ex parte* and did not attempt to conceal the fact. Yet this in itself does not mean that his writings can be treated as mere propaganda. The results which Hyde Clarke presented in *Physical Economy* could not have been reached without extended research and computation; better propaganda could have been produced with less effort. It would seem more reasonable simply to see Hyde Clarke as an engineer with a somewhat unusual cast of mind who on the one hand was led by his mathematical and scientific studies to a lasting interest in the phenomena of cycles and their possible economic implications and on the other, by his railway interests to attempt a pioneer account of the real processes which railway investment involved.

Writing in the boom conditions of 1846, the view which Hyde Clarke took of the effects of railway investment at the time was certainly unduly optimistic. While those effects have been a subject of some controversy among economic historians, few if any would now suggest that investment in railways did not contribute in some measure to the crisis of 1847. Nevertheless, writers like Gary Hawke have stressed that time lags in railway-investment outlays at this period ensured that much of it was contracyclical, while spending on maintenance was little affected by trade conditions (Hawke, 1970, pp. 363-73). So the results of modern research do afford some support for Hyde Clarke's defence of investment in railways.

## V

In conclusion, we may return to the question posed at the beginning of this paper—how far can Hyde Clarke be properly regarded as a precursor of Kondratieff, and indeed of more recent long-wave theorists?

If we look first at this from the point of view of the perception and measurement of the cycle, it seems that there is a strong case for regarding Hyde Clarke as genuinely anticipating later presenters of the long-wave hypothesis. At a time when only a few thinkers outside the mainstream of contemporary political economy had even grasped the concept of a decennial cycle, Hyde Clarke made the intellectual leap involved in realising that this might only be part of a larger cycle. He followed this up with considerable empirical research as far as the distinctly sketchy data available to him would allow and succeeded in working out the basic chronology in a manner which later and more sophisticated research has not contradicted. This alone should have been enough to earn Hyde Clarke a more prominent place in the history of economic thought than he has so far been conceded.

On the more specific question of a comparison between the work of Hyde Clarke and that of Kondratieff, there is first of all a noticeable resemblance between their views on periodic movements in the economic and other spheres. In 1924 Kondratieff published a paper entitled "On the Notion of Economic Statics, Dynamics and Fluctuations," a section of which appeared in an English translation in the following year (Kondratieff, 1925).[11] Comparatively little attention has been paid to this article in the West, probably because of the very general terms in which the translated section was cast. In it he divided dynamic processes "into the evolutionary (or nonreversible) processes on the one hand, and the wave-like or fluctuating one the other.... By "wave-like" or "fluctuating" processes are meant processes of variation which are changing their direction in the course of time and are subject to repetition and reversion.... The conceptions of reversible and nonreversible processes, as well as those of statics and dynamics, belong, strictly speaking, to the domain of natural science in the narrower sense of the word, such as physics, chemistry and biology.... But if the necessary caution is exercised in making use of the conceptions in economics, there would appear to be no obstacles to their application in this field as well; and the use of the conceptions of reversible and nonreversible processes in economics may be looked upon as an application of a general idea to a specific class of cases. Attentive empirical, and especially statistical, analysis shows, further, that there exist both regular and irregular reversible processes. Regular processes in turn, may be either seasonal or cyclical. As to cycles, the processes may again be different"—which leads Kondratieff to the identification of the various types of cycles (Kondratieff, 1925, pp. 579-81).

All this casts light on the way in which Kondratieff thought about the problem of the long waves. Similarities with the mind-set which Hyde Clarke had displayed in his 1838 and 1847 writings are apparent. There is the same central concern with periodicity, with "wave-like fluctuations," the same recognition that these occur in the domains of both the natural and the social sciences, and the same realisation that in economic activity more than one cycle can be identified. Turning to the question of the causation of the cycle, we can again note a resemblance between the writings of Hyde Clarke and Kondratieff, in that both were distinctly cautious and reticent in what they wrote on this point.

Hyde Clarke came no closer to a definitive statement about it than his comment that "Mr. Mackenzie has alluded to the shifting or oscillation of the magnetic poles in connection with the periods of the weather, and my own impressions and observations go far to persuade me that the great causes of the phenomena manifested in the seasons and the harvests at present are referable to fluctuations in the electromagnetic condition of this globe" (Clarke, 1847b, p. 9).

In his paper "The Long Waves in Economic Life," which has become the version of his work most familiar to Western economists, Kondratieff rejected the idea that long waves "are conditioned by casual extra economic circumstances and events" but did not go beyond saying that "in asserting the existence of long waves and in denying that they arise out of random causes, we are also of the opinion that the long waves arise out of causes which are inherent in the essence of the capitalistic economy" (Kondratieff, 1935, 1944, pp. 41-2).

After penetrating beyond the caution and reticence which both authors displayed in formulating their hypotheses, a fundamental difference between them is apparent in that ultimately Hyde Clarke's explanation of the long cycle was exogenous, whereas Kondratieff's was endogenous. The essence of Hyde Clarke's concept of "Physical Economy" was that "the operation of physical phenomena as affecting mankind and society" must be taken into account by economists as well as "the moral laws which influence society" and which formed the subject matter of political economy as he knew it. As to the mechanisms by which physical phenomena affected economic activity, he never committed himself to any single and simple hypothesis and his thinking on this seemed to become more tentative in his later years.

Here Hyde Clarke's approach is in notable contrast to that of Jevons, whose belief in the truth of his sun-spot explanation of decennial crises seemed to grow ever stronger, and who to the end of his life was "sufficiently convinced of the truth of the theory though it may not be possible at present to meet every difficulty" (Black, 1977, Vol. V, p. 194). Hyde Clarke, on the other hand, was sceptical of the value of sun-spot research: "instead of assisting the economical investigation or the meteorological discussion, it had rather interfered with our obtaining clear results," he argued. This was because "in all these discussions with regard to sun-spots, periods had been laid out almost in some cases like minutes and seconds" (Clarke, 1884a, p. 66), while in a situation where so many disturbing factors were involved, such precision was not to be expected in cause and effect sequences.

In the papers which he presented to the British Association between 1884 and 1887 and which are fully discussed in Professor Henderson's article (1992a), Hyde Clarke made clear that, partly because of innovations affecting the relative prices and transport costs of industrial and agricultural products, the conditions of trade in the later nineteenth century were very different from those which had existed in its earlier years, and the growth of international exchange reduced the importance of fluctuations in the yield of single crops. Yet even apart from this, "it was the interference of the larger cycles...which would prevent them from predicting so readily as some persons thought what would be the incidents of agriculture and industry all over the world, or in any one region" (Clarke, 1884a, p. 67). So Hyde Clarke's belief that there were at least two cycle patterns observable in the price data led him to think that "it would always be beyond their power absolutely to predict what the result would be;" but all these reservations did not lead him to doubt that there was a long cycle in economic activity and that it had an exogenous, physical cause.

In the paper on "Major Economic Cycles" which he first read before the Economic Institute in Moscow in 1926, but of which an English translation was not available until 1984, Kondratieff "set forth briefly...a first attempt—a first hypothesis—to explain those cycles" (Kondratieff, 1984, p. 89). Central to this explanation was the idea "that the material basis for the long cycles is the wear and tear, replacement and increase in those basic capital goods requiring a long period of time and tremendous investments for their production." (According to Kondratieff, "these include such capital goods as big construction projects, the building of major railroads, the construction of canals, big land-improvement projects, etc."). "*The replacement and expansion of the fund of these goods does not take place smoothly but in spurts, and the long waves in economic conditions are another expression of that*" (Kondratieff, 1984, pp. 92-93, emphasis in original).

Kondratieff went on to argue "that the dynamics of the long cycles possess an inner regularity. Therefore, strictly speaking, we cannot regard this or that link of the cycle as the cause of the whole cycle. We can only say that the rhythm of the long cycles reflects the rhythm in the process of the expansion of society's basic capitalist goods" (Kondratieff, 1984, p. 99).

Thus Kondratieff offered an explanation of the "rhythm of the long cycles" which traced its source to major capital projects such as railroads—those very projects which Hyde Clarke had sought to show were only passively involved because the rhythm of long cycles came from exogenous physical factors. It follows from this that Schumpeter's attribution to Hyde Clarke of "a striking anticipation of the major cycles or spans of later days, especially of Kondratieff's long waves" has to be interpreted with caution. So far as the concept of the long wave and its dating are concerned, Hyde Clarke did indeed anticipate Kondratieff; so far as its causation is concerned, he did not.

However, if we extend comparison beyond the work of Kondratieff himself to the many other research studies of the long wave phenomenon which have been made more recently, the case appears somewhat differently. On the basis of such research, J.J. van Duijn has recently suggested that "Two different long cycles...appear to exist: one, a Kondratieff price cycle whose course is determined by discontinuities in the expansion of productive capacity in agriculture and raw material production; the other, a long wave in industrial production, which results from fluctuations in innovations over time and the way in which these innovations give rise to the establishment of growth sectors" (van Duijn, 1983, p 91). If we accept this view, it would seem possible to regard Hyde Clarke's work (although based on product yields rather than productive capacity in agriculture) as anticipating the idea of the first of these two types of long cycle, if not also the second.

## ACKNOWLEDGMENT

The author is Emeritus Professor of Economics, Queen's University of Belfast. He is indebted to Mrs. J. Wright for valuable research assistance in connection with an earlier unpublished version of this paper, prepared in 1979-80. He would like also to thank Professor James P. Henderson for many useful suggestions and for allowing him to see an advance copy of his paper on Hyde Clarke; Dr. Nigel F. Allington and Dr. J.W. Taylor of the University of Wales Institute of Science and Technology, Cardiff, for advice and assistance in regard to John Rooke and to early English railway development; his colleague, Dr. Alun Davies, of Queen's University, Belfast, for bringing to his attention the interest in periodicity among horologists and astronomers in England in the 1830's; Dr. Joyce Brown, of Imperial College, London, for assistance on the question of Hyde Clarke's Indian career; and participants in the discussion when this paper was read at the History of Economic Thought Conference in Manchester, England in September 1987, whose comments prompted several improvements in it. He also gratefully acknowledges the helpful comments of three anonymous referees for this volume.

## NOTES

1.   For an example of semi-popular literature on the subject, see Shuman and Rosenau (1972), and for a Marxist interpretation, Mandel (1975 and 1980). Perhaps the most comprehensive recent treatment is van Duijn (1983).

2.  The article was reprinted in Jevons (1884, pp. 221-243). Hyde Clarke had been known to Jevons since at least 1871, but their first exchange of views was on a very different topic, the geographical distribution of intellectual qualities (cf. Black, 1977, Vol. III, p. 243).

Although Hyde Clarke objected to being called "Doctor" by Jevons, he frequently appended the letters D.C.L. to his name. However, he is not included as a Doctor of Civil Law in the alumni lists of any of the British universities of his time, nor have I been able to discover any evidence that he held the rank of Colonel in any army.

3.  The notice in the *Annual Register* refers to "Hyde Clarke Nyndeen" but it has not proved possible to find any explanation for or corroboration of this curious additional name.

4.  Boase (1892/1965, Vol. I, p. 676) describes Hyde Clarke as "son of H. Clarke of Sandford House." This may well have been the same Sandford Manor House which Baedeker listed among "famous old houses of Chelsea," noting that Addison occasionally resided there (Baedeker, 1902, p. 380). This, like a number of other points in Hyde Clarke's biography, seems to suggest that his background was one of some affluence.

5.  I am indebted to the Assistant Curator of the Royal Engineers Museum, Brompton Barracks, Chatham, Kent, who checked through the Royal Engineers Lists on my behalf for Hyde Clarke's name and concluded "it is safe to say that he was not a Royal Engineer" (Letter dated 18 February 1980). See also Duncan (1877, pp. 41-51, 82).

6.  Lonsdale's actual words on the connection between Rooke and Hyde Clarke were: "For many years Rooke had been an observer; the railway interests made him an author on geology. Mr Hyde Clarke, the projector of a railway across Morecambe Bay, had induced Rooke to survey and report of the practicability of effecting that object: and this circumstance gave rise to a long discussion on the nature and influence of tidal action in sedimentary disposition" (Lonsdale, 1872, p. 256).

7.  I am indebted to the Archivist of the National Westminister Bank (into which the London and County Bank was ultimately absorbed), the Institute of Bankers, Professor R.S. Sayers and Dr. A.B. Cramp for having patiently dealt with my enquiries about Hyde Clarke's supposed connection with the London and County Bank; all agreed that there is no evidence for it. (See Gregory, 1936, Vol. I, pp. 322-91.)

8.  India Office Records, Railway and Telegraph Department 1847-1858, [2/ L/PWD/2/4]—Northern Bengal—Electric Telegraphs and Railways, Letters 133, 235, 345, 528. I am indebted to Mr. T. Thomas of the India Office Records section, Foreign and Commonwealth Office, London, for these references.

9.  Information kindly supplied by Mr. Peter W. Evans, Secretary of the Newspaper Press Fund, London.

10.  I am grateful to Professor James P. Henderson for drawing my attention to this reference.

11.  The chronology of Kondratieff's papers and their translations into German and English is fully set out in Garvy (1943).

# REFERENCES

Ambirajan, S. 1978. *Classical Political Economy and British Policy in India.* Cambridge, England: Cambridge University Press.

*The Annual Register: A Review of Public Events at Home and Abroad for the Year 1895.* 1896. London: Longmans, Green & Co.

Baedeker, Karl. 1902. *London and its Environs.* Leipzig: Baedeker.

Bennett, J.A. 1980. "George Biddell Airy and Horology." *Annals of Science* 37: 269-85.

Black, R.D. Collison, ed. 1977. *Papers and Correspondence of William Stanley Jevons* Vol. III: Correspondence, 1863-1872; Vol. IV: Correspondence, 1873-1878; Vol. V: Correspondence, 1879-1882. London: Macmillan.

Boase, Henry. 1892/1965. *Modern English Biography.* 6 vol. London: Frank Cass. (Originally published 1892).

[Brewster, David]. 1818. "An Account of the System of the Weather of the British Islands, Discovered by Lieut. George Mackenzie." *Blackwood's Edinburgh Magazine* IV(October): 84-7.

Clarke, Hyde? 1838. "On the Mathematical Law of the Cycle." *The Railway Magazine and Annals of Science* V(November): 378-80.

Clarke, Hyde. 1838. "On the Political Economy and Capital of Joint-Stock Banks." *The Railway Magazine and Annals of Science*, IV, no. xxvii, 288-93, no. xxviii, 360-62.

Clarke, Hyde. 1846. *Theory of Investment in Railway Companies.* London: John Weale.

————. 1847a. "Contribution to the Discussion on G.B. Wheeler Jackson's paper, "Description of the Great North Holland Canal," read February 9, 1847. *Minutes of Proceedings of the Institution of Civil Engineers* 6: 112, 118, 131.

————. 1847b. *Physical Economy: A Preliminary Inquiry into the Physical Laws governing the periods of Famines and Panics.* NP.

————. 1847c. *Practical and Theoretical Considerations on the Management of Railways in India.* London.

————. 1865. "On a Form of Savings Banks among the Christians of Asia Minor." *Journal of the [Royal] Statistical Society* 28: 321-3.

————. 1878. "On the Debts of Sovereign and Quasi-Sovereign States, owing to Foreign Countries." *Journal of the [Royal] Statistical Society* 41: 299-347.

————. 1878-79. "Contribution to the Discussion on J. Purser Griffith's paper, 'The Improvement of the Bar of Dublin Harbour by Artificial Scour,' read May 20, 1879." *Minutes of Proceedings of the Institution of Civil Engineers* 58: 126-7.

————. 1881. "The English Stations in the Hill Regions of India: their Value and Importance, with some Statistics of their Products and Trade." *Journal of the [Royal] Statistical Society* 44(September): 529-63.

————. 1884. Discussion on J.H. Poynting's paper, "A Comparison of the Fluctuations in the Price of Wheat and in the Cotton and Silk Imports into Great Britain." *Journal of the [Royal] Statistical Society* 47(March): 65-68.

————. 1884b. *Morecambe Bay Railway and Reclamation in 1836 and 1883*. London: Lord and Gill.

Coats, A.W. 1968. "The Origins and Early Development of the Royal Economic Society." *Economic Journal* 78(June): 349-371.

de Foville, Alfred M. 1879. "Les Tâches du Soleil et les Crises Commerciales." *L'Economiste Français* (15 Fevrier): pp. 191-3.

Dubbey, J.M. 1978. *The Mathematical Work of Charles Babbage*. Cambridge: Cambridge University Press.

Duncan, F. 1877. *The English in Spain*. London: John Murray.

Ekelund, Robert B., and Hérbert, Robert F. 1975. *A History of Economic Theory and Method*. New York: McGraw Hill.

Garvy, George. 1943. "Kondratieff's Theory of Long Cycles." *Review of Economic Statistics* 25(November): 203-220.

Gregory, Theodore E. 1936. *The Westminster Bank through a Century*. London: Westminster Bank.

Hawke, Gary R. 1970. *Railways and Economic Growth in England and Wales 1840-1870*. Oxford: Clarendon Press.

Henderson, James P. 1992a. "Astronomy, Astrology and Business Cycles: Hyde Clarke's Contribution." *Research in the History of Economic Thought and Methodology*, 9.

————. 1992b. "Hyde Clarke's Publications...," *Research in the History of Economic Thought and Methodology*, 9.

Henderson, W.O. 1934. *The Lancashire Cotton Famine 1861-65*. Manchester: Manchester University Press.

Hudson, Derek, and Luckhurst, K.W.1954. *The Royal Society of Arts 1754-1954*. London: John Murray.

Jenks, Leland H. 1927/1963. *The Migration of British Capital to 1975*. London: Nelson. (First edition, 1927, New York: A Knopf).

Jevons, W. Stanley. 1884. *Investigations in Currency and Finance*, edited by H.S. Foxwell. London: Macmillan and Co.

————. 1977. *Papers and Correspondence of W.S. Jevons*, Vol. IV. London: Macmillan.

Kendall, Maurice George. 1948. *The Advanced Theory of Statistics* (2nd ed.). London: C. Griffin and Co.

Kondratieff, Nikolai D. 1925. "The Static and the Dynamic View of Economics." *Quarterly Journal of Economics* 39(August): 575-83.

————. 1935/1944. "The Long Waves in Economic Life." (Translated from the German by W.F. Stolper). *Review of Economic Statistics* 17(November): 105-115. (Reprinted in American Economic Association. *Readings in Business Cycle Theory*. Philadelphia: Blakiston, pp. 20-42.)

————. 1984. *The Long Wave Cycle*. (Translated by Guy Daniels.) New York: Richardson and Snyder.

Link, Raymond G. 1959. *English Theories of Economic Fluctuations, 1815-1848*. New York: Columbia University Press.

Lonsdale, Henry. 1872. *The Worthies of Cumberland: The Howards, Rev. R. Matthews, John Rooke, Captain Joseph Huddart*. London: Routledge.

Mackenzie, George. 1818. *The System of the Weather of the British Islands: discovered in 1816 and 1817 from a Journal commencing November 1802.* Edinburgh: W. Aitken.

————. 1829. *Manual of the Weather for the Year MDCCCXXX.* Edinburgh: W Blackwood.

Mandel, Ernest. 1975. *Late Capitalism.* London: New Left Books.

————. 1980. *Long Waves of Capitalist Development: the Marxist interpretation.* Cambridge: Cambridge University Press.

Mitchell, Wesley C. 1930. *Business Cycles, The Problem and its Setting.* New York: National Bureau of Economic Research.

Moon, G. Washington, ed. 1891. *Men and Women of the Time: A Dictionary of Contemporaries* (13th ed.). London: Routledge.

Ridley, Jasper G. 1970. *Lord Palmerston.* London: Constable.

Sanders, Lloyd C. (ed.). 1887. *Celebrities of the Century.* London: Cassell.

Schumpeter, Joseph A. 1939. *Business Cycles.* 2 vols. New York: McGraw Hill.

————. 1954. *A History of Economic Analysis.* London: G. Allen and Unwin.

Seligman, Edwin R. A. 1903. "On Some Neglected British Economists." *Economic Journal* 13: 335-63, 511-35.

Shuman, James B. and Rosenau, David. 1972. *The Kondratieff Wave.* New York: World Publishing Company.

Simmons, J. 1978. *The Railway in England and Wales, 1830-1914.* Leicester: Leicester University Press.

van Duijn, Jacob J. 1983. *The Long Wave in Economic Life.* London: G. Allen and Unwin.

Wright, William. 1884. *The Empire of the Hittites.* London: James Nisbet and Co.

# HYDE CLARKE'S PUBLICATIONS:
## PAPERS PRESENTED AT MEETINGS OF
## SCIENTIFIC SOCIETIES, AND OTHER
## NOTES AND LETTERS OF INTEREST

James P. Henderson

---

## I. *NATIONAL UNION CATALOG* LISTINGS
### (hereafter N.U.C.)

*Colonization, Defence, and Railways in our Indian Empire.* London: J. Weale, 1857.

*Contributions to Railway Statistics, in 1845.* London: J. Weale, 1846.

*Contributions to Railway Statistics, in 1846, 1847 & 1848.* London: J. Weale, 1849.

*Dante and Italian Colonies in England in the Time of Chaucer.* 1892.

Research in the History of Economic Thought and Methodology, Volume 9, pages 59-72.
Copyright © 1992 by JAI Press Inc.
All rights of reproduction in any form reserved.
ISBN: 1-55938-428-X

"The Early History of the Mediterranean Populations, &c., in Their Migrations and Settlements Illustrated from Autonomous Coins, Gems, Inscriptions, &c." *Transactions of the Royal Historical Society*, n.s., vol. 10: 134-202. London, 1882.

*The Early History of the Mediterranean Populations, &c., in Their Migrations and Settlements. Illustrated from Autonomous Coins, Gems, Inscriptions, &c.* London: Trubner & Co. 1882.

*Ephesus; Being a Lecture Delivered at the Smyrna Literary and Scientific Institution.* Smyrna: G. Green (etc., etc.), 1863.

*Examination of the Legend of Atlantis in Reference to Protohistoric Communication With America.* London: Longmans, Green & Co., 1885.

"Examination of the Legend of Atlantis in Reference to Protohistoric Communication with America." *Transactions of the Royal Historical Society*, n.s., vol. 3: London, 1886, 1-46.

*Examination of the Legend of Atlantis in Reference to Proto Historic Communication with America.* London: Longmans, Green & Co., 1886.

*Excerpts From Various Journals, etc.* Constantinople, 1861. Contents: "The Imperial Ottoman Smyrna and Aidin Railway," "The Inhabitants of Asia Minor," "On the Propagation of Mining and Metallurgy," "On Public Instruction in Turkey," "On the Supposed Extinction of the Turks and Increase of the Christians in Turkey," "Discussion From the Insurance Record."

*The Geography of Great Britain.* (Society for the Diffusion of Useful Knowledge). London: R. Baldwin, (1850?).

*The Globe Dictionary of the English Language as it is Spoken and Written.* Boston: Aldine Book Publishing Company, 1887.

*Gold in India.* (A paper read before the Indian Section of the Society of Arts.) London: Effingham Wilson, 1881.

*A Grammar of the English Tongue, Spoken and Written; for self-teaching and for schools.* London: J. Weale, 1853.

*A Grammar of the English Tongue, Spoken and Written; for self-reading and for schools.* London: J. Weale, 1859.

*A Grammar of the English Tongue, Spoken and Written, With an Introduction to the Study of Comparative Philology.* London: Virtue; New York: Virtue and Yorston, ca. 1860.

*A Grammar of the English Tongue, Spoken and Written, With an Introduction to the Study of Comparative Philology.* London: Lockwood & Co., 1874.

*Grammar of the English Tongue, Spoken & Written, With an Introduction to the study of Comparative Philology.* 4th edition. London: J. Weale, 1879.

*A Help to Memory in Learning Turkish.* Constantinople, 1862.

*Himalayan Origin and Connection of the Magyar and Ugrian.* London: Harrison and Sons, 1877.

"The Iberian and Belgian Influence and Epochs in Britain." *Transactions of the Royal Historical Society*, n.s., vol. 1: pp. 158-192. London, 1883.

*The Imperial Ottoman Smyrna & Aidin Railway, its Position and Prospects.* Constantinople, Koehler Brothers (etc., etc.), 1861.

*The Khita and Khita-Peruvian Epoch: Khita, Hamath, Hittite, Canaanite, Etruscan, Peruvian, Mexican, etc.* London: N. Trubner & Co., 1877.

*Life of Richard Trevithick...-[Life of George Stephenson...].* n.p., 1848?.

*Memoir on the Comparative Grammar of Egyptian, Coptic, & Ude.* London: Trubner & Co., 1873.

*Metropolitan Fire Assurance and Fire Police.* London: printed by Kelly & Co., 1856. (First published in the *Building News*, n.d.).

*A New and Comprehensive Dictionary of the English Language; as Spoken and Written.* London: Weale, 1855.

*A New and Comprehensive Dictionary of the English Language; as Spoken and Written.* 2nd ed., corrected. London: J. Weale, 1861.

*A New and Comprehensive Dictionary of the English Language; as Spoken and Written.* 5th ed., London: Virtue & Co. and New York: Virtue and Yorston, 1869.

*A New and Comprehensive Dictionary of the English Language; as Spoken and Written.* 7th ed. London: Lockwood & Co., 1872.

*A New and Comprehensive Dictionary of the English Language.* London: Lockwood & Co., 1873?.

*New and Comprehensive Grammar and Dictionary of the English Language, as Spoken and Written.* 8th ed., London: C. Lockwood & Co., 1881.

*New and Comprehensive Grammar and Dictionary of the English Language, as Spoken and Written.* Philadelphia: G.T. Stockdale, 1855.

"Notes on the Ligurians, Aquitanians, and Belgians." *Transactions of the Royal Historical Society*, n.s. vol. 1: 62-69. London: 1883.

"Note on the Order of Domesday Book." *Domesday Commemoration*, Vol. 2, edited by P.E. Dove. 1891.

*On Cold Harbours.* London, 1859.

*On Copper Smelting.* London: Mining Journal Office, 1858.

"On Geological Surveys: An Address, Delivered Before the Geologist's Association, February 1859." London, 1859.

"On Public Instruction in Turkey." *Journal of the Statistical Society of London.* London, 1867.

"On the Epoch of Hittite, Khita, Hamath, Canaanite, Lydian, Etruscan, Peruvian, Mexican, etc.." *Transactions of the Royal Historical Society*, n.s., vol. 6: 1-85. London: 1877.

"On the Settlement of Britain and Russia by the English Races." *Transactions of the Royal Historical Society*, n.s., vol. 7: 249-308. London: 1878.

*On the Statistics of Fire Assurance.* London: 1853?.

"On the Turkish Survey of Hungary & its Relation to Domesday Book." *Domesday Commemoration, 1888-1891*, Vol. 1, edited by P.E. Dove.

*Physical Economy: A Preliminary Inquiry into the Physical Laws Governing the Periods of Famines and Panics.* n.p., 1847.

"The Picts and Preceltic Britain." *Transactions of the Royal Historical Society*, n.s., vol. 3: 243-280. London: 1886.

*Practical and Theoretical Considerations on the Management of Railways in India.* London: 1847?.

"Preface." *Domesday Commemoration, 1888-1891*, vol. 1, edited by P.E. Dove.

*Researches in Prehistoric and Protohistoric Comparative Philology, Mythology, and Archaeology, in Connection with the Origin of Culture in America and the Accad or Sumerian Families.* London: N. Trubner & Co., 1875.

*Serpent and Siva Worship and Mythology, in Central America, Africa, and Asia.* London: N. Trubner & Co., 1877.

*Serpent and Siva Worship and Mythology, in Central America, Africa, and Asia. And the Origin of Serpent Worship.* Two Treatises by Hyde Clarke and C. Staniland Wake. Edited by Alexander Wilder. New York: J.W. Bouton, 1877.

*A Short Handbook of the Comparative Philology of the English, Anglo-Saxon, Frisian, Flemish or Dutch, Low or Platt Dutch, High Dutch or German, Danish, Swedish, Icelandic, Latin, Italian, French, Spanish, and Portuguese Tongues.* London: J. Weale, 1859.

*A Short Handbook of the Comparative Philology of the English, Anglo-Saxon, Frisian, Flemish or Dutch, Low or Platt Dutch, High Dutch or German, Danish, Swedish, Icelandic, Latin, Italian, French, Spanish and Portuguese Tongues.* 2nd ed. London: Lockwood, 1873.

*Sovereign and Quasi-Sovereign States: Their Debts to Foreign Countries.* London: E. Wilson, 1878. (Reprinted from the *Journal of the Statistical Society*, June 1878.)

*Sovereign and Quasi-Sovereign States: Their Debts to Foreign Countries.* 2nd ed. London: E. Wilson, 1878. (Reprinted from the *Journal of the Statistical Society*, June 1878.)

*The Statistics of Belgian Railway Traffic in 1844 and 1845.* London: 1846.

*The Statistics of Fire Assurance.* London: Land and Building News, 1854.

*The Statistics of Fire Assurance.* London: Land and Building News, 1855?.

*Theory of Investment in Railway Companies.* First published in the fourth volume of the *Railway Register.* London: J. Weale, 1846.

*The Turanian Epoch of the Romans, as also of the Greeks, Germans and Anglo-Saxons, in Relation to the Early History of the World.* Printed for private circulation, London: 1879.

"The Turanian Epoch of the Romans, as also of the Greeks, Germans, and Anglo-Saxons, in Relation to the Early History of the World." *Transactions of the Royal Historical Society*, n.s., vol. 8: 172-222. London: 1880.

*Two Articles on the Gage Question, and on the Performance of the Great Western Leviathan Locomotive.* London: J. Weale, 1846. (Reprinted from the *Railway Register*, no. XX.)

"The Warings, or Waranghians." *The Levant Quarterly Review* 1861(2): 147-166. Pera.

## II.  JOHN WEALE ARCHITECTURAL AND ENGINEERING LIBRARY

(From an advertisement appearing in *Theory of Investment in Railway Companies*. London: J. Weale, 1846.) (First published in the fourth volume of the *Railway Register*.)

*Contributions to Railway Statistics in 1845*. (Also cited in *N.U.C.*)

*Hydrostatic and Hydraulic Docks of the United States*.

*Engineering of Holland. On the Construction of Dykes. From Dutch and Original Authorities*.

*Two Articles on the Gage Question. With Experiments on the Great Western Locomotive*. (Also cited in *N.U.C.*)

*Astronomical Discoveries of La Place*. From the French of M. Arago. Translated by Hyde Clarke With Notes.

*Lectures of Colour*. With Engravings.

*Life of Watt, and History of the Steam Engine*. By M. Arago. Translated by Hyde Clarke.

*Notes on Railways. Railway Traffic and Statistics. The Gage Question. The Great Western Engine*.

*The Theory of Railway Investments explained, on Practical and Politico-Economical Principles*. (Also cited in *N.U.C.*)

*The Railway Register*. (Volumes I, II, and III, for 1844-5-6.) (Also cited in *N.U.C.*)

## III.  JOURNAL OF THE (ROYAL) STATISTICAL SOCIETY

1865

"Supposed Extinction of the Turks, and Increase of the Christians in Turkey." Vol. XXVIII (June): 261-293. (Read before the Statistical Society, April, 18, 1865.)

"Savings Banks among Christians in Asia Minor." Vol. XXVIII (June): 321-323.

## 1867

"On Public Instruction in Turkey." Vol. XXX (December): 502-534. (Read before the Statistical Society, November 19, 1867). (Reprinted as a pamphlet, see *N.U.C.*)

## 1871

"Geographical Distribution of Intellectual Qualities in England." Vol. XXXIV (September): 357-373. (Read before the Statistical Society, June 1871.)

## 1878

"On the Debts and Liabilities of Sovereign and Quasi-Sovereign States Due to Foreign Creditors." Vol. XLI (June): 299-341; discussion of the paper pp. 342-347. (Read before the Statistical Society, 16 April, 1878.) (Also presented before the 1877 meeting of Section F of the B.A.A.S.; also reprinted as a pamphlet, see *N.U.C.*)

Discussion of a paper by A. J. Mundella, "What are the conditions on which the Commercial and Manufacturing Supremacy of Great Britain depend...?" Vol. XLI: 123-124.

## 1881

"On the Progress of the English Stations in the Hill Regions of India; their value and importance, with some Statistics of their Products and Trade." Vol. XLIV (September): 528-563, discussion of the paper pp. 563-573. (Read before the Statistical Society, 21 June, 1881.) (Also presented before the 1880 meeting of Section F of the B.A.A.S.)

## 1884

Clarke's contribution to the discussion of a paper by J. H. Poynting, "A Comparison of the Fluctuations in the Price of Wheat and in Cotton and Silk Imports into Great Britain." Vol. XLVII (March): 65-68.

## IV. PROCEEDINGS OF THE INSTITUTION OF CIVIL ENGINEERS

Discussion on a paper by G. B. Wheeler Jackson, "Description of the Great North Holland Canal." Vol. VII (1847): 112, 118, 131.

Discussion on a paper by J. Purser Griffith, "The Improvement of the Bar of Dublin Harbour by Artificial Scour." Vol. LVIII (1878-79): IV: 126-127.

# V.  TRANSACTIONS OF THE ROYAL HISTORICAL SOCIETY

1877

"...On the Epoch: Khita, Hamath, Hittite, Canaanite, Etruscan, Peruvian, Mexican, etc." Vol. 6: 1-85. (Probably also reprinted as a pamphlet with the title, "The Khita and Khita-Peruvian Epoch: Khita, Hamath, Hittite, Canaanite, Etruscan, Peruvian, Mexican, etc." see *N.U.C.* Probably also presented at the 1877 meeting of the B.A.A.S., under the title: "On Hittite, Khita, Hamath, Canaanite, Lydian, Etruscan, Peruvian, Mexican, &c.")

1878

"On the Settlement of Britain and Russia by the English Races." Vol. 7: 249-308.

1880

"The Turanian Epoch of the Romans, as also of the Greeks, Germans and Anglo-Saxons, in Relation to the Early History of the World." Vol. 8: 172-222. (Also reprinted as a pamphlet "printed for private circulation," see *N.U.C.*)

1882

"The Early History of the Mediterranean Populations, &c., in Their Migrations and Settlements Illustrated from Autonomous Coins, Gems, Inscriptions, &c.." Vol. 10: 134-202. (Also reprinted as a pamphlet, see *N.U.C.*. May also have been presented as a series of papers and an exhibition at the 1881 meeting of the B.A.A.S. under the titles: "On the Numerical and Philological Relations of the Hebrew, Phoenician, or Canaanitic Alphabet and the Language of the Khita Inscriptions," "The Early Colonisation of Cyprus and Attica and its Relation to Babylonia," and "Exhibition of Stone Implements From Asia Minor.")

1883

"Notes on the Ligurians, Aquitanians, and Belgians." Vol. 1: pp. 62-69.

1884

"The Iberian and Belgian Influence and Epochs in Britain," Vol. 1: 158-192.

**1886**

"The Picts and Pre-Celtic Britain." Vol. 3: 243-280. (Also presented at the 1885 meeting of the B.A.A.S.)

"Examination of the Legend of Atlantis in Reference to Protohistoric Communication With America." Vol. 3: 1-46. (Also reprinted as a pamphlet, see *N.U.C.*)

## VI.   THE RAILWAY MAGAZINE AND ANNALS OF SCIENCE

**1838**

"On the Political Economy and Capital of Joint-stock Banks." New series, Vol. IV, (XXVII): 288-293 and (XXVIII): 360-362.

"Plan for Running Vessels on Canals by Locomotives on the Banks." New series Vol. IV, (XXVIII): 353-355.

Probably also authored: "On the Mathematical Law of the Cycle." New series, Vol V, (XXXIII): 378-380.

"Political Economy of Joint Stock Banks of Circulation." New series, Vol. V, (XXIX): 5-9.

"On the Principles of Administration of Works of Public Enterprise." New series, Vol. V, (XXXV): 528-32.

"On the Threatening State of Geological Phenomena." New series, Vol. V, (XXXVI): 607-09.

"On the Principles of Administration of Works of Public Enterprise." New series, Vol. V(XXXVI): 611-17 (Apparently a second piece on this topic, but not so numbered).

"Observations on the Statistical Law of Births, in opposition to Malthus and Quetelet." New series, Vol. VI(XXXVIII): 129 (Written in the form of a letter to the editor, occupying only half a page).

"On Atoms and Dimorphism." New series, Vol. VI(XXXIX):218-19.

"On a New Method of Printing by Electricity." New Series, Vol. VI(XL).

# VII.  PAPERS PRESENTED AT MEETINGS OF THE B.A.A.S.

*[Section F where noted by (F)]*

## 1864

On the Iberian Population of Asia Minor Anterior to the Greeks.

## 1868

On the Western Asia Minor Coal—and Iron-basins, and on the Geology of the District.

On the Progress of Turkey. (F).

## 1869

On the Want of Statistics on the Question of Mixed Races. (F).

On the Distinction Between Rent and Landtax in India. (F).

On variations in the Rapidity and Rate of Human Thought. (F).

## 1870

Note on the Distribution of Names in Prehistoric Times.

Proposition for a Census of Local Names. (F).

## 1872

On the Ethnological and Philological Relations of the Causasus.

On the Mangnema or Manyema of Dr. Livingstone.

On Polygamy as Affecting Population.

On the Progress of the Through Railway to India.

## 1873

On Prehistoric Names of Weapons.

On the Comparative Chronology of the Migrations of Man in America in Relation to Comparative Philology.

On the Ashantee and Fantee Languages.

On the Report Concerning Bushman Researches of Dr. W.H. Bleck, Ph.D.

On the Influence of Large Centres of Population on Intellectual Manifestation. (F).

On the Progress of the Through Railway to India.

## 1874

On the River-Names and Populations of Hibernia, and their Relation to the Old World and America.

On the Phoenician Inscription of Brazil.

On the Agaw Race in Caucasia, Africa, and South America.

On Circassian and Etruscan.

On the Classification of the Akka and Pygmy Languages of Africa.

## 1875

On Prehistoric Culture in India and Africa.

Further Note on Prehistoric Names of Weapons.

On the Himalayan Origin of the Magyar and Fin Languages.

## 1876
On the Prehistoric Names for Man, Monkey, Lizard &c.

On Hittite, Khita, Hamath, Canaanite, Lydian, Etruscan, Peruvian, Mexican, &c.

On the Part in the Operation of Capital Due to Fixed or Limited Amounts Invested in Trade. (F).

## 1877

On the Debts and Liabilities of Sovereign and Quasi-Sovereign States Due to Foreign Creditors. (F).

## 1878

On the Prehistoric Relations of the Babylonian, Egyptian, and Chinese Characters and Cultures.

## 1879

On the Yarra and the Languages of Australia in Connection With Those of the Mozambique and Portuguese Africa.

On High Africa As the Centre of a White Race.

On Credit as an Asset of a State. (F).

## 1880

On Drum-Signaling in Africa.

On a Manuscript, Perhaps Khita, Discovered by Capt. Gill in Western China.

Recent Doubts on Monosyllabism in Philogical Classification.

On the Pre-Cymric Epoch in Wales.

On the Antiquity of Gesture and Sign Language, and the Origin of Characters and Speech.

On the Discovery of a Bi-Lingual Seal in Cuneiform and Khita.

Further Researches on the Prehistoric Relations of the Babylonian, Chinese and Egyptian Characters, Language and Culture, and Their Connection With Sign and Gesture Language.

On the 'Vei Syllabary' of Liberia, West Africa.

On the Progress of the English Stations in the Hill Regions of India. (F).

## 1881

On the Numerical and Philological Relations of the Hebrew, Phoenician, or Canaanitic Alphabet and the Language of the Khita Inscriptions.

The Early Colonisation of Cyprus and Attica and its Relation to Babylonia.

Exhibition of Stone Implements From Asia Minor.

On the Relation of the Gold Standard in England to the International Money market. (F).

## 1882

The Names Britannia and Hibernia, With Their Iberian Relations.

The Lolo Character of Western China.

On the Formula of Alfred R. Wallace in its Relations to Characters and Alphabets.

On Some Influences Affecting the Progress of our Shipping and Carrying Trade. (F).

## 1883

The Yahgan Indians of Tierra Del Fuego.

The English-Speaking Populations of the World. (F).

The Growth of Barrow-in-Furness, &c. (F).

A Comparison of Morecambe Bay, Barrow-in-Furness, North Lancashire, West Cumberland, &c. in 1836 and 1883.

## 1884

Prospective Prices in Europe, America and Asia. (F).

Observations on the Mexican Zodiac and Astrology.

Notes on Researches as to American Origins.

## 1885

On Depression of Prices and Results of Economy of Production, and on the Prospect of Recovery. (F).

The Picts and Prae-Celtic Britain.

## 1886

The Causes Affecting the Reduction in the Cost of Producing Silver. (F).

Remarks on the Principles Applicable to Colonial Loans and Finance. (F).

## 1887

Effective Consumption and Effective Prices in Their Economical and Statistical Relations. (F).

## 1889

The Increase in Europe and America of Nominal or Fictitious Capital. (F).

The Right or Property in Trees on Another's Land, as an Origin of Rights of Property.

# VIII.  OTHER LETTERS AND NOTES OF INTEREST

In support of Jevons's November 14, 1878 sunspot paper, Clarke submitted a letter: "The Drought," *Nature*, Vol. 19 (November 21, 1878): 53.

Report of a meeting of the Society of Arts, includes Clarke's comments on Jevons's sunspot theory of the business cycle and Clarke's contributions, *Nature*, Vol. 19(January 30, 1879): 299-300.

Three letters between Clarke and Jevons in *Papers and Correspondence of William Stanley Jevons*, edited by R. D. Collison Black.

Jevons to Clarke, 24 June, 1871. (Letter number 339, Vol. III: 243-244).

Clarke to Jevons, 31 August, 1878. (Letter number 541. Vol. IV: 274-276).

Clarke to Jevons, 18 November 1878. (Letter number 560. Vol. IV: 295-296).

Letter of Hyde Clarke to Sir James C. Melville, written from "Simla Railway Office, 42 Basinghall Street, E.C." (London), June 29, 1857. Advocates the building of railways to hill stations in India. India Office Records, London, Ref. L/PWD/2/57.

# USES OF THE TERM "NATURAL" IN ADAM SMITH'S *WEALTH OF NATIONS*

Edward Puro

In *The Wealth of Nations*, Adam Smith (1937) uses the term "natural" in a variety of ways. An analysis of the different usages will be worthwhile for two reasons. First, such an analysis is helpful in evaluating the internal consistency of important portions of Smith's discussion. Second, since the term "natural" is used extensively by various authors in other contexts, it is of general interest to identify and discuss some possible meanings of the term. The present analysis will identify and give examples of eight distinct usages of the term "natural" in *The Wealth of Nations*, and will identify possible inconsistencies in Smith's discussion based on these different usages. The order in which we will discuss these usages has been chosen for ease of exposition only and is unrelated to the order they appear in the book.

Research in the History of Economic Thought and Methodology, Volume 9, pages 73-86.
Copyright © 1992 by JAI Press Inc.
ISBN: 1-55938-428-X

The first use of the term natural is to *denote the innate characteristics of a thing or person.* This can be expressed in two ways. A characteristic can be called natural if it is innate, or the innate characteristic can be identified as the nature of the thing or person. This is straightforward when Smith discusses the innate characteristics of some inanimate object, such as when he refers to the "perishable nature" of corn (p. 494).

More common and potentially troublesome are the cases where Smith applies this concept to mankind and to that part of human behavior embodied in institutions and historical events. In the most acceptable cases of this sort, he uses the term without specifying which exact innate characteristics he is referring to. Consider, for example, the following: "Wherever the law allows it, and the nature of the work can afford it, therefore, he will generally prefer the service of slaves to that of freemen" (p. 365). Here, since he does not identify which characteristics he means, the modern reader can envision any plausible scheme of classifying work by its compatibility with slave labor. The statement's generality thus renders it acceptable.

There are a number of comparable examples, including "If their trade should be of such a nature that one of them exported to the other nothing but native commodities..." (p. 456). The most extreme examples of references to unspecified characteristics are those in which Smith refers merely to the nature of things in general. An example is when he refers to the divisions of ancient Greek philosophy as being "perfectly agreeable to the nature of things" (p. 723). Elsewhere he makes the following statement concerning the apparent inability of England to be politically united with her American colonies. "The principal perhaps arise, not from the nature of things, but from the prejudices and opinions of the people both on this and on the other side of the Atlantic" (p. 589).

Problems begin when Smith begins drawing conclusions based on unspecified characteristics that may not agree with the conclusions a modern reader might reach. This has the effect of making Smith's statements appear overly strong. An example of this is, "The station of a farmer besides is, from the nature of things, inferior to that of a proprietor" (p. 371). Even when one understands Smith's usage of inferior, some readers might find basing the relationship on an unspecified innate characteristic, rather than on a particular social framework, say, as a bit stronger than warranted. Another example, in which he discusses the role of the East India Company in India, is the following: "No other sovereigns ever were, or, from the nature of things, ever could be, so perfectly indifferent about the happiness or misery of their subjects..." (p. 710).

In other cases, some readers might find Smith's statements not overly strong, but incorrect. An example occurs when he discusses the plight of the natives of the East and West Indies after their discovery by the Europeans. Smith writes, "These misfortunes, however, seem to have arisen rather from accident than from any thing in the nature of those events themselves" (p. 590). Some modern readers might wish to disagree with Smith about what the nature of those events did in fact entail. Another example is a passage where Smith states that the work menial servants perform "is not of a nature" to repay the expense of their maintenance (p. 639).

Problems of this sort reach their most obvious form when Smith discusses the nature of mankind. To take an example, consider his discussion of the probability of using the various instruments of government: "...yet such, it seems, is the natural insolence of man, that he almost always disdains to use the good instrument, except when he cannot or dare not use the bad one" (p. 751).

A recurring theme that often leads to questionable statements of this sort is the implicit notion that an innate characteristic of individuals is their desire to promote their own self-interest. The rigor with which Smith pursues this idea leads him to proclaim natural a wide variety of behavior which a modern reader, by envisioning other plausible innate characteristics, might consider unnatural. To clarify this point, note that the problem typically encountered in this and the following definition of natural are not due to any ambiguities in the usage itself. They are due to the fact that modern readers, familiar with the social theorizing of the last two centuries, are apt to disagree with Smith about what are and are not the innate characteristics of mankind, and about which of these characteristics are of primary importance in various situations.

Let us postpone discussion of the innate desire to promote one's self-interest until we get to our second definition of natural, for reasons which we will shortly make clear. First, however, it might be wise to bring up a problem that may occur when one considers Smith's discussion of human nature in his earlier work, *The Theory of Moral Sentiments*. As Henry Spiegel explains, "In Smith's ethics, sympathy and the desire for approval cause us 'to restrain our selfish, and to indulge our benevolent effections.' This 'constitutes the perfection of human nature...'" (Spiegel, 1983, p. 229).

This last sentence, which is Spiegel quoting Smith, is remarkable in that it seems to indicate the existence of contradictory innate characteristics both of which are to be considered natural. That is, human nature apparently includes both the innate characteristic of promoting one's self-interest and that of restraining one's attention to self-interest. This raises the problem of determining which aspect of human nature is to be operative at any particular time. Since the issue here is the use of the term "natural" in *The Wealth of Nations* specifically, we will not pursue this idea further. However, it should be noted that if human nature is considered to include contradictory influences, Smith's argument in *The Wealth of Nations* may run into some problems in terms of its internal logic, a point which will be made clear later.

The second usage of the term natural is to *denote behavior that is in accord with the set of innate characteristics that individuals possess*. Clearly these statements could also be interpreted using our first definition to mean that the behavior itself is an innate characteristic. More appealing to the modern reader, however, is the notion that the behavior is natural because it is in accord with some implicit innate attitude or desire. This latter interpretation seems more appealing because, for the modern reader at least, it seems odd to say that a person has the innate characteristic of performing a given action. It seems much more acceptable to say that a person has innate attitudes or desires, which is an idea fully compatible with the developments of modern psychology. Since it is unclear which interpretation Smith had in mind, we will choose the one that seems the most reasonable today. Before considering behavior based on the desire to promote one's self-interest, let's consider behavior based on some other postulated innate characteristics.

For Smith, one innate characteristic individuals possess is the desire to grant authority to various people. Thus, for example, teachers have "that natural authority, which superior virtue and abilities never fail to procure from young people..." (p. 731). This quote is typical of this usage and will therefore stand some explication. First, it is unlikely that the authority in question is to be considered an innate characteristic of teachers. That is, teachers are not seen as being born with natural authority, irrespective of whether young people recognize it or not. Thus, we do not have an instance of the first usage. Second, it seems clear from the text that the authority is natural because young people provide it without it having to be enforced in any way. Thus, the behavior of young people is the crucial factor. Since we have elected to separate actual behavior from the desire to behave in a certain way, with only the latter considered an innate characteristic, we are left with the notion that the authority is natural because the behavior that generates it follows from an innate characteristic of young people.

In another case, Smith postulates a sort of authority which, in contrast to a council of merchants, "naturally over-awes the people, and without force commands their willing obedience" (p. 603). Once again, the aspect of this sort of authority which seems to be associated with its being natural is that it is granted in response to people's innate desire to do so rather than being legislated and enforced.

Along the same lines is the notion that birth and fortune "are the two great sources of personal distinction, and are therefore the principal causes which naturally establish authority and subordination among men" (p. 673). Once again, the point is probably that the authority and subordination are the result of the intrinsic desires of those involved.

Another innate characteristic, besides that of the desire to grant authority in certain situations, is the bestowing of kindness in certain situations. For example: "The common people look upon him with that kindness with which we naturally regard one who approaches somewhat to our own condition, but who, we think, ought to be in a higher" (p. 762). We also find that "Their kindness naturally provokes his kindness" (p. 762).

An example which may or may not be appropriate here is the following: "As soon as writing came into fashion, wise men, or those who fancied themselves such, would naturally endeavor to increase the number of those established and respected maxims..." (p. 724). This may imply that it is human nature to desire to write maxims or, in a generalized sense, to pursue knowledge. On the other hand, it may imply that the maxims are being written for the rewards they bring the writer, in which case we are implying the innate characteristic of desiring to promote one's self-interest.

Let us now consider this most important instance of this use of the term natural, which is succinctly stated in the passage where Smith refers to "The natural effort of every individual to better his own condition..." (p. 508). There are a variety of examples of this idea.

For instance, after discussing the advantages of the home-trade, Smith writes that "upon equal or nearly equal profits, every wholesale merchant naturally prefers the home-trade" (p. 421). Later he states that when a demand for some trade develops, some merchants "naturally turn their capitals towards the principal, and some towards the subordinate branches of it..." (p. 598).

A very important case is the idea that monopolists are acting naturally by undertaking actions that are in accord with their innate desire to promote their own self-interest. Thus, "In all trades, the regular established traders ... naturally combine to raise profits..." (p. 695). A supporting passage, which is really an example of the first usage, is the one in which we find that "monopolizing spirit ... is natural to the directors of a regulated company" (p. 696). This is interesting because it seems to identify an innate characteristic besides the desire to seek one's self-interest as the source of monopolizing behavior, namely, "monopolizing spirit." Rather than pursue this idea, we will assume that monopolizing spirit is itself an artifact of the desire to promote one's self-interest.

This second definition of natural is used in yet another way. Here, Smith implicitly imputes a set of innate beliefs to the reader and then finds that these beliefs lead not to any particular behavior, but to various specific expectations about things or events. This allows him to make statements such as, if an immense capital was divided among an immense number of proprietors, then it was "naturally to be expected, therefore, that folly, negligence, and profusion should prevail in the whole management of their affairs" (p. 703). Observe that this does not mean that the folly itself is necessarily natural, but that our expectations given the facts are. Another example is the passage where he states that "We naturally expect more splendor in the court of a king, than in the mansion-house of a doge or burgomaster" (p. 767). These statements can appear troublesome to modern readers if they do not possess the required set of beliefs which make these expectations natural.

The third usage of the term natural is closely related to the second. Here, "natural" refers to *behavior that is consistent with stated characteristics of the actors, regardless of whether those characteristics are themselves innate or natural.* This presents fewer difficulties for the modern reader than the previous usage because Smith in this case does not go so far as to impute innate characteristics or beliefs. These statements can thus be read as conditional statements, as far as the word natural is concerned, even though Smith does not always present them in this way. Consider the following: "The ambition of every clergyman naturally led him to pay court, not so much to his sovereign, as to his own order, from which only he could expect preferment" (p. 752). Observe that what is natural here is not the ambition of the clergyman, but the behavior given the ambition. Another example occurs when Smith discusses the fact that merchants cannot afford to spend time in martial exercises and that "his attention to his own interest naturally leads him to neglect" those exercises (p. 659).

There are a few problematic cases here as well. Typically these occur when Smith is insufficiently specific when stating the postulated characteristic. A good example of this is when he states that "common humanity naturally disposes" slave owners to give protection to their slaves (p. 554). Whether one agrees with this statement or not obviously depends on one's conception of common humanity, an entity Smith does not feel the need to elaborate upon.

This is a good time to interrupt the flow of our discussion to consider the quite distinct fourth usage of the term natural. In this case, *natural denotes a characteristic or operation of the physical world, construed so as to exclude mankind.* This definition includes the use of the word "nature" to denote the set of forces or principles that underlie the physical world. As an example consider the following: "It is the work of nature which remains after deducting or compensating every thing which can be regarded as the work of man" (p. 345). On the same page we find that in manufacturing "nature does nothing, man does all." There are also numerous references to natural fertility, which is the level of fertility obtaining in the absence of man. We have, for example, the statement that "An inland country naturally fertile and easily cultivated, produces a great surplus of provisions..." (p. 382). A related phrase using the word natural rather than nature is Smith's reference to "natural and moral philosophy" (p. 724). Observe that under this definition, man himself is not considered natural. That is, mankind's behavior is not a characteristic of the physical world.

Let us now return to the first three definitions and consider a related usage of the term natural. This fifth usage of the term natural *identifies a certain form of liberty, namely natural liberty.* It is with this usage, especially, that modern readers are apt to encounter problems. Of course, this usage did not originate with Smith, but with various preceding social theorists, most prominently John Locke. Rather than going into the details of the development of this concept, let us consider what Francis Hutcheson, a professor at the University of Glasgow and an important influence on Smith, had to say about it: "As nature has implanted in each man a desire of his own happiness, and many tender affections towards others in some near relations of life, and granted to each one some understanding and active powers, with a natural impulse to exercise them for the purposes of these affections; tis plain each one has a natural right to exert his powers, according to his own judgment and inclination, for these purposes in all such industry, labour, or amusements as are not hurtful to others in their persons or goods, while no more publick interest necessarily requires his labours, or requires that his actions should be under the direction of others. This right we call *natural liberty*" (quoted in Mitchell, 1967, p. 123).

Hutcheson's definition suggests that if natural liberty holds, people will be able to behave in a manner which is in accord with their innate characteristics, with certain restrictions. Smith, who does not provide an actual definition of the term as such, probably has something similar to this in mind. There is, however, some evidence that Smith makes the notion more consistent by omitting the restrictions from his notion of natural liberty. Consider the following: "...those exertions of the natural liberty of a few individuals, which might endanger the security of the whole society, are, and ought to be, restrained by the law of all governments..." (p. 308). Thus, it is not contradictory to say that exertions of natural liberty can be harmful to others. Unfortunately, Smith is inconsistent on this point and later comes out with statements to the effect that all violations of natural liberty are to be avoided. An example is his characterization of certain laws as "evident violations of natural liberty, and therefore unjust" (p. 497). Another example, which also illustrates his definition of natural liberty, occurs when Smith discusses his desire to restore to "all his majesty's subjects" the "natural liberty of exercising what species of industry they please" (p. 437). Smith seems torn between the rhetorical impact of an unrestricted notion of natural liberty, and the suspicion that this notion might promote behavior that he does not wish to condone.

Another context in which this term is used is in the expression "system of natural liberty." This is a system of law in which natural liberty is promoted. Now the same problem which we just discussed in reference to natural liberty arises here as well. Specifically, if restrictions are not put on whose natural liberty the system is promoting, and if an unrestricted notion of natural liberty is used, then it is possible that monopolists, for example, will exert their natural liberty to restrict trade and create monopolies. We have already seen that this would be in accordance with their innate desire to further their own interest. This is definitely not what Smith has in mind. He addresses this problem with the following: "All systems either of preference or restraint, therefore, being thus completely taken away, the obvious and simple system of natural liberty establishes itself of its own accord" (p. 651). Thus, under the system of natural liberty, there are some who are legally prevented from exercising their natural liberty, that is, from acting according to their innate desire to promote their own self-interest. Now Smith is trying hard to avoid this implicit notion of political conflict. This is probably the reason he states that once his legal system is in place, the system of natural liberty will take place "of its own accord." This appears to buttress his use of the word "natural," by introducing yet another definition of natural which we will discuss shortly. Of course, there would be no problem if one used a restricted notion of natural liberty; however, in that case the link between natural liberty and the expression of innate characteristics is lost. In such a situation it is difficult to see in what sense the liberty is natural.

It should be stressed that the system of natural liberty is not that system which takes place in the state of nature, that is, in the absence of civil government. We have, in addition to the passage just cited, the famous passage: "According to the system of natural liberty, the sovereign has only three duties to attend to..." (p. 651). Thus the sovereign, in addition to the legal framework mentioned earlier, plays a part in the system of natural liberty.

We can now consider the sixth usage of natural, which is to *denote an event that takes place of its own accord, which in this case means in the absence of human action except insofar as that action is in accordance with mankind's innate characteristics.* This is a very important usage because it provides a link between the second and fourth definitions. It is different from the second usage because in this case the emphasis is not on mankind's behavior being natural, but on the event taking place of its own accord, an allusion to the fourth usage. It is different from the fourth usage because it implies that people acting in accordance with their innate characteristics are equivalent in a sense to the physical laws of the fourth usage, an idea that comes from the second usage.

This sixth usage is a very common usage and underlies the numerous statements in which various equilibrating actions are said to occur naturally. Thus, in discussing two channels into which capital might flow, Smith states that the capital will "naturally flow into them of its own accord" (p. 353). He means, of course, that if the owners of capital pursue their innate desire for self improvement, they will allocate capital to the channels under consideration. A related example is the following: "If a nation, therefore, is ripe for the East India trade, a certain portion of its capital will naturally divide itself among all the different branches of that trade" (p. 598).

This usage is closely related to the previously discussed notion of a system of natural liberty, since this is the system under which people act in the manner necessary for the current usage to hold. In this context, Smith occasionally links the words natural and free, as in discussing the colony trade in its "natural and free state" (p. 574). Here, Smith is using the term "free" to refer to the absence of the systems of preference or restraint he mentioned as a necessary condition for the establishment of the system of natural liberty. Of course, this usage is subject to the same criticism that was applied to the system of natural liberty, which was that under this system not everyone is acting in accordance with their innate characteristics. Thus, if monopolists act in their self-interest the various equilibrating events may not occur. Smith is quite explicit on this point and makes frequent references to the unnatural events that will occur if monopolists are not legally prevented from acting in their self-interest. For example, he refers to manufactures that have grown in the presence of monopolistic restrictions as being "artificially raised up to an unnatural height" (p. 571). Another example is his statement that the monopoly of the colony trade forces toward it "a much greater proportion of the capital of Great Britain than what would naturally have gone to it... " (p. 570).

The modern reader may well wonder why Smith is so intent on describing as natural what we would now simply describe as the working of a perfectly competitive market, given the problem we have been discussing. The reason probably has to do with the historical context in which Smith wrote. As Smith inherited the notion of natural liberty, so he inherited the notion that nature was in some sense designed to promote the welfare of mankind. This notion could be traced back to ancient Greek philosophy and beyond. Two forces that made this idea particularly appealing when Smith was writing were the influences of Rousseau's notion of mankind thriving in a state of nature, and of Newton's discovery of natural laws. The combination of these forces led credence to the already existing idea that one could discover natural laws governing human behavior, which would by being natural promote mankind's welfare more effectively than could the corrupt and artificial designs of man. This idea was certainly present in the writing of the Physiocrats, with which Smith was well acquainted. Hutcheson also held this view. Spiegel (1983, p. 228) quotes Hutcheson as saying that a law of nature is "no more than a conclusion from observation of what sort of conduct is ordinarily useful to society." It is well accepted that Smith held a comparable view. Thorstein Veblen wrote that Smith held the conviction that "The Creator has established the natural order to serve the ends of human welfare; and he has very nicely adjusted the efficient causes comprised in the natural order including human aims and motives, to this work that they are to accomplish..." (quoted in Mitchell, 1967, p. 150).

Thus, when Smith uses the term "natural" in the sense we are now considering, he does not mean merely to use an arbitrary term that he himself has defined, such as perfect competition would be had he coined that expression. He means to say that this usage of natural is fully comparable with the fourth usage, in which natural referred to the set of forces underlying the physical world. This is most likely because he conceived of this set of forces, perhaps God, as being the same which causes mankind to have the innate characteristics it does:

> ...in the political body, the natural effort which every man is continually making to better his own condition, is a principle of preservation capable of preventing and correcting, in many respects, the bad effects of a political economy, in some degrees both partial and oppressive.... In the political body...the wisdom of nature has fortunately made ample provision for remedying many of the bad effects of the folly and injustice of man..." (p. 638).

The problem here is with reconciling an argument about the need for a specific legal arrangement with the argument based on the naturalness of the result illustrated in this quote. Another example is Smith's statement that a system of hurtful regulations "is not always capable of stopping altogether the natural progress of a nation towards wealth and prosperity ... " (p. 638). The idea here seems to be that the progress is natural because it is implied by the existence of innate characteristics which are not subject to human control or influence. An example of the former argument, concerning the need for a specific legal arrangement, is the passage where capital is allocated in the "natural, healthful, and proper proportion which perfect liberty necessarily establishes, and which perfect liberty can alone preserve" (p. 572). In this case mankind's influence is apparently needed for the innate characteristics to lead to progress and the sense of natural expressed in the fourth usage is lost. Observe that the naturalness of the innate characteristics does not establish the naturalness of the progress, since the progress depends on both the innate characteristics and the specific legal arrangements being promoted. What is missing in this case is an argument concerning the naturalness of the legal arrangement.

The seventh usage of the term natural is in the expressions "*natural price.*" The primary meaning of natural price is the price that results under the system of natural liberty. For example, Smith discusses regulations which lower the price of a commodity "below what may be called its natural and proper price" (p. 616). By implication, the natural price would be that forthcoming in the absence of these regulations.

What probably led to the further development of this idea is that Smith's scheme of a naturally equilibrating economy is necessarily dynamic. This implies that at any given point in time, the observed market price may not be the natural price, even when we are operating under the system of natural liberty. This led Smith to consider the natural price as the average or ordinary price that would exist in a system of natural liberty. Thus, for example, he discusses the circumstances that cause the components of price to differ from their "natural or ordinary rate" (p. 29). A more famous example is the passage, "The natural price, therefore, is, as it were, the central price, to which the prices of all commodities are continually gravitating" (p. 58).

There is at least one passage in which Smith is somewhat inconsistent in this regard. In discussing the exchange rate between England and Scotland, he refers to the "natural rate, or to what the course of trade and remittances might happen to make it" (p. 310). This is similar to the earlier idea of the natural rate as that which would hold under a system of natural liberty. In this form, however, it does not seem fully compatible with the notion of the natural rate being the average rate which would hold under such a system. Note, incidentally, that although our discussion of this term was based mostly on a discussion of natural price, the terms "natural rate" and "natural profit" can be analyzed in exactly the same manner.

Another definition of the natural price follows from the naturally equilibrating economy Smith is discussing and is contained in the following passage: "The natural price, or the price of free competition ... is the lowest which can be taken, not upon every occasion indeed, but for any considerable time together" (p. 61). This definition can be viewed as an implication of the previous definition and the general argument set out in *The Wealth of Nations.*

The eighth usage of the term "natural" is as a *synonym for ordinary*, in reference to things besides the natural price. This is obviously related to the seventh usage discussed above. However, by treating natural price as one usage, we are led to treat this case as a separate case. An example of this rather rare usage is Smith's discussion of "what may be called the natural state of those employments," which occurs when the demand for that type of labor is neither greater nor less than usual (p. 115).

Having finished the enumeration of the major uses of the term "natural," let us quickly review the most serious problems that arise from the point of view of the modern reader: First, the imputation to various people of various innate characteristics or beliefs, some of which may appear questionable today. Second, the potentially inconsistent relation of natural liberty to the system of natural liberty, or of natural liberty to the expression of innate characteristics. Recall that the point here was that if natural liberty means the capacity to act in accordance with one's innate characteristics, then not everyone exercises their natural liberty under the system of natural liberty. On the other hand, if this is not the definition of natural liberty, then it unclear in what sense the liberty can be called natural. Third, Smith's rather strained attempt to link the legally enforced system of natural liberty to nature conceived to be the set of forces underlying the physical world. Fourth and last, the historical notion of a providential nature, defined again as the set of forces underlying the physical world.

In addition to these major problems, there is the usually minor problem of not being able to discern exactly which usage Smith is invoking on various occasions. In some cases, it is possible that passages may admit of more than one interpretation. This is a minor problem because typically, if a passage can admit of more than one interpretation consistent with Smith's discussion, it is not crucial to discover the exact usage Smith himself had in mind.

In conclusion, Smith uses the term "natural" in at least eight major ways in *The Wealth of Nations*. Many of these usages follow from others in a straightforward manner. Some usages represent quite distinct ideas. Various problems can occur when these different usages are combined in the way Smith does. If the modern reader is to follow Smith's discussion, it is clearly important that these various uses be adequately understood and kept in mind.

## REFERENCES

Mitchell, Wesley C. 1967. *Types of Economic Theory*, Vol. I. New York: Augustus M. Kelley.

Smith, Adam. 1937. *The Wealth of Nations*. New York: Modern Library.

Spiegel, Henry. 1983. *The Growth of Economic Thought*. Durham: Duke University Press.

# FRANK H. KNIGHT ON
# THE CONFLICT OF VALUES
# IN ECONOMIC LIFE


Ross B. Emmett

---

In his recent essay on Frank Knight in *The New Palgrave*, George Stigler (1987) suggested that there was a fundamental difference between the way Knight approached economics and the way most other twentieth-century economists have approached their discipline:

> For most present-day economists, the primary purpose of their study is to increase our knowledge of the workings of the enterprise and other economic systems. For Knight, the primary role of economic theory is rather different: it is to contribute to the understanding of how by consensus based upon rational discussion we can fashion [a] liberal society in which individual freedom is preserved and a satisfactory economic performance achieved. This vast social undertaking allows only a small role for the economist, and that role requires only a correct understanding of the central core of value theory (Stigler, 1987, p. 58).

Research in the History of Economic Thought and Methodology, Volume 9, pages 87-103.
ISBN: 1-55938-428-X

Although in the course of this paper we will see that there is at least one aspect of the basic orientation of Knight's work that is not captured by Stigler's remark, his identification of the centrality of the relation of economics to political life in Knight's work is a useful starting point because it highlights the two major themes of this paper and points us toward the nature of their relation in Knight's work. The first theme is Knight's belief in the fundamental indivisibility of the intellectual and moral aspects of social problems. Knight was highly critical of the line of reasoning regarding the relation of the positive and normative which has become the conventional wisdom in twentieth-century economic thought because of its implicit acceptance of the idea that there is widespread agreement regarding the goals of social policy and, hence, that solutions for our social problems are to be found primarily in the improvement of our present social and economic knowledge.[1] Believing that disagreement over social policy changes within society emerged as much from disagreement over, and conflict among, the relevant values affected by the policy as from any disagreement over the facts regarding the policy's consequences, Knight continually emphasized the unity of the intellectual and moral aspects of social problems and the indivisibility of the positive and normative;

> The social problem is not one of fact—except as values are also facts—nor is it one of means and end. It is a problem of values. And the content of social science must correspond with the problem of action in character and scope. (Knight, 1956a, p. 134).

The second theme highlighted by Stigler's remark is the important role that value theory played in Knight's thought, especially in terms of the relation of economic value theory to ethical or social value theory. The conventional wisdom regarding the relation of the positive and normative is built, in part, upon the assumption that the ethical commitments of individuals in society can be treated functionally as the correlates of the individuals' tastes and preferences because there is no rational means by which we can resolve conflict among the values of competing individuals. For values, as for tastes and preferences, economists assume that *de gustibus non est disputandum*. Following the methodological argument articulated most clearly by George Stigler and Gary Becker (1977) in an article bearing that Latin expression as its title, the conventional wisdom also tends to downplay the social significance of differences in values among the members of society, and changes in an individual's values over time, in favor of an emphasis upon the importance of differences, and changes, in our perceptions of the relative costs of various social policies. Knight, on the other hand, believed that all of our intentions had a inner, creative dynamism which made almost any choice, individual or social, a problem of ends as well as means. Social policy changes incite dispute, argued Knight, not only because they change the relative cost of achieving one's objectives—producing additional potential benefits for some at the expense of others, but also because they initiate institutional changes which shape the kind of people we are becoming and, therefore, either support or undermine our differing conceptions of who we should be:

> The broad crucial task of free society is to reach agreement by discussion on the kind of civilization it is to create for the future; hence it must agree on the meaning of progess.... Discussion of...change must run in terms of general values or ideals. The politics of democracy cannot be a contest between individuals or interest groups in getting what they want at the cost of others.... One of the worst verbal confusions is using the same term, "value," for both subjective desires and ideals which, in seeking agreement, must be recognized as objectively valid, hence "cognitive." Social problems arise out of conflicts at either of the two levels, but they can be discussed only as differences in critical-intellectual judgment of norms. Mere assertion of opposed claims cannot tend toward agreement, but must intensify conflict (Knight, 1956b, p. 26).

The purpose of this paper is to examine the way in which Knight developed his understanding of the inseparability of the intellectual and moral dimensions of social problems by investigating his approach to the conflict among social values and his insistence on the difficulty of achieving consensus over the ethical ideals for a liberal democracy. In order to show the relation between Knight's value theory and his understanding of social problems, I will begin by taking up the hint provided by Stigler when he said that Knight understood the role of the economist in social discourse to be circumscribed by economic value theory, and look first at Knight's discussion of the moral dimension of economizing problems.

# THE ECONOMIZING PROBLEM AS
# A MORAL PROBLEM

At the center of Knight's economic value theory was the same
fundamental ambiguity in the word *value* that he berated as one of
our worst verbal confusions in the comment, quoted above, regarding
the nature of social problems. Early in his career as an economist,
Knight explored the ambiguity of the term as it is used in economics
in an important series of articles. (See Knight, 1935, pp. 19-147, and
237-50; 1925). In those articles, Knight argued that, if human
preferences and ethical ideals are simply scientific data, "givens" to
be accepted as static and unavailable for rational discussion and
dispute, then economics *is* ethics, because the only possible evaluation
of "given" interests is the one created by the coordinating mechanism
itself. For a market society, this implies that price theory is value
theory, because the pricing system provides the basic mechanism for
the social coordination of individual interests. In Knight's own words:

> In so far as the ends are viewed as given, as data, then all activity is economic.
> The question of the effectiveness of the adaptation of means is the only
> question to be asked regarding conduct, and economics is the one and all-
> inclusive science of conduct. From this point of view the problem of life
> becomes simply the economic problem, how to employ the existing and
> available supplies of all sorts of resources, human and material, natural and
> artifical, in producing the maximum *amount* of *want-satisfaction*, including
> the provision of new resources for increased value production in so far as
> the present population finds itself actually desiring future progress. The
> assumption that wants or ends are data reduces life to economics, and raises
> again the question with which we started out, Is life all economics or does
> this view require supplementing by an ethical view of value? (Knight, 1935,
> pp. 34-35) (italics in original).

Knight's subsequent insistence upon the possibility of evaluating
wants, desires, and ethical ideals *outside* of society's coordinating
mechanisms focused upon the limitations of the view that such
interests could be taken as scientific data. In Knight's estimation,
human intentionality has an inner, creative dynamism which makes
our preferences and values unstable, immeasurable, and individually
unique. Economic principles have only a limited scope of application
to human conduct, because it is only within a very narrow range of
human activity, if at all, that our interests can be taken as given.

Furthermore, the price system, which Knight believed to be the most effective mechanism for the coordination of competing "given" interests, would, in his estimation, quite likely prove to be an ineffective coordinator of competing "dynamic" interests, because it provided no standards by which to measure their moral progress:

> The chief thing which the common-sense individual wants is not satisfactions for the wants which he has, but more, and *better* wants (Knight, 1935, p. 22) (italics in original).

For Knight, therefore, the economizing problem itself was seldom simply a problem of means, for people want to know what constitutes "better wants," and, hence, there is a need for an independent, or non-price, evaluation of our personal interests. "It is," Knight said, "the higher goal of conduct to test and try these values (i.e., interests), to define and improve them, rather than to accept and 'satisfy' them" (Knight, 1935, p. 40). The job of ethics is to develop value standards which assist us in that task; standards which help us to exercise wise judgment without establishing absolute rules based upon values that are arbitrarily taken as absolute. Those ethical standards, Knight believed, would come closer to the standards by which we judge great literature and art, than it would to those standards by which we evaluate scientific theories.[2]

The necessity of an independent ethics for the real world of dynamic interests implied two things for Knight. First, it implied that price and value theory could never be completely severed. Commenting once upon Gustav Cassel's repudiation of utilitarian value theory in favour of a pure exchange model in his *Theoretische Socialoekonomie*, Knight warned that:

> ...the "repudiation of value theory" is very good, and the writer is altogether in favor of it—for the first stage in the discussion of economic problems. But should it not be kept in mind also that the ultimate object of economic theorizing is a criticism in ethical and human terms of the workings of the economic machine, and that a theory of value as well as price is indispensable? (Knight, 1921, p. 146).

Second, the necessity of an independent ethics implied for Knight that efficiency was not the chief criterion by which societies should judge coordination mechanisms; instead, they should be judged primarily in terms of the kind of wants and desires they create, and the character of the people they form. When Knight, in his justly famous essay "The Ethics of Competition," turned the standards of two major ethical systems (Aristotelian and Christian) regarding the nature of our interests and the quality of our character on the market mechanism itself, he found it wanting:

> [Because] the social order largely forms as well as gratifies the wants of its members...it must be judged ethically rather by the wants which it generates, the type of character which it forms in its people, than by its efficiency in satisfying wants as they exist at any given time.... [T]he competitive system, viewed simply as a want-satisfying mechanism, falls far short of our highest ideals. To the theoretical tendencies of perfect competition must be opposed just as fundamental limitations and counter-tendencies, of which careful scrutiny discloses a rather lengthy list. Its standards of value for the guidance of the use of resources in production are the prices of goods, which diverge widely from accepted ethical values; and if the existing order were more purely competitive, if social control were reduced in scope, it seems clear that the divergence would be enormously wider still. Moreover, untrammelled individualism would probably tend to lower standards progressively rather than to raise them. "Giving the public what it wants" usually means corrupting popular taste (Knight, 1935, pp. 51, 57).

The really interesting thing about the two sides of Knight's economic value theory, however, is the fact that they are never clearly reconciled in his work. We have to remember that the man who wrote "Ethics and the Economic Interpretation" also wrote "Some Fallacies in the Interpretation of Social Cost" (see Knight, 1935, pp. 19-40, 217-36); that the man who said that price theory could never adequately encompass the realities of a world of dynamic intentionality was in no small measure responsible for the initiation of the "Chicago School" tradition of deliberately explaining actual human conduct solely in terms of price theory; and that the man who said that there was no ethical foundation upon which one could justify the market later turned the statement around to say that the market was a social institution which no ethical system had yet adequately comprehended (see Knight, 1947, pp. 55-153).

James Buchanan recently pointed out the perpetual presence of this tension between price and value theory in Knight's work in his rational reconstruction, along catallactic lines, of Knight's ethical critique of the capitalist order. After suggesting that Knight failed to recognize the possibility of separating price and value theory, and therefore underrated the ethical support for free markets, because he failed to escape completely the maximizing element of traditional economic theory, Buchanan concludes with the admission:

> It is, of course, possible that it was precisely the methodological ambiguity that created the tension in Knight's analysis and that it is this tension that allows us to remain fascinated with his works (Buchanan, 1987, p. 74).

Despite his desire to resolve the tension within Knight's work by reeducating Knight in such a way as to convince him of the separability of price and value theory, Buchanan has clearly recognizes that to do so would result in a vision of social and economic problems which is somehow smaller than Knight's own. The tension between the two concepts of value theory within Knight's work may frustrate the reader's desire for a coherent account of economics and its relation to ethics, but it also entices the reader to think more deeply about the problems of economic organization. Before moving from Knight's consideration of the economizing problem as a moral problem to his consideration of social problems as moral problems, we need to pause and consider the place that this type of tension had in Knight's thought.

## II. THE THERAPEUTIC ORIENTATION OF KNIGHT'S WORK

Most economists familiar with Knight's work recognize that he often played a role which one author has described as that of a "Socratic gadfly" (Purcell, 1973, p. 43)—seeking more to ask questions which explore the various limitations and constraints under which our ideas operate than to set out an improved system of ideas. His writings on economic and social philosophy, in particular, were marked by a question-oriented mode of thinking which sought to edify by raising questions more than to construct by answering them. In the words of F.A. Hayek (1978, p. 51, n. 1), Knight was "a puzzler if there ever was one."

Despite widespread recognition of the "puzzling" or edifying quality of Knight's work, most interpreters are still tempted to distill out of his "Socratic" ruminations a clearly articulated philosophical doctrine on economics and society. Without denying that his work is shaped by certain philosophical commitments, I wish to suggest that it is nevertheless a major mistake to categorize his work by reference to those commitments. The inclination to discover a coherent system of ideas within a past thinker's work emerges from our desire to classify thinkers and place them within intellectual categories which serve our contemporary purposes. Although this is often useful, it must be recognized that it almost completely ignores the past thinker's own intentions as they were expressed in the interaction between the thinker's ideas and the audience to which they were addressed (See Pocock, 1971, pp. 3-41; Rorty, 1984; Skinner, 1969; and Wood, 1979). For the purposes of interpreting Knight, such a perspective is almost fatal because a systematic exposition of his work will miss the main point, which is that his primary contribution to the development of a more coherent economic and social philosophy lay in the way in which he endeavored to show economists and other inquirers into human society their inability to encompass human experience within the confines of a single intellectual system and the necessity of accepting the moral responsibility their intellectual limitations placed upon them. As Warner Wick said at Knight's memorial service, to speak of Knight as a philosopher is to say that he practiced philosophy:

> ...in its ancient character as an activity which has no end, and produces no authoritative doctrines, just because it reflects critically on the aims, inter-relations, limitations, and inevitable distortions of all doctrines (Wick, 1973, p. 513).

Knight's work, then, is not some giant jigsaw puzzle, which, when finally put together, reveals a picture of a comprehensive system of thought about the economy or society; it is, rather, an assortment of ruminations which seek to destroy systems of thought because they are seen as inimical to the continued health of that great conversation we call human society.

In order to distinguish Knight's intentions from those of the great systematic thinkers on economic and social philosophy, I suggest that we describe his work as therapeutic in orientation. This term is borrowed from Rorty's recent description of the difference between modern philosophers such as Nietzsche, Dewey, Wittgenstein and Heidegger, whose works are disturbing and paradoxical because they resist the effort to classify them according to traditional philosophical categories, and the great systematic thinkers of this century who provide cogently argued and systematically organized presentations of new approaches to the basic problems of philosophy (Rorty, 1979, pp. 5-6, 357-94). The works of these therapeutic thinkers, Rorty argues, are disturbing and paradoxical because they deliberately refuse to follow the generally accepted notions of what it means to do philosophy. By resisting reduction, classification, and institutionalization, they strive to keep us from interpreting their work as an incremental contribution to a progressive philosophical research program and prevent us from reducing human conversation to scientific argument—*edification* rather than *construction* is their primary goal. By pointing out that the search for truth is merely one of many human projects (Knight added that the search for truth was subject to diminishing returns[3]), they speak of the conflicts which emerge between it and other human occupations and remind the philosopher and social scientist of the need for humility in the face of the creative complexity and novelty of human experience. And by offering stories, satires, and aphorisms in reaction to the prevailing currents of philosophical opinion, they parody the systematic philosopher's desire for sound logic and conclusive arguments and remind us of the need for the love of wisdom as well as knowledge. Knight himself captured the edifying message of the therapeutic philosophers when he said in his presidential address to the American Economic Association:

> ...the right principle is to respect all the principles, take them fully into account, and then use *good judgement* as to how far to follow one or another in the case in hand (Knight, 1956a, p. 256) (italics in original).

Recognition of the therapeutic orientation of Knight's work helps us to appreciate his personal refusal to specify any kind of resolution for the prioritization and coordination of competing dynamic interests and, hence, to understand why he appeared to drop us off at exactly the point at which we should really begin. A more systematic thinker, of course, would try to guide us through the task of prioritizing and coordinating our ethical ideals with our economic interests, as the work of more recent thinkers as various as John Rawls, Amartya Sen, Robert Nozick, Hal Varian, and James Buchanan have done. Knight did not lead us through such an exercise because, ultimately, he believed that the quest for better interests was our responsibility and that the prioritization and coordination of interests required for that quest could only emerge from the actual *practice* of individuals and societies. His task was merely to bring us to the point where we recognized the moral nature of our practice and accepted the difficulty of fulfilling our responsibility. In turn, it was the need to fulfill that purpose that led Knight to expand his focus beyond the relation of the two sides of value theory in economics to their relation in the broader context of social practice. And it is to his therapeutic ruminations on that broader context that we now turn.

## III.  SOCIAL PROBLEMS AS MORAL PROBLEMS

Like most social philosophers who follow in the tradition of classical liberalism, Knight saw democracy as the most compatible political partner of free markets because the mechanisms of democratic political activity allowed for the coordination of individual interests in collective decisions in a manner similar to the coordination of individual choices by the market. Given the centrality of the tension between the two sides of value theory in his exploration of the market system, it is not surprising that the same tension emerged as a dominant theme in his exploration of liberal democracy.

One side of the tension in Knight's social thought was essentially contractarian and emerged from his recognition of the fact that, when our ethical ideals are taken up as interests, they play the same role within our collective decision making as do our economic interests in our individual decision making. Because interests conflict, their interaction within the context of collective choices requires a type of coordination similar to that provided by the market's coordination of tastes and preferences to ensure that the eventual outcomes are mutually beneficial, within the limits imposed by scarcity, for all participants. From this perspective, democratic action is simply a coordination mechanism (much like the market) for resolving the conflicting interests of freely associating individuals regarding collective choices, and the central political problem is the specification of an institutional structure for the coordination of interests which resolves those conflicts efficiently.

A good example of this side of Knight's social thought can be found in his critical review of two books by Michael Polanyi (Knight, 1949). Despite his general agreement with Polanyi regarding the nature of scientific discussion and the organization of the quest for scientific truth, Knight takes Polanyi to task for trying to apply the model of freedom in scientific discussion to the problems raised by free discussion in democratic society. Social problems, Knight tells us, do not involve the search for truth, in any sense of that word comparable to its usage in science, rather, they involve the search for agreement among individuals who hold competing evaluations of the outcomes of policy changes. Better (i.e., more efficient) agreements may be reached through intelligent discussion of the issues involved, but even if unanimity is achieved, it could not be said that a "true" judgment had been made. The terms "true" and "false" are simply irrelevant to political decision making. In the words of James Buchanan, Knight's criticisms of Polanyi emerge from a perspective which holds that:

> Politics is the collective counterpart of individual choice and nothing more.... [It] is the process through which the initial preferences [of individuals] are expressed, discussed, compromised, and, finally, resolved in some fashion (Buchanan, 1967, p. 306).

Despite the prominence that the contractarian side of Knight's social thought has reached through its extension in Buchanan's work, there was another theme in Knight's thought which, if we are to fully understand him, must be held in tension with the contractarian theme. This second theme emerges from the other side of his value theory—from the view that the creative dynamism of our intentions necessitates the development of a set of intersubjectively valid ethical standards.

On this second side of Knight's thought, values exist, not only as the subjective interests of individuals, but as supra-individual expressions of our understanding of the common good for humanity. Put differently, our values reflect our corporate understanding of the kind of people we want to be. Furthermore, social institutions are not only coordination mechanisms, but embodiments of our values, albeit in imperfect ways. Social policy changes become problems for our society because they initiate institutional changes which directly participate in forming the kind of people we are becoming, and therefore support or undermine our differing understandings of who we should be.

From this perspective, collective choices are similar to individual choices, not because they both represent the resolution of conflict among various given interests but, rather, because they both embody in human practice the quest for higher ethical ideals. In a book review written early in his career, Knight described the goal in the following terms:

> The larger problem is to arrange things so that people will find their lives interesting and will grow into such personalities that they can respect themselves, admire others and enjoy their society, appreciate thought and beauty, and in general look upon creation and call it good (Knight, 1919, p. 806).

Because actual social practice never realizes this goal, it can, in a sense, be described as a lengthy conversation about nature of a good society, and the fact that a specific conflict has been resolved is not as important as the fact that the conversation which that society represents has been continued and carried forward.[4]

The tension between values as the subjective interests of individuals and values as supra-individual ideals for the common good—or, to say the same thing in a different way, the tension between democracy as a coordination mechanism and democracy as a conversation—lies behind Knight's emphasis upon the conflicts between freedom and justice, and freedom and order, within a liberal democratic society. Knight generally identified freedom as the central value of a liberal society because, in keeping with the contractarian side of his thought, the absence of coercion implied the rights of individuals to pursue their interests by making changes, and to associate together with others for purposes of mutual betterment. Keeping within the boundaries of the contractarian side of his thought for the moment, we can see that the need for an orderly process for making changes that promote individual and group interests and also ensure equality of treatment among individuals conflicts with, and places limitations upon, the desire to maximize the freedom of the individual. Without agreement on constitutional principles establishing rules for the coordination of individual and group interests, collective actions could only become the setting for social strife, conflict and chaos.

But there is more to Knight's discussion of the conflict among the values of freedom, order, and justice than a call for constitutional rules to coordinate our contractarian society, for social *practice* will always be pushing at the limits of those constitutional rules from two different directions. On the one hand, the imperfections and limitations of any particular constitutional rules will focus social discussion on adaptations and changes to the rules which will make them truer embodiments of the society's vision of the common good. The difficulty of this task is, of course, compounded by the evolving nature of our understanding of a just society—the central problem, Knight suggested, "is that of defining the social good, or "justice" in the widest sense, by describing the social order which embodies the ideal in the highest degree" (Knight, 1949, p. 281).

At the same time as our social practice requires us to reformulate our conceptions of the common good and reform our existing constitutional rules in an effort to promote progress toward those ideals, it also has a restraining effect upon progress because of the requirement to conserve the personal and institutional integrity found in the existing order of society. If social institutions are the embodiments of ethical ideals and significantly shape the kind of people we become then, no matter how imperfectly they reflect their ideals, there is a need to conserve them for the sake of preserving our present personal and social character. Order, therefore, is the supreme value of society (Knight, 1960b, p. 30), viewed from an institutional perspective, because through the conservation of existing institutions, society strives to ensure that changes made in the name of freedom and justice will not undermine the existing character of our society and the gains already made.

Knight's own "conservatism" can be placed in perspective by these comments. Systematic thinkers and social reformers who desire progress on our major social problems find Knight's refusal to tackle the resolution of value conflicts frustrating and often decide, after considering his willingness to let the tension among various values simply exist, that it represents a basic unwillingness to change the status quo.[5] This view seriously misreads Knight. His conservatism arises, not out of a love of tradition, but out of the almost paralyzing tension created by a strong belief in the need for social progress and an equally strong belief in the essential tragicness of human existence. Here was man who desperately desired a better world, but whose study of economics and society had brought him face-to-face with the terrible constraints scarcity places upon us and fact that even our best-intentioned efforts fail to draw us closer to a better world. In a letter to none other than Richard Tawney, in 1939, Knight described the path along which his thoughts had taken him and the reluctance and disappointment he felt as a result:

> When I took up Economics as a career, I thought of it in terms of doing good in the world. But it seems as if the first step in any direct effort along this line is to choose between any high degree of accuracy and impartiality in dealing with the facts, and the possibility of cooperation with other people who declare themselves interested in social-economic betterment. It is certainly with reluctance and disappointment that I have felt myself forced to adopt a position of neutral, in most of the great discussions of issues currently going on—knowing that neutrality means being treated as an enemy by both sides, or escaping this fate only by being regarded as utterly insignificant, or being actually unheard of (Knight, 1939).

The development of a therapeutic orientation seems to have been Knight's only defense against the reality of scarcity. The line of tension between the two sides of the conflict among freedom, justice, order, and other values runs throughout most of Knight's work after 1935, with almost no suggestions as to how the tensions can be resolved. Once again, we find that Knight brings us to the essential tension within the social discourse of a liberal society, without attempting to guide us through it. With reluctance, he realized that it was only in actual social practice that resolutions would be found, and that his role, as critic and philosopher, was to bring us to realize the limitations of our values and accept the responsibility for working out their resolution. As he often said: "(My) aim is merely to raise certain questions, without attempting to give them final answers" (Knight, 1956a, p. 179; Knight, 1960a, pp. 121-22).

## ACKNOWLEDGMENT

The author is Assistant Professor of Economics, Augustana University College, Camrose, Alberta, Canada, T4V 2R3. He wishes to thank Anthony Waterman, Warren Samuels, and Bryce Jones for their comments on an earlier draft, and the University of Chicago Library for permission to quote from unpublished material in the Frank H. Knight Papers. The paper was prepared for presentation at the annual meeting of the Association for Social Economics in New York, 30 December 1988 while the author was a Visiting Fellow at St. John's College, The University of Manitoba.

# NOTES

1. The view that Knight opposed was summarized succinctly by his student Milton Friedman in the introduction to his famous essay on economic methodology when he said: ". . . differences about economic policy among disinterested citizens derive predominantly from different predictions about the economic consequences of taking action—differences that in principle can be eliminated by the progress of positive economics—rather than from fundamental differences in basic values, differences about which (we) can ultimately only fight" (Friedman, 1953, p. 5).

2. I cannot resist adding two asides at this point: First, Knight's arguments against the possibility of using absolute rules for the guidance of human conduct go a long way toward explaining his negative reaction to the monetary rules proposed by his student, Milton Friedman. Knight was never very much of a monetarist! Second, Knight once commented that the authors of great imaginative literature were "always indefinitely better psychologists than the psychologists so-called" (Knight, 1935, p. 31). I cannot help but think that he would also believe that they were "always indefinitely better *ethicists* than the *ethicists* so-called."

3. "It is the nature of interests to conflict, ultimately, to be subject to a law of diminishing importance or power. The interest in truth is no exception.... We cannot live on truth alone, or the discussion and quest of truth" (Knight, 1925, p. 250). This theme was repeated in many of his later writings.

4. Knight often quoted with approval Lord Bryce's definition of democracy— that is, "government by discussion"—because it gave him a way to lead up to the idea that it is the continuation of the discussion, rather than the resolution of a particular disagreement, which is of central importance (Frank H. Knight, 1952, pp. 5-7, 1955, pp. 49-56).

5. Many share the view expressed by Ben Seligman (1962, p. 665): "Despite all his protestations to the contrary, Knight was more of a traditionalist than he knew."

# REFERENCES

Buchanan, James M. 1967. "Politics and Science: Reflections on Knight's Critique of Polanyi." *Ethics* 77 (July): 303-10.

———. 1987. "The Economizing Element in Knight's Ethical Critique of Capitalist Order." *Ethics* 98 (October): 61-75.

Friedman, Milton. 1953. "The Methodology of Positive Economics." In *Essays in Positive Economics*, pp. 3-43. Chicago: University of Chicago Press.

Hayek, F.A. 1978. "Two Kinds of Minds." In *New Studies in Philosophy, Politics, Economics and the History of Ideas*, pp. 50-56. Chicago: University of Chicago Press8.

Knight, Frank H. 1919. "Review of *Cooperation and the Future of Industry*, by L.S. Woolf." *Journal of Political Economy* 27 (November): 805-6.

———. 1921. "Cassel's Theoretische Sozialoekonomie." *Quarterly Journal of Economics* 36 (November): 145-53.

————. 1925. "Fact and Metaphysics in Economic Psychology." *American Economic Review* 15 (June 1925): 247-66.

————. 1935. *The Ethics of Competition and Other Essays.* Essays selected by Milton Friedman, Homer Jones, George Stigler, and Allen Wallis. London: George Allen & Unwin.

————. 1939. Letter to Richard H. Tawney, 28 April 1939, Box 62, Folder 9, Frank H. Knight Papers, Special Collections, Joseph Regenstein Library, University of Chicago, Chicago.

————. 1947. *Freedom & Reform: Essays in Economics and Social Philosophy,* pp. 55-153. Essays selected by Hubert Bonner, William Grampp, Milton Singer, and Bernard Weinberg. New York: Harper & Bros. (Reprint 1982, Indianapolis: Liberty Press).

————. 1949. "Virtue and Knowledge: The View of Professor Polanyi." (Review article on *Science, Faith and Society* and *The Foundations of Academic Freedom,* by Michael Polanyi). *Ethics* 59 (July): 271-84.

————. 1952. "Economic Freedom and Social Responsibility." Emory University School of Business Administration. Studies in Business and Economics, No. 7.

————. 1955. "Economic Objectives in a Changing World." In *Economics and Public Policy,* pp. 49-80. (Brookings Lectures, 1954). Washington, DC: The Brookings Institution.

————. 1956a. *On the History and Method of Economics: Selected Essays.* Essays selected by William L. Letwin and Alexander J. Morin. Chicago: University of Chicago Press.

————. 1956b. "Science, Society, and the Modes of Law." In *The State of the Social Sciences,* pp. 9-28. (Papers presented at the 25th Anniversary of the Social Science Research Building, The University of Chicago, November 10-12, 1955). Edited by Leonard D. White. Chicago: University of Chicago Press.

————. 1960a. *Intelligence and Democratic Action.* Cambridge: Harvard University Press.

————. "Social Economic Policy." *Canadian Journal of Economics and Political Science* 26 (February): 19-34.

Pocock, J.G.A. 1971. *Politics, Language and Time: Essays on Political Thought and History.* New York: Atheneum.

Purcell, Edward A., Jr. 1973. *The Crisis of Democratic Theory: Scientific Naturalism and the Problem of Value.* Lexington: University Press of Kentucky.

Rorty, Richard. 1979. *Philosophy and the Mirror of Nature.* Princeton, NJ: Princeton University Press.

————. 1984. "The Historiography of Philosophy: Four Genres." In *Philosophy in History: Essays in the Historiography of Philosophy,* edited by Richard Rorty, J.B. Schneewind, and Quentin Skinner, pp. 49-75. Cambridge: Cambridge University Press.

Seligman, Ben B. 1962. "Frank H. Knight and Abstractionism." In *Main Currents in Modern Economics,* Vol. 3, *The Thrust Toward Technique,* pp. 646-665. Glencoe, IL: The Free Press. 1962. (Reprint 1971. Chicago: Quadrangle Books).

Skinner, Quentin. 1969. "Meaning and Understanding in the History of Ideas." *History and Theory* 8: 3-53.

Stigler, George J. 1987. "Frank Hyneman Knight." In *The New Palgrave: A Dictionary of Economics*, edited by John Eatwell, Murray Milgate, and Peter Newman, Vol. 3, pp. 55-59. New York: Stockton Press.

Stigler, George J., and Gary S. Becker. 1977. "De Gustibus Non Est Disputandum." *American Economic Review* 67 (March): 76-90.

Wick, Warner. 1973. "Frank Knight, Philosopher at Large." *Journal of Political Economy* 81 (May/June): 513-15.

Wood, Gordon S. 1979. "Intellectual History and the Social Sciences." In *New Directions in American Intellectual History*, edited by, John Higham and Paul K. Conkin, pp. 27-41. Baltimore: Johns Hopkins University Press.

# EVER SINCE ADAM SMITH:
## THE MYTHICAL HISTORY OF INDIVIDUAL RATIONALITY IN ECONOMIC ANALYSIS

Mary K. Farmer

## THE CONTINUITY MYTH

*The view has been maintained, with some justification, that ever since its emergence in the late seventeenth and early eighteenth century, orthodox modern economic theorising has been built around, or has mainly consisted of, one central model of maximisation and self-equilibriation. It has been claimed regarding modern political economy and economics that though there have been "unsuccessful rebellions... its basic maximising model has never been replaced," that is neither its maximising statics nor its self-adjusting dynamics.....The self-adjusting, self-equilibriating model or "system," was generalised and consummated in The Wealth of Nations.*

—Terence Hutchison
(1978, p. 200)[1]

Research in the History of Economic Thought and Methodology, Volume 9, pages 105-127.
Copyright © 1992 by JAI Press Inc.
All rights of reproduction in any form reserved.
ISBN: 1-55938-428-X

To the outsider or the new student, economics displays a remarkably monolithic appearance. Across university and college syllabuses and textbooks, there appears striking agreement on the core principles, central theoretical constructions, and fundemental methods of analysis which any intending practitioner must master, and in almost every case the student is early on impressed with the distinguished and ancient origins of this consensus. McKenzie and Tulloch put it in typical fashion when they state, in the opening pages of their *New World of Economics* that the economist's starting point is the rational actor, which generates "a model, which has been developed and refined since the days of Adam Smith, and it is because we employ this model in our discussion that we consider this to be an economic treatise" (McKenzie and Tulloch, 1978, p. 4).

Orthodox modern economics (or what I will henceforth refer to as "modern mainstream economics"),[2] has of course a very particular concept of rational individual action as utility-maximizing behaviour. Making the claim that economic analysis has been built around a concept of rational individual action "ever since Smith" thus entails, as the quotation from Hutchison makes clear, a claim that the *utility-maximizing model* of action is the one which can be found in the writings of mainstream economists back to Smith and his contemporaries, even if in a "less-developed" form. Such claims contain the clear suggestion that economists must either embrace the modern utility-maximizing model of economic analysis, or abandon any concept of individuals as rational actors, and thereby cut all ties with the grand two-hundred-year-old tradition of Western economic thought and start again.

It has been argued elsewhere that the view exemplified in my quotation from Hutchison plays a powerful definitional and integrative role in contemporary economics (Farmer, 1988). It is not only mainstream economists, but also many of their strongest critics, who subscribe to the belief that the utility-maximizing model is an essential component of what economics *is*. The imperative, "explain whatever you choose to try to understand using a model based on individual utility maximizers," undoubtedly constitutes a fundemental part of the positive heuristic of the mainstream research programme in the discipline. The further belief that it has *always* been an essential part of the core of the discipline, (or at least "ever since Adam Smith," which to all intents and purposes means the same thing as far as most economists are concerned) ensures that those who attempt to abandon, or indeed even to modify the assumption of individual utility maximization, are viewed as putting themselves beyond the pale as "not really economists at all."

Conversely, the claim to be extending the rational choice framework, or to be taking it to its logical conclusion, (the argument from authority as Donald McCloskey would undoubtedly classify it (McCloskey, 1986) has, in the twentieth century, come to be seen as a powerful weapon in the rhetorical armoury of any economist attempting a theoretical or substantive innovation. The weapon has been powerfully deployed by the "new home economists" grouped around Gary Becker and his co-workers (see Becker 1976), by those working on the microfoundations of macrotheory, and most recently by the "new classical rational expectations theorists," led by John F. Muth and Robert E. Lucas (see Sheffrin 1983, p. 5). Critics of these positions have undoubtedly found them harder to deal with because of the aura of theoretical purity which surrounds them; their air of doing what all economists agree we should be doing, but doing it more wholeheartedly. All too easily, those who express unease about these developments are cast in the role of snipers from the fringes of the discipline whose commitment to its core principles must be viewed as in some doubt.

## II. THE MYTH AND THE REALITY

In this section, I will argue that the concept of rational action as utility-maximizing behavior, and the approach to explanation that this entails, cannot be traced back directly to Adam Smith. To argue, (as, for example, George Stigler has done) that Smith's concept of individuals as rational pursuers of self-interest has simply been "relabelled 'utility-maximizing behavior'" (Stigler in Smith, 1976, p. xi) is to impose a significant distortion on the history of economic thought. Indeed, a number of research traditions now treated as on the margins of the subject will be shown to have more in common with Smith's treatment of human action than the modern mainstream tradition.

If successful, such a demythologising attempt will not constitute a critique of the explanatory framework adopted by contemporary mainstream economists, but it should remove some spurious defensive barriers currently obstructing the paths of those who seek to provide such critiques or to change current mainstream theoretical practice.

Let us begin by briefly establishing how rational action is characterised in modern mainstream economics and what role it plays in that research programme. For the modern economist, "rational action" is homologous with "utility-maximizing behaviour." In a typical, textbook-level exposition of this notion, Richard McKenzie explains that when economists assume that individuals act rationally, they are assuming that "people know what they want, are able to order their wants from most preferred to least preferred, and are able to act consistently on the basis of that ordering so as to maximize some welfare notion such as utility, which Becker often calls 'full income'" (McKenzie, 1983, p. 29).

Of course, economics students are soon exposed to refinements of this basic concept of rational action. Criticisms that it is unrealistic to assume that actors have perfect knowledge are countered with the riposte that what is maximized is, of course, *expected* utility (though this refinement is conveniently ignored in much routine work). Further, they learn that "(i)f people are not in fact rational in all their endeavors, then, for theoretical purposes, they can be treated *as if* they are" (McKenzie, 1983, p. 29).

Thus, in modern mainstream economics the world is viewed as (or as if it were) made up of individuals who have a clear and consistent ranking of the things they want, and whose actions consist of attempts, based on the most efficient possible use of available knowledge, to get them. Rational actors, thus conceived, have a number of notable characteristics: first, the well-ordered set of preferences of which they are the proud possessors are both objectively given (i.e., conceivably available for inspection and comprehension by an outsider) and relatively stable. (*How* stable is a matter of some dispute, but certainly all mainstream economists view giving any explanatory efficacy to changes in actors' tastes as something of a defeat for "the economic model of analysis.") Second, given their preferences, the rational actors' actions are entirely dictated by the external environment. If some change in the constraints they face allows them to act so as to increase their utility, they will unerringly do so. When no conceivable action can further improve their position, they cease to act. Thus in equilibrium, there is no reason why they should ever act at all—and since equilibrium points are what mainstream neoclassical analysis is all about, there is considerable weight to the complaint that neoclassical economics has no real theory of *action* at all. The Austrian critic, Rothbard, has referred rather strikingly to the behaviourist/determinist utility-maximizing model of the neoclassicals as the "reflexive or knee-jerk" concept of action (Rothbard, 1976, p. 19). Less critically but in the same vein, Latsis has described it as "situational determinism" (1972, p. 16). In principle, the behaviour of such rational actors is fully predictable—all that is required to predict it successfully is the "correct theory," that is a "correct" model of the actors' objectives and of the constraints they face.

A further characteristic of the modern mainstream concept of the rational actor is that it is embedded in an approach to explanation which is individualistic, which builds up from individual rational actors. As McKenzie and Tulloch put it "(t)he focal point of the study of economics is the *individual*. It is the individual who possesses values, makes choices, and, if given the freedom, takes actions. All group decisions and actions are thought of in terms of the collective decisions and actions of individuals..." (McKenzie and Tulloch, 1978, p. 8).

In this model, social institutions are merely the aggregate results of the choices of individuals each acting to maximize his or her own utility. Such social structures are unambiguously the *product* of individual action—individuals or their preferences are givens, never themselves seen as the socially constructed products of a particular familial, class, or cultural environment, and institutions which appear in the analysis are also seen as givens, faced by individuals as constraints on their actions, never viewed as, for example, the products of the exercise of class power. (Thus, in the "economics of crime" literature, for example, definitions of "crime"—that is, of what is or is not viewed as criminal behaviour—are not treated as cultural variables, the product of, for example, a history of struggles between different interest groups or classes but merely as external "facts" faced by the actor.)

Is this really the model of economic analysis which was introduced by Adam Smith and which has characterised the economic tradition ever since? In fairness to those who claim it is, the quotation must first be clarified. No one, not even the most hard-nosed economic imperialist, claims that ever since Adam Smith all good economists (i.e., those whose practice is now emulated) have solely and consistently operated with the utility-maximizing, rational-actor-based model. Rather, the claim is usually that the *best practice* of all "good" economists has followed this model. Thus, Gary Becker insists that "(t)he economic approach to human behavior is not new, even outside the market sector. Adam Smith often (but not always!) used this approach to understand political behavior" (Becker, 1976a, p. 8).

So the question becomes: *when* Adam Smith and his successors used a rational action model in the explanation of social phenomena, was it the same model which the modern economist adopts, one which has been simply relabelled "utility-maximizing"?

If the reader is already steeped in the utility-maximizing approach it is not difficult to read it into the text of *The Wealth of Nations*. But there are in fact crucial differences between this approach and Smith's mode of economic analysis. There are, of course, many passages in which Smith elegantly illustrates the mileage which can be got by explaining social phenomena as the outcomes of the actions of actors acting out of perceived self-interest. Some of the most striking deal, in ways of which modern economic imperialists would be proud, with "non-economic" phenomena, where the actors' objectives are far removed from crude wealth-accumulation. For example, when discussing education, he suggestively comments that "(t)he discipline of colleges and universities is in general contrived, not for the benefit of the students, but for the interest, or more properly speaking, for the ease, of the masters" (Smith, 1976, Bk. V, ch. I p. 287). In the same section, he explains why "(i)n the University of Oxford, the greater part of the public professors have, for these many years, given up even the pretence of teaching" (p. 284).

Some might be tempted to view Smith as having identified some subrational behaviour which might lend itself to explanation in terms perhaps of Herbert Simon's "bounded rationality" (1982) or Harvey Leibenstein's "X-efficiency" (1980). But Smith has no need of such notions. He explains the situation simply as the result of the behavioral principle (i.e., assumption about actors' objectives) that it is "(i)n the interest of every man to live as much at his ease as he can," and the institutional circumstance that "the teacher is prohibited from receiving any honorary or fee from his pupils, and his salary constitutes the whole of the revenue which he derives from his office." Since he gets it whether he bothers to teach or not, he has no incentive to teach. Of course, the plausibility of the explanation depends on another, culturally specific, assumption, which Smith has smuggled in, no doubt unawares—the assumption that there were neither significant psychic costs attached to failing to teach nor psychic benefits from teaching, for an eighteenth-century professor.

So Smith certainly does construct explanations in which individuals are viewed as acting so as to try to do the best they can for themselves, given their objectives and given the situational constraints they face. But in the context of the work as a whole it is evident that Smithian actors, though certainly *purposive actors*, are not the *utility-maximizers* of modern economic theory.

In *The Wealth of Nations* individuals are not assumed to necessarily or unerringly go for individually optimal solutions to discrete decision problems. They neither invariably seek to achieve a result which is their own best interest, nor do they invariably achieve a result they intended. Smith does of course claim, in one of his most famous passages, that "(i)t is not from the benevolence of the butcher or the brewer or the baker that we expect our dinner, but from their regard to their own interest" (Smith, 1976, Bk. I, ch. II, p. 18). But even on the same page, he says, slightly more equivocally, "man has almost constant occasion for the help of his bretheren, and it is in vain for him to expect it from their benevolence *only*. He will be *more likely* to prevail if he can interest their self-love in his favour" (my emphases).

Ignoring the question of the relationship between the theory of the individual in *The Wealth of Nations* and *The Theory of Moral Sentiments*, it is clear that, even in the former, self-love is not seen as a totally reliable predictor of individual actions, even in those situations in which self-love is the primary motivation for action. However, as Sen has pointed out in commenting on related aspects of the misinterpretation of Smith by modern economists, "there are many... activities inside economics and outside it in which the simple pursuit of self-interest is not the great redeemer, and Smith did not assign a generally superior role to the pursuit of self-interest in any of his writings. The defence of self-interested behavior comes in specific contexts, particularly related to various contemporary bureaucratic barriers and other restrictions to economic transactions which made trade difficult and hampered production" (Sen, 1987, p. 25).

We might say that, for Smith, individuals are rational actors (though this is not his terminology) in the sense that they have purposes which they pursue in the course of their activities. Perhaps we might say that they were "zweckrational" or instrumentally rational as defined by Max Weber and understood by modern sociologists, (though in Smith there is more of a sense of action as a continuous process rather than a discrete event of Weber). In some institutional settings, these purposes are primarily selfish; in others, qualities such as humanity, justice, generosity, and public spirit are more dominant motivations. Further, quite apart from the possibility of error, which Smith readily allows, it is clear that he believed that, rather than having given and fixed preferences, individuals could learn by doing and action could change individuals—their tastes and desires, and indeed (to use a modern term) their whole personalities. A well-known passage, usually read as an argument about the aliqenating effects of the division of labor, suggests that, unlike modern economists, Smith had a theory of the social construction of the individual: he says that the understandings of the greater part of men are necessarily formed by their ordinary employments. "The man whose whole life is spent in performing a few simple operations... has no occasion to exert his understanding, or to exercise his invention.... He naturally loses, therefore, the habit of such exertion, and generally becomes as stupid and ignorant as it is possible for a human creature to become" (1976, Bk. V, ch. I, pt. III. art. II pp. 302-303). (In order to counteract this effect Smith advocates a limited form of universal primary education.) Further evidence that Smith does not adopt a presocial or asocial concept of the individual is found in Book I, where he states, "The difference of natural talents in different men is, in reality, much less than we are aware of; and the very different genius which appears to distinguish men of different professions, when grown to maturity, is not upon many occasions so much the cause, as the effect of the division of labour" (1976, Bk. I, ch. II, p. 19).

In the modern utility-maximizing model, objective givenness and stability of preferences are required for the economic model to generate (ideally, determine) predictions, and to generate them independently of any other theory. But Smith wrote before economics had been influenced by a desire to conform to the positivist/instrumentalist (what Habermas would call the empirical/analytic), prediction-obsessed model of good scientific practice drawn from physics,[3] and before it had developed strict lines of demarcation between itself and the other social sciences. He clearly did not view human behaviour as totally determined or its outcomes as completely predictable; human beings were far too complex in their motivations, too fallible, and too changeable for that. He merely expected economic theory to be able to help statesmen make better informed judgements about likely effects of their policies. Thus he had no *need* to impose restrictive assumptions such as modern economics imposes in its theory of action.

The passages from Smith discussed above also serve to illustrate a larger point: Smith was not an individualist in the sense that the term can be applied to modern economists. "Individualism" is a tricky concept, but for modern economists it primarily represents a methodological principle. Methodological individualism asserts that social explanations should be reducible to (or, possibly, "ultimately reducible to") statements about individuals. For example, the attempt by Stigler and Becker (1977) to ground the explanation of apparent changes in the tastes of individuals within price theory, is clearly in part a strategy to cut the ground from under the kinds of "holistic" attempts that sociologists make to account for taste changes as the products of changes at the level of social structure.[4] Yet that was precisely what Smith was doing in arguing that the process of the division of labor, which had reduced many jobs to a few simple operations, had increased the stupidity and ignorance of parts of the working population. Further, Smith did not merely assume that social structures and institutions affected individuals in their behaviour, he explicitly studied the development of and the relationships between such structures and institutions in their own right. Thus, in Book I, chapter XI, of *The Wealth of Nations*, he considers the relationships between social classes, or what he calls "the great, original and constituent orders of every civilised society," concluding that the interests of landowners and wage-earners are "strictly and inseparably connected with the general interest of society" but that this is not true of the third order, "those who live by profit" (Smith, 1976, p. 276).

Smith was not alone. Many of the major subsequent figures in the discipline, Malthus, Ricardo, Mill and Marx included, studied the relationships between economic institutions and social classes (defined in terms of property rights over the means of production), attempting to answer questions about the consequences of new knowledge and new techniques, new markets and new resources, for these relationships. (That Smith and Marx addressed similar questions is not of course at all the story that purveyors of the mythical version of the history tell.)

Similar structural and institutional interests can be found among mainstream economists right into this century. Marshall laid great stress on the need for us, as social scientists, to understand the ways in which activities *give rise to* wants, arguing that "much that is of chief interest in the science of wants" (i.e., economics) "is borrowed from the science of efforts and activities" (Marshall, 1949, p. 76) This view will no doubt be found puzzling by many modern mainstream economists. Only among those working in alternative research traditions—Marxists, post-Keynsians, radicals, institutionalists and subjectivists—is there sympathy with Marshall's dictum, only in these marginal fields is work being done which at least treats seriously the need to explain the social processes behind changing and culturally variable human wants.

I have argued that Smith was not a methodological individualist, building up his analytical model from atomistic individuals with presocially given wants, but a social scientist who took seriously the way in which the historical and institutional context moulds individuals and affects their actions. Further, I have stressed that for him, though individuals were purposive actors, self-love was not the sole motivation for action. Rather, action was clearly a learning process (in which error might of course occur), in the course of which changes might feed back into individuals' preferences.

Must we therefore abandon the well-established picture of Smith as the first great innovator of an explanatory model of the social world with the rational actor as its foundation and centerpiece? The answer must be no. As the example of Smith's explanation of the laziness of Oxford professors illustrates, Smith was a master of a form of explanation based on a concept of individuals as rational actors. But his concept of rational action and the role it played in his analysis was not the concept of the utility-maximizer which animates (or at any rate mechanically powers) most contemporary economic analysis. It is indeed much closer to the concepts of rational action found in the writings of modern subjectivists.

The subjectivist position is put very clearly by Peter Earl (1983) in the conclusion to his recent book *The Economic Imagination* in which he says of his central theme "(i)t is that the conventional economist's view of rationality is one which it is irrational to accept if the aim is to have a theory which is neither dangerously misleading nor impossible to operationalise." This is because "the world is a very sophisticated place, full of interdependencies between events in the past, present and future... Furthermore, events themselves, if we dare to isolate them, are complex structures." Earl thus argues that we must reject "neoclassical notions of rationality, but... not the idea that decision makers have reasons for their choices" (Earl, 1983, p. 188).

The subjectivists' insistence that they are not abandoning rationality as a central organising concept, but simply interpreting it in a more useful way, is put in its strongest form by Austrian writers, who of course do see themselves as the legitimate descendants of the Smithian tradition, and who place great importance on the idea that individuals are rational actors. (Though as von Mises has pointed out, given *his* claim that "(h)uman action is necessarily always rational... (t)he term "rational' is... pleonastic and must be rejected as such" (von Mises, 1949, p. 18)).

For the politically libertarian Austrians, the utility-maximizing model of action is condemned at the outset by its inability to leave any scope for human freedom of action, but they have also been the source of a powerful associated critique of its *explanatory* shortcomings. They stress in particular the failure of such a model to treat action as a process taking place in real time, in the course of which the environment, and knowledge about it, not merely *changes*, but (this is stressed particularly in the work of the veteran subjectivist George Shackle) is continuously *created*. This idea of novelty is found puzzling, I think, by many economists who, when they do attempt to build "real time' into their models, do so in a rather mechanical way, but it is very much in line with the concept of action as central to the process of social reproduction found in much contemporary sociology. Shackle would undoubtedly be more at home than most economists with Anthony Giddens' definition of action as "a stream of actual or contemplated causal interventions of corporeal beings in the ongoing process of events-in-the-world" where the term action "does not refer to a series of discrete acts combined together, but to a *continuous flow of conduct*" (Giddens, 1979, p. 55) (emphasis in the original).

## III. THE EMERGENCE AND FUNCTION OF THE MYTH IN MODERN ECONOMICS

It has been argued that the claim that "ever since its emergence in the late seventeenth and early eighteenth century, orthodox modern economic theorising has been built around... one central model of maximisation and self-equilibriation" (Hutchison, 1978) needs to be re-examined. The widespread acceptance of such a concept of the history of the discipline, by mainstream practitioners and critics alike, has clearly been associated with the strikingly monoparadigmatic nature of economics as compared with all other social sciences. (Indeed it would not be much of an exaggeration to say that in economics you're either within the mainstream tradition, or many doubt whether you should be counted as a real economist at all.)[5] While Kuhn, and many economists themselves, might view this monoparadigmatic state of affairs as indicative of the position of economics as the most "mature" of the social sciences, it could alternatively be argued that it simply, or at least partly, represents the power of the "occupiers of the high ground" in the subject to effectively police the discipline. In such a policing operation, maintaining, and convincing their opponents of the validity of, a reading of history which endorses the historical superiority, via direct descent from the founders, of the currently dominant position, is of course a valuable weapon for the dominant group. The weapon has been very effectively deployed, consciously or unconsciously, by modern economists, who have succeeded in getting many of their critics to accept their own misreading of history, with the result that many have misdirected their attacks at the whole mainstream tradition of Western economic thought, with its supposed central bogey-figure, rational economic (utility-maximizing) man. One can only surmise that economists' well-known antipathy to reading history of thought has contributed to the successful spread of this myth.

Just as the claim that the utility-maximizing model of action has a history in economics going back more than two hundred years is false, so many of the attendant weaknesses of the approach for many of its critics—individualism, a failure to attend to the social environment and ahistoricalism—are likewise less endemic in pre-twentieth century economic thought than many, including critics, seem to believe. They certainly cannot be indiscriminately attributed to the whole tradition of "bourgeois economic thought" from Smith to the present day. On the contrary, an economics comprehensively committed to a methodologically individualist epistemology, and to an ahistorical nomotheticism largely blind to the social environment in which action takes place, is a modern development. Its proponents can of course find all these tendencies illustrated at one time or another in pre-twentieth century writers (individualism in Mill or ahistorical nomotheticism in Ricardo for example), but it was not until this century that they became, in combination, a *requirement* of "good practice" mainstream economics. To a large extent, those groups of economists (notably institutionalists, post-Keynsians, radicals and subjectivists) who have attempted to maintain a "parliamentary opposition" to this hegemonic force within the discipline, have grouped themselves around opposition to one or more of these requirements.

Like utility maximization itself, abstraction from the social environment, ahistoricalism, and individualism are protected from significant critical examination within the modern mainstream research programme. They are clearly elements of the hard core. Thus "exogenous structural change" (i.e., change in other parts of the social structure) is introduced only as a last resort to explain shifts in time-series data in econometric work, and macrotheories which cannot be satisfactorily reduced to theories of individual utility-maximizing behaviour are deemed deficient and in need of "microfoundations" (see Phelps, 1971). In both cases, a plausible and intellectually coherent rationale could be offered for such positions, but it is significant that they seldom are, and that the majority of economists could certainly not produce them. (Only Hayek (1976), for example, has developed a serious and coherent defence of individualism in economics which has any significant currency among mainstream economists, and he is a leading member of the Austrian school.)[6]

The best that many economists can offer in defence of the hard core features of modern economic theory we have been discussing is to claim that they are "what economics is all about." The implication is of course that what it's all about and how it should go about it have been settled long since (since Adam Smith in fact!), and modern economists are therefore under no obligation to continue wasting time refighting old battles. But the battles have never really been fought to a conclusion, though skirmishes have taken place from time to time—over ahistoricalism and individualism during the German Methodenstreit at the end of the nineteenth century, over abstraction from the social environment in debates provoked by the American institutionalists early in this century, and again over individualism in the wake of logical positivism in the 1930s for example. All these are relatively recent skirmishes, which of course gives the lie to the belief that such issues have been resolved since the earliest period of modern economics. And they are, of course, very much live methodological issues in the rest of the social sciences. Somehow economics has, in the twentieth century, managed to successfully cocoon itself from the fierce debates between rival methodological positions which continue to rage in the rest of social science, and to convince itself that *it* successfully resolved them long ago. (Economists have not been notable for their zeal in offering their solutions to other social scientists still struggling to resolve these issues for themselves, perhaps because many economists are not actually very confident that they could articulate the arguments in favour of their hard core methodological, principles themselves).[7]

It is arguable that a principal cause of the emergence of the present comfortable methodological consensus in economics, alone among the social disciplines, was the introduction and spread of mathematical modeling centered on the use of calculus. This development was much influenced by the scientific desire, evident for example in the key figures of Walras and Jevons, to reconstruct economics along the lines of the successful model of late nineteenth century. This has, as Mirowski has noted, imposed an "analytical regimen" on economics (1984, p. 368) which helps explain, among other things, "the preference for techniques of constrained maximisation over any other analytical techniques," "the persistent use of an unobservable and unmeasurable value determinant—utility," and the modern controversy over "the necessity for a "microfoundations for macroeconomics" (p. 372) (the physical theory is essentially atomistic). Further, Mirowski argues that it is to the desire to model economics on pre-entropy physics that we must trace modern economics' commitment to the assumption that history does not matter, and its view that one can "practically ignore the question of how a market actually functions in real time, paying attention only to putative "eventual' outcomes" (p. 374). Mirowski's analysis begs the question of why a model with such characteristics attracted economists (they could for example have turned to evolutionary biology for their model instead), but his argument is nevertheless interesting and illuminating as far as it goes.

Mirowski pinpoints, correctly I believe, a number of detailed weaknesses in modern mainstream theory which he believes are directly attributable to the adoption by key theorists of a model for mathematical theory derived from nineteenth century energetics. My point here concerns more general methodological aspects of mainstream economics' development. A historicalism, individualism and abstraction from the rest of the social environment were not introduced into economics ab initio along with the mathematics by those who attempted to reconstruct economic theory along the lines of a metaphor borrowed from physics: all three had long been established positions in economics. It was simply that the form that mathematization took made such positions seem natural. Once they had been adopted by the mainstream, these methodological principles became established too and ceased to be viewed as problematic. The new direction in which economics had turned was accorded the status of "only legitimate heir" to the tradition founded by Adam Smith, and this new status served to put a stop to serious debate over methodological first principles.[8]

The curtailment of methodological debate did not, however, follow immediately in the train of the Marginal Revolution in the 1870s. As has already been noted, for example, someone as "mainstream" as Alfred Marshall (1949) was arguing for a more socially and institutionally situated, and less individualistic, economics in his *Principles of Economics* of 1890, a book which continued to have widespread currency as a textbook at least until the late 1930s. I believe that the new concept of rational action and its concomitant methodological principles cannot really be said to have become dominant in the mainstream of the subject until the 1930s.

In the establishment of this change, Lionel Robbins' classic *The Nature and Significance of Economic Science* (1932) must be seen as a crucial milestone. Robbins was of course responsible for the definition of economics which is taught to every student and which has almost universal currency: "(e)conomics is the science which studies human behaviour as a relationship between ends and scarce means which have alternative uses" (Robbins, 1932, p. 16).

Of course, though it seems seldom to be noticed, this definition is pretty vacuous without some specification of the mechanism by which means and ends are related. Robbins makes clear that it is *rationality of action* which plays this role. But the form of rationality which Robbins assumes is closer to the older tradition in economics: people *choose* among scarce means in order to achieve their desired ends: and "it is arguable that if behaviour is not conceived as *purposive*, then the conception of the means-ends relationship which economics studies has no meaning" (1932, p. 93) (my emphasis). What is more, Robbins made quite clear both that the purposes the rational actor pursued were to be understood as the actor's *subjectively formulated* ends ("(t)he idea of an end, which is fundamental to our conception of the economic, is not possible to define in terms of external behaviour only" (p. 89), and that rational action in this sense was not to be confused with consistent action ("this is not to say in the least that all purposive action is completely consistent," p. 89). Thus, the explanatory practices of Smith (as illustrated by his explanation of the lazy habits of Oxford professors), and indeed, though I have no space to document this claim here, with the explanatory practice of the majority of economists up until this century. What makes this matter so peculiar is that Robbins's definition of economics was adopted by those who were in the process of abandoning the earlier concept of rational action in favour of the "knee-jerk" utility-maximizing version. That is to say that most of those who adopted Robbins' definition of economics did so at the same time as they were abandoning the concept of action as subjectively purposive, which he viewed as implicit in his definition and necessary to give it meaning.

The adoption of a deterministic model of action in place of the earlier purposive concept fitted in with the desire of a growing number of economists for a predictively successful theory which would match the contemporary concept of satisfactory science—the same objective which had led theoretical innovators such as Walras to borrow physics' mathematical apparatus in the first place. Adoption of the apparatus of differential calculus required that individuals be seen as consistent maximizers with well-defined utility functions, and this is what the actors became (subsequent modifications notwithstanding).[9]

## IV.  CONCLUSION

Unmasking the "ever since Adam Smith" myth does not constitute an argument against the methodologically individualist, asocial, and ahistorical orthodoxy of modern mainstream economics. But, at present, "the weight of tradition" serves to obscure the need for an intellectually respectable rationale for the hard core. And such a rationale is sorely needed, not least by those working at the imperialist frontiers of the subject who have been brave enough to take on sociologists and political scientists on their own ground. Other social scientists have not been trained to see individualism et al as unquestionably necessary components of satisfactory social explanation and are prone to ask searching questions of economists who stray into their territories.

It will, however, by now be apparent that I believe economists would do well to consider the readoption of a less mechanically deterministic, more purposive, concept of rational individual action. Those economists committed to a thoroughgoing instrumentalist concept of the subject, which places ability to produce reliable predictions above all other criteria of good theory, and who are also committed to methodological individualism, would undoubtedly find such a shift hard to contemplate, for only a deterministic model of action is compatible with such a position.[10] Indeed, many economists appear fearful of abandoning mechanistic utility-maximizing models for fear that in their absence theoretical chaos would break out, simultaneously undermining their scientific respectability and their ability to play the role of policy scientists (not to say their lucrative consultancies).

On the other hand, defenders of the status quo have signally failed to provide good grounds for believing that social systems exhibit the characteristics necessary for them to be the objects of theories in which explanation entails prediction. On the contrary, social systems exhibit novelty rather than invariant empirical regularities through time. They are not, and cannot be experimentally transformed into, the closed systems which are necessary for the purposes of testing theories by their predictions. And if this is the case, then even the instrumentalist let-out (that it is prediction rather than explanation with which the social scientist should be primarily concerned) ultimately fails, for if and when a previously predictively successful theory stops generating reliable predictions, theoretical chaos breaks out anyway. (Indeed, in principle this sort of theoretical chaos is the worst sort possible, since if an established theory has been adopted purely for its predictive success, once it ceases to predict well scientists are left with no signposts to tell them where to begin constructing a replacement.)

There is reason to believe, however, that those economists fearful of losing their scientific status and claims to policy relevance along with their mechanical model are unduly anxious. Many natural scientists, notably evolutionary biologists, study phenomena which constitute open systems in which, while retrodiction may provide some test of a theory, *pre*diction is impossible. (For example, The nature of genetic mutation and its interaction with a changing environment makes the evolution of a species in future time quite unpredictable, but does not thereby render its past evolution inexplicable.) Inability to make determinate predictions (already the reality of economic policy analysis) need be no bar to using the theory as a basis for theoretically informed policy analysis and (nondeterministic) forecasting. (It is worth remembering that Smith was first and foremost a successful policy scientist.)[11]

Such forecasting is more likely to succeed if the economist draws on the work of other social scientists, in order to make use of their analyses of the processes at work in the institutional environment in which economic activity takes place, and of the effects of such processes on individuals' objectives and aims.

Some economists accept the value of paying more attention to the work of sociologists, psychologists, and other social scientists. But this is hardly the direction in which most mainstream theorists are going. This is by no means to say that all their work is uninteresting or unimportant. But each theoretical development should be assessed for the contribution it makes to our theoretical tools for explaining and understanding reality, and none should be spared critical attention on the basis of a spurious claim to be logical developments of a tradition stretching back to Adam Smith.

What is worrying about modern mainstream economics is how narrow the focus of many theorists has become, and how much attention is addressed to problems within the theory which are themselves the legacy of the formalization and mathematization process of recent history, rather than being concentrated on the problems of explaining real social phenomena in the world. The "problem" of producing simpler and more elegant axioms of choice epitomises this whole tendency. Those who concern themselves with it are remarkably uninformative about how their attempts to refine the axioms will improve economists' ability to explain real world phenomena. Some (though not all) critics of the current mainstream orthodoxy in economics do, in contrast, address themselves to the problems of explaining economic phenomena as they really exist. Of course, the readoption of the earlier concept of rational action inevitably means moving away from the grand universal theories which have come to *be* twentieth-century economics for many people and toward explanation which is temporarily and culturally grounded.[12] This kind of economics is of course closer to the vision of Alfred Marshall, who insisted:

> (t)he function... of analysis and deduction in economics is not to forge a few long chains of reasoning, but to forge rightly many short chains and single connecting links (Marshall, 1949, p. 638).

## ACKNOWLEDGMENT

An earlier version of this paper was presented at the George Shackle Conference, University of Surrey, Guildford, U.K., in September 1984. In addition to the audience on that occasion (and in particular George Shackle), I am grateful to John Dearlove, Roger Farmer, Mark Matthews and Warren Samuels for various kinds of help and constructive criticism in the course of the development of this article. The argument, and any mistakes therein, remain indubitably my own.

## NOTES

1. In fairness to Hutchison, who has a far greater sensitivity to the history of the discipline than many of those whose views he is summarising, it should be noted that he continues "(b)ut by Adam Smith the model was not carried to extremes of unrealistic abstraction, and was based on historical and psychological evidence and analysis, including a view of man" (1978, p. 200).

2. This term is intended to have a wider reference than "neoclassical economics," which might be viewed as the most orthodox part of the mainstream. The term "neoclassical" has a confused history and a confused contemporary usage. Perhaps, as Aspromogourgos suggests (following Hicks) it would be better if the term were entirely expunged from the language (Aspromogourgos, 1986).

3. Philip Mirowski has discussed the influence of physical science models on the development of marginalist economics (Mirowski, 1984).

4. It is striking that, a year before the publication of that article, Becker was arguing (1976a, p. 14) that "the preferences that are given and stable in the economic approach, are analysed by the sociologist, psychologist, and probably most successfully by the sociobiologist." Sociobiology would of course not pretend to explain changes in "preferences" in a time scale shorter than the many millenia it takes for natural selection to produce evolutionary change, and if it is argued that sociobiology gives the "most successful" explanations of tastes, then it follows that it must be being assumed that fundemental tastes are unchanging within the time scales of interest to social scientists. Nevertheless, Becker goes on to argue that "(t)he value of other social sciences is nor diminished even by an enthusiastic and complete acceptance of the economic approach." But by 1977 it has clearly occurred to him that this generous-hearted pluralism is inconsistent. Stigler and Becker (1977) claim

to use the economic approach to explain observed changes in preferences as compatible with underlying tastes which are "stable over time and similar among people." They hence directly challenge sociological accounts of, for example, historical, cultural, or class-based differences among people in their wants, desires, or concepts of what is good for them, and so forth (see Sahlins, 1974; Douglas and Isherwood, 1980; Elias, 1978), while interestingly no longer even mentioning sociology in their list of competing sources of explanatory frameworks. It may be noted that Stigler and Becker's individualistic starting point for accounting for "differences of tastes between people" does not necessarily follow from a recognition of the biological basis of human behaviour. The neurobiologist Steven Rose, for example argues that the individual's development in a particular social environment determines "an individual's behaviour pattern and mode of thought" and argues for "a recognition by neurobiologists of this individuality and social conditioning at the cellular and biochemical level" (Rose, 1976, p. 32).

5.   In an attempt to study the correctness of the "widespread feeling that modern economics has established itself as a science enjoying a high degree of consensus" Bruno Frey et al. (1984) have attempted an empirical, cross-cultural, study of economists' views. They produced a less than clear-cut picture, with significant dissensus on some questions and notable national differences. (The highest degree of consensus was found on the effectiveness and desirability of the price system as a social choice mechanism.) It should, however, be pointed out that the propositions put to respondents concerned policy issues rather than economic methodology. It is surely with regard to method rather than outcomes of analysis that economics is a such a strikingly consensual discipline.

6.   This point is echoed by Boland, who says "there is little methodological discussion of why economics *should* involve only explanations that can be reduced to the decision-making of individuals—except, perhaps, for Hayek's arguments for the informational simplicity of methodological individualism" (Boland, 1982, p. 28).

7.   The favour is reciprocated. Few philosophers and social scientists writing on the methodology of the social sciences make mention of economics. In fact, its absence from countless books claiming to deal with the philosophy of social science, social explanation, the foundations of social theory and so forth, is seldom even remarked, perhaps because so few economists read them. In a review of two volumes of collected papers on topics in the philosophy of social science by Charles Taylor (Hands, 1987, p. 172), D. Wade Hands remarks that the papers "seem systematically to avoid economics." What he doesn't say is that it's rare to find a work in this area of which that could not be said.

8.   Kenneth Arrow is one of the very few mainstream economists to have noted that, although "(e)conomic theory, since it has been systematic, has been based on some notion of rationality," it has not always been based on the same notion of rationality. He points out that it was not until "the great pioneers of the marginalist revolution, Jevons, Walras, and Menger (anticipated... by H.H. Gossen)" that the rationality hypothesis for the consumer became "the maximisation of utility under a budget constraint," a formulation which allowed demand to be defined as a function of all prices and made possible the formulation of the general equilibrium of the economy (Arrow, 1987, p. 204).

9. The widely acknowledged low level of predictive success of the consequent body of theory has not, in the main, led economists to question their adoption of a deterministic concept of action. Rather, they have responded either in the optimistic mode—"let's have a tighter definition of rational behaviour" (e.g., the rational expectations theorists)—or in the resigned mode—"maybe we'll just have to accept that there are more things we can't explain than we thought." Arrow illustrates both responses: "the next step in analysis, I would conjecture, is a more consistent assumption of computability in the formulation of economic hypotheses. This is likely to have its own difficulties because, of course, not everything is computable, and there will be in this sense an inherently unpredictable element in rational behaviour. Some will be glad of such a conclusion" (Arrow, 1987, p. 214).

10. This is not to say that the deterministic model of action has to be held to be "really true," the instrumentalist defence—that it be treated "as if" it is true—will do perfectly well.

11. Policy-relevant work based on ideal-typical scenarios rather than deterministic predictions is perfectly possible. For an illustration with accompanying methodological justification, see Farmer and Barrell (1981).

12. This need not of course invalidate the continuing development of formal models which can be "set to work" in particular socially and institutionally specified environments.

# REFERENCES

Arrow, Kenneth. 1963. *Social Choice and Individual Values*. New Haven: Yale University Press. (First published 1951).

————. 1987. "Rationality of Self and Others in an Economic System." In *Rational Choice: The Contrast Between Economics and Psychology*, edited by Robin M. Hogarth and Melvin W, Reder. Chicago: University of Chicago Press.

Aspromogourgos, Tony. 1986. "On the Origins of the Term 'Neoclassical'," *Cambridge Journal of Economics* 10(September):265-270.

Becker, Gary S. 1976a. *The Economic Approach to Human Behavior*. Chicago: University of Chicago Press.

————. 1976b. "Altruism, Egoism and Genetic Fitness." In *The Economic Approach to Human Behavior*. Chicago: University of Chicago Press.

Bhaskar, Roy. 1979. *The Possibility of Naturalism: A Philosophical Critique of the Contemporary Human Sciences*. Brighton: Harvester.

Boland, Lawrence. 1982. *The Foundations of Economic Method*. London: George Allen and Unwin.

Buchanan, James. 1972. "Toward Analysis of Closed Behavioral Systems." In *Theory of Public Choice*, edited by J. Buchanan and R. Tollison. Ann Arbor: University of Michigan Press.

Caldwell, Bruce. 1982. *Beyond Positivism*. London: George Allen and Unwin.

Coats, A.W. 1983. "The Revival of Subjectivism in Economics." In *Beyond Positive Economics,* edited by J. Wiseman. London: Macmillan.

Dolan, Edwin G. 1976. *The Foundations of Modern Austrian Economics*. Kansas City: Sheed and Ward.

Douglas, Mary, and Baron Isherwood. 1980. *The World of Goods: Towards an Anthropology of Consumption*. Harmondsworth, England: Penguin.

Earl, Peter. 1983. *The Economic Imagination*. Brighton: Wheatsheaf Books.

Elias, Norbert. 1978. *The History of Manners*. Oxford: Basil Blackwell.

Elster, Jon. 1979. *Ulysses and the Sirens: Studies in Rationality and Irrationality*. Cambridge: Cambridge University Press.

————. 1983. *Sour Grapes: Studies in the Subversion of Rationality*. Cambridge: Cambridge University Press.

Farmer, Mary K. 1988. "The Rationality Totem: Some Thoughts on the Past and Present Role of the Rationality Postulate in Economics." University of Sussex mimeo.

Farmer, Mary K., and Ray Barrell. 1981. "Entrepreneurship and Government Policy: The Case of the Housing Market." *Journal of Public Policy* 1(August): 307-332.

Frey, Bruno S., et al. 1984. "Consensus and Dissension Among Economists: An Empirical Enquiry." *American Economic Review*, 74(December): 986-984.

Friedman, Milton. 1953. "The Methodology of Positive Economics." In *Essays in Positive Economics*. Chicago: University of Chicago Press.

Giddens, Anthony. 1979. *Central Problems in Social Theory*. London: Macmillan.

Hands, D. Wade. 1987. Review of two books by Charles Taylor. *Economics and Philosophy* 3(April): 172-75.

Hayek, F.A. 1976. *Individualism and Economic Order*. London: Routledge and Kegan Paul.

Hollis, Martin, and Edward Nell. 1975. *Rational Economic Man*. Cambridge: Cambridge University Press.

Hollis, Martin, and Steven Lukes. 1982. *Rationality and Relativism*. Oxford: Basil Blackwell.

Hutchison, Terence. 1978. *On Revolutions and Progress in Economic Knowledge*. Cambridge: Cambridge University Press.

Klammer, Arjo. 1984. *The New Classical Macroeconomics*. Brighton, England: Wheatsheaf Books.

Latsis, Spiro. 1972. "Situational Determinism in Economics," *British Journal for the Philosophy of Science* 23(August): 207-245.

Leibenstein, Harvey. 1980. "Microeconomics and X-efficiency Theory." *The Public Interest* (Special Issue).

Loasby, Brian. 1978. "Whatever happened to Marshall's Theory of Value?" *Scottish Journal of Political Economy* 25(February): 1-12.

McCloskey, Donald. 1986. *The Rhetoric of Economics*. Brighton, England: Wheatsheaf Books.

McKenzie, Richard B., and Gordon Tullock. 1978. *The New World of Economics*. 2nd edition. Homewood, IL: Richard D. Irwin.

McKenzie, Richard B. 1983. *The Limits of Economic Science*. Boston: Kluwer Nijhoff.

Marshall, Alfred. 1949. *Principles of Economics*. 8th edition. London: Macmillan.

Mirowski, Philip. 1984. "Physics and the Marginalist Revolution." *Cambridge Journal of Economics*. 8(December): 361-379. (Reprinted in 1988. *Against Mechanism*. Totowa, NJ: Rowman & Littlechild.)

Phelps, E.S., ed. 1971. *Microeconomic Foundations of Employment and Inflation Theory*. London: Macmillan.

Robbins, Lionel. 1932. *An Essay on the Nature and Significance of Economic Science*. London: Macmillan.

Rose, Steven. 1976. *The Conscious Brain*. Harmondsworth: Pelican.

Rosenberg, Alexander. 1981. *Sociobiology and the Preemption of Social Science*. Oxford: Basil Blackwell.

Sahlins, Marshall. 1974. *Stone Age Economics*. London: Tavistock.

Samuels, Warren. 1977. "The Political Economy of Adam Smith." *Ethics* 87(April): 189-207.

Schutz, Alfred. 1964. "The Problem of Rationality in the Social World." In *Collected Papers II*, edited by A. Broderson. The Hague: Martinus Nijhoff.

Sen, Amartya, and Bernard Williams, eds. 1982. *Utilitarianism and Beyond*. Cambridge: Cambridge University Press.

Sen Amartya. 1987. *On Ethics and Economics*. Oxford: Basil Blackwell.

Sheffrin, Steven. 1983. *Rational Expectations*. Cambridge: Cambridge University Press.

Simon, H.A. 1982. *Models of Bounded Rationality*, 2 vols. Cambridge, MA: M.I.T. Press.

Smith, Adam. 1976. *The Wealth of Nations*, edited by Edwin Cannaan. Chicago: University of Chicago Press.

Stigler, George J., and Gary S. Becker. 1977. "De Gustibus non est Disputandum." *American Economic Review* 67(March): 2, 76-90.

Taylor, Charles. *Philosophy and the Human Sciences: Philosophical Papers II*. Cambridge: Cambridge University Press.

von Mises, Ludwig. 1949. *Human Action*. London: Hodge.

Ward, Benjamin. 1972. *What's Wrong with Economics?* London: Macmillan.

Weber, Max. 1968. *Economy and Society*, 2 vols. Edited by Guenther Roth and Claus Wittich. Berkeley: University of California Press.

Winch, Donald. 1978. *Adam Smith's Politics*. Cambridge: Cambridge University Press.

Wiseman, Jack. 1983. *Beyond Positive Economics*. London: Macmillan.

# KEYNES' CRITIQUE OF WAGE CUTTING AS ANTIDEPRESSIONARY STRATEGY

John E. Elliott

An examination of Keynes' critique of wage-cutting as an antidepressionary strategy, approximately a half century after publication of *The General Theory of Employment, Interest and Money* (1936, hereinafter referred to as *GT*), is pertinent to contemporary economics for several main reasons. First, this critique is integral to Keynes' critical assessment of neoclassical economics in general and thereby is a strategic complement to his own alternative theory. Second, Keynes' own views on the inefficacy of wage (and price) cuts as means to overcome depression are significantly different from standard "textbook Keynesianism," and, thus, are essential to the broader issue of differentiation between "Keynes and the Keynesians." Third, through Keynes' critical discussion of wage and price cutting, it is possible to infer anticipatory responses to

Research in the History of Economic Thought and Methodology, Volume 9, pages 129-169.
Copyright © 1992 by JAI Press Inc.
All rights of reproduction in any form reserved.
ISBN: 1-55938-428-X

contemporary new classical and other criticism of "Keynesian" theories of unemployment. This reinforces the insight that criticism of Keynesian" theory is not ipso facto applicable to Keynes (or to contemporary theory rooted in Keynes', as differentiated from Keynesian, thought).

In the first three sections of this essay, I endeavor to clarify the basic character of Keynes' argument in terms of his critical differentiation between postulates and theories in neoclassical economics as related to the demand for and supply of labor, both in *GT* (notably chapter 2) and as subsequently emended in his *Economic Journal* article of 1939. The fourth section examines his more extended critique of the neoclassical theory of wage and price cutting and unemployment in chapter 19 of *GT*. The final section returns to chapter 2 of *GT* to consider Keynes' rejection of a secondary aspect of both the postulate and the theory of the neoclassical supply of labor and to assess the role of "sticky" wages in Keynes critical analysis.

## I.  KEYNES' TWO LEVELS OF CRITICISM OF NEOCLASSICAL UNEMPLOYMENT THEORY

In one, very broad sense, Keynes' critique of the classical/neoclassical perspective concerning unemployment is a challenge to its scope and assumptions. At one level, the standard theory of value and resource allocation "*assumes* full employment." In the received theory of value, a "whole dimension of affairs has been neglected." How, then, "could it offer any hint or hope of a theory to explain unemployment" (Shackle, 1967, p. 146)?

Keynes appears to be writing at this very broad level in chapter 1 of *GT*, where he presents the socially bold, but analytically mild, claim that the "classical" theory's "postulates" are applicable to:

> a *special case only* and not to the general case, the situation which it *assumes* being a *limiting point* of the possible positions of equilibrium (*GT*, italics added).
>
>   Moreover, the classical theory is discordant with the empirical realities of the actual economic society, so that the theory's teaching is "misleading and disastrous if we attempt to apply it to the facts of experience" (*GT*, p. 3).

Keynes continues in this broad vein in his famous rejection of the "false division" between the theory of value and distribution and the theory of money and prices (the latter presented in "Volume II, or more often in a separate treatise"), and proposes instead a "right dichotomy" between a theory of firm and industry with a "*given* quantity of resources" and a theory of output and employment "*as a whole,*" or, alternatively, between a theory of "stationary equilibrium" and that of "shifting equilibrium," the latter being a terrain of uncertain and changing expectations and monetary linkages between present and future (*GT*, pp. 292-93).

At this level of critique, Keynes, in effect, identifies an error of *omission*, or at least misplaced emphasis and relative neglect, in neoclassical theory, which he proposes to rectify. This requires a modification in both the scope of economics and its assumptions. Economics must now systematically encompass a study of output and employment "as a whole," including, notably, time, uncertainty, and "shifting equilibria," with no prelimiting assumption of full employment equilibrium. In such a project, the novelty lies "as much in the question as in the answer" (Ackley, 1961, p. 218).

From this perspective, also, the "young and innocent" are warned "away from Book I (especially the difficult Chapter 3)" and are urged on to the core of Keynes' positive contribution in Books III and IV, and policy implications in Book VI, especially chapter 24 (Samuelson, 1946, p. 149). If criticism of the accepted theory lies "not so much" in "logical flaws in its analysis" as in the fact that its "tacit assumptions are seldom or never satisfied," it "cannot solve the economic problems of the actual world" (*GT*, p. 378).

The "classical theory comes into its own again," however, if full employment is achieved, through Keynesian-style policies. Supposing the volume of output is given at a full employment level, Keynes raises "no objection" to the classical microeconomic analysis of resources allocation and income distribution (*GT*, pp. 378-79). Thus, hints of Samuelson's (1967, p. 361) "grand neoclassical synthesis," wherein the microeconomic theory of value and distribution is perceived in neoclassical terms and Keynesian analysis provides the practical macroeconomic arguments for expansionary monetary and fiscal policy, finds some foundations in Keynes' *GT* itself, presupposing that Keynes' critique is restricted to the scope of received theory and its prevailing assumption of full employment.

At a second level of critical analysis, however, Keynes clearly perceives full employment as a conclusion from a theoretical argument, resting in turn on more fundamental assumptions. At this second level of critique, Keynes challenges neoclassical theory, not merely its scope and assumptions. For example, Keynes presents a conception of equilibrium as a "point of rest" or balance between contending forces, which may be or may not involve market-clearing or equality between supply and demand (*GT*, p. 243; Chick, 1983, p. 21). Similarly, he postulates a general tendency toward self-adjustment (for example, for the marginal efficiency of capital to become equal to the rate of interest), but denies the inevitability or plausibility of self-adjustment "at the optimum level" (*GT*, p. 339; Milgate and Eatwell, 1983, p. 256). Finally, as shall be elaborated shortly, Keynes rejects (or substantially modifies) the neoclassical theory of the labor supply and demand functions. In embarking on his task, Keynes modifies or abandons some neoclassical assumptions perceived as impediments to his task, notably assumptions concerning perfect (as distinguished from atomistic and free) market processes—that is, perfect foresight, price flexibility, and mobility, and unlimited markets—but goes out of his way to retain (and emphasize the retention of) several others, notably, the traditional triad of diminishing returns, profit-maximization, and (atomistic and free, if not perfect) competition.

Keynes' first level of critique might be called "external," in the sense that it supplements or complements the neoclassical theoretical framework. His second level of argument is "internal," in that it questions received theory itself, to a considerable extent on its own grounds. In intellectual strategy, Hegel once remarked, if one wishes to best one's opponents in debate, one must enter their lair, and confront them in their own domain, on their own terms. If this is not done, one's opponents may simply reply, "Ah, but those are not my assumptions." In accepting several prominent neoclassical assumptions, Keynes adopts Hegel's proposed strategy and takes on his neoclassical opponents partly on their own ground. He thereby protects the integrity of his theory from the counterargument that he has simply substituted alternative assumptions, thus rendering it less vulnerable to counterattack, and leaves to subsequent discussion—both in *GT* and elsewhere (1939)—the demonstration that adoption of more descriptively realistic assumptions does not alter the core of his critique and alternative theory.

Keynes' own perspective consequently contrasts sharply with other popular interpretations of contending perspectives on wages, prices, and unemployment. For example, in one representative discussion, neoclassical and "neo-Keynesian" economists are perceived to "both accept the same basic theoretical apparatus," including neoclassical labor demand and labor supply functions, "differing only in the assumptions they make before they operate it" (Crouch, 1972, p. 163). From this viewpoint, unemployment is derived strictly by substituting such (neo-Keynesian) assumptions as price, wage, or interest rate rigidity, or money illusions, for such (neoclassical) assumptions as perfect flexibility in all prices and the absence of money illusions. Although useful for differentiating between neoclassicism and some versions of neo-Keynesian analysis, this typology is definitely misleading if extended to an interpretation of neoclassicism versus Keynes.

Insofar as Keynes develops a second level of critique, he, in effect, identifies an error of *commission* in neoclassical theory. The corollary is that an alternative theory is feasible and needed on neoclassicism's own terms, not simply by virtue of the substitution of different assumptions. From this perspective also, it is some of the relatively neglected chapters of Keynes' *GT* that are most relevant, notably chapters 2 and 19.

## II. EMPLOYMENT AND REAL WAGES: POSTULATES VERSUS THEORIES

Although departing fundamentally from the "classical" theory's explanation of labor market-clearing and thereby full-employment-equilibrating behavior, Keynes' exposition, in chapter 2 of *GT*, emphasizes one "important point of agreement" with that theory's underlying assumptions. With a "given organization, equipment, and technique, real wages [$W/P$] and the volume of output [$O$] (and hence employment [$N$]) are uniquely correlated..." (*GT*, p. 17). Supposing diminishing returns to labor, an increase (decrease) in employment, caused by an expansion (contraction) in aggregate demand ($D$), will, indeed must, elicit a reduction (increase) in the real-wage. This follows from the "classical" theory's "first postulate"—which Keynes accepts—that, for profit-maximizing firms under competitive conditions, the "wage is equal to the marginal product of labor" [$W/$

$P = MPL]$ ($GT$, p. 5). Hence, in the event of diminishing returns to labor, the line of causation, for Keynes, would be roughly as follows:

$$\uparrow\downarrow AD \rightarrow \uparrow\downarrow O \rightarrow \uparrow\downarrow N \rightarrow \downarrow\uparrow MPL \rightarrow \uparrow\downarrow MC \rightarrow \uparrow\downarrow P \rightarrow \downarrow\uparrow W/P$$

In short, according to Keynes, it is not real wages which determine the demand for labor (and thereby output). It is "other forces (that is, aggregate demand for output and thereby labor) which determine the general level of real wages" ($GT$, p. 13). As Keynes summarizes it in chapter 3 of $GT$,

> the propensity to consume and the rate of new investment [$AD$] between them determine the volume of unemployment [$N$], and the volume of employment [via $MPL$, $MC$, and $P$] is uniquely related to a given level of real wages—not the other way around ($GT$, p. 30).

By contrast, Keynes subsequently characterizes the neoclassical argument concerning the labor market as based on a "demand schedule for labour in industry as a whole relating the quantity of employment to different levels of wages" ($GT$, p. 259). At the level of the individual firm, the neoclassical demand function for labor is, of course, derived from the marginal product of labor, via the "first postulate" of the competitive market, profit-maximizing rule ($W/P = MPL$). But the neoclassical theorem (that $Nd = f(W/P)$, wherein $N$ varies inversely with changes in $W/P$) differs from and presents a stronger claim than the assumption concerning variable proportions of inputs upon which it is based (that $MPL = f(N)$, where $MPL$ varies inversely with $N$).

Consequently, beginning from an initial position of unemployment, reductions in money wages, in Keynes' summary of orthodox theory ($GT$, p. 257), via lower costs and lower prices elicited thereby, cause increases in demand, which thus validate higher output and employment, albeit, because of diminishing returns, with an ensuing lower marginal product of labor and therefore lower real wages (which implies that prices fall less than wages do).

Keynes' summary of the neoclassical argument thus starts with money (and thereby real) wage reductions and, via an aggregate demand for labor function derived from marginal product of labor schedules, concludes with higher employment and aggregate demand.

Keynes' exposition of his own position commences with increases in aggregate demand and employment, and, via the marginal product of labor schedule, concludes with reductions in real-wages. Thus, the "revolutionary break that Keynes made with classical theory was to turn it on its head. At the aggregate level, it is not the real-wage that determines employment; rather, it is the level of employment, determined by aggregate demand, which determines the real-wages" (Thirwall, 1981).

According to Meltzer, Keynes "accepts the classical theory of the demand for labor" (1981, p. 53). The textual evidence given to support this interpretation, however, is simply Keynes' acceptance of the "first postulate," under conditions of diminishing returns (*GT*, pp. 5, 17). It is Keynes' acceptance of diminishing marginal productivity of labor, Meltzer states, which suggests that "Keynes' demand for labor is obtained from the first-order condition of the neoclassical production function" (1983, p. 74). In his summary of the neoclassical theory, Keynes observes that the "first postulate" gives us the demand for labor schedule (GT, p. 6). What Meltzer here implies is that by accepting the underlying assumptions of neoclassical theory associated with the "first postulate" Keynes has thereby also accepted the theorem concerning the demand for labor derived from those assumptions.

But, in effect, this conflates (1) $W/P = MPL$ and $MPL = f(N)$ with (2) $Nd = f(W/P)$. It is true that if (2) is accepted, (1) is logically consistent with it. But it does not follow that if (1) is accepted, (2) may validly be derived from it at the aggregate level. As illustrated in Figure 1, for example, if employment is $N2$ (because of a higher level of $AD$), condition (1) is met at point B and the real-wage is $(W/P)2$. If employment, by contrast, is $N1$ (because of a lower level of $AD$), condition (1) is met at point A and the real-wage is $(W/P)1$. A reduction in real wages for example, from $(W/P)1$ to $(W/P)2$, however, may or may not be accompanied by an increase in employment (for example, from $N1$ to $N2$) (as implied by condition (2)). In accepting the "first postulate" of neoclassical economics, Keynes does not thereby commit himself to its associated demand for labor function. More precisely, as shall be discussed more fully in section IV, he expressly rejects as "invalid" the simple derivation of condition (2) at the macro level from condition (1) for individual firms (GT, p. 259).

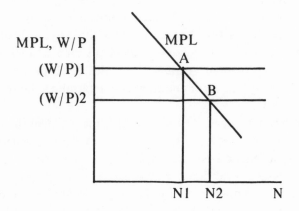

*Figure 1.*

It thus seems clear that, for Keynes, as Davidson (1967, 1981, 1983a) and others (for example, Tuchscherer, 1979, pp. 102-103) aptly put it, the *MPL* curve is not (Keynes' view of) the (aggregate) demand for labor curve. Although a demand for labor curve may be derived that is consistent with Keynes' argument (Weintraub, 1958; Davidson and Smolensky, 1964), that argument is logically cohesive without it. Given aggregate demand and supply functions (delineated, by Keynes, in wage units), employment may be derived directly. Given employment and a marginal product of labor schedule, the associated profit-maximizing, real-wage level may be designated.

## III. KEYNES' MODIFICATIONS OF THE ASSUMPTIONS UNDERLYING THE "FIRST POSTULATE"

The argument in the preceding paragraph is reinforced by Keynes' emendations to the assumptions underlying the "first postulate," both in *GT* and elsewhere. If one or more of the assumptions embodied in the first postulate is abandoned or modified without requiring alterations in Keynes' own theory, the argument which derives the neoclassical theorem of the demand for labor function as a matter of logical necessity from the originally joint neoclassical/Keynes assumptions is clearly problematic.

This is certainly the view of the matter taken by Keynes. Although Keynes was resistive to abandoning the assumption of diminishing returns, apparently on grounds of perceived descriptive accuracy— even in the light of empirical studies by Dunlop (1938) and Tarshis (1939) that money wages and real wages tend to fluctuate together— this resistance was in no way based on a perceived necessity of diminishing returns for the cohesion of his own theory:

> That I was an easy victim of the traditional conclusion (that is, that $W/P$ falls, because of diminishing returns, when $W$ rises under conditions of rising $AD$ and expanding $N$) because it fitted my theory...this conclusion was inconvenient, since it had a tendency to offset the influence of the main forces ($AD$ and $N$) I was discussing and made it necessary for me to introduce qualifications...(1939, p. 40).

Indeed, if

> it proves right to adopt the contrary generalization (that is, that $W$ and $W/P$ rise together as $AD$ and $N$ expand, presumably because diminishing returns are circumvented), it would be possible to simplify considerably the more complicated version of my fundamental explanation which I have expounded in my "General Theory" (p. 40).

Suppose, for example, that the marginal product of labor remains constant, at least over a substantial range of output, under conditions of significant unemployment. Abstracting momentarily from changes in money wages, real wages would also remain unchanged. As illustrated in Figure 2, an increase in employment from $N1$ to $N2$ (caused by an expansion in aggregate demand, under conditions of constant marginal productivity of labor), would leave real wages unchanged, at $W/P$). If, to take a second example, as illustrated in Figure 3, the marginal product of labor schedule shifts upward (for example, from $MPL1$ to $MPL2$), an increase in employment (for example, from $N1$ to $N2$), caused by an expansion in aggregate demand, would result in an increase in real wages (for example, from $(W/P)1$ to $(W/P)2$).

For Keynes' purpose, an explanation of why the marginal product of labor and hence real wages might remain constant (or rise) rather than fall as employment increases would be interesting, but not essential. Whatever the theoretical rationale, abandonment of the assumption of diminishing returns considerably simplifies the "more

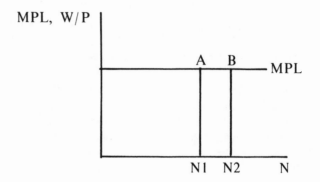

*Figure 2.*

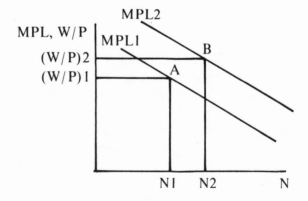

*Figure 3.*

complicated version" of Keynes' "fundamental explanation"
expounded in *GT*. Comparing Figures 1 through 3, the central core
of Keynes' theoretical argument and its line of causation remains
unchanged in each instance. All that differs is the outcome for real-
wages. This does not affect Keynes' theoretical acceptance of the "first
postulate" of neoclassical economics as illustrated by the fact that
$MPL = W/P$ at points A and B in each diagram, or his critique as

invalid of the neoclassical derivation of an aggregate demand for labor function from that postulate. All (!) that would change in these different circumstances of labor's marginal productivity would be Keynes' "practical conclusions" which would have "a fortiori force":

> If we can advance farther on the road towards full employment that I had previously supposed in the *GT* without seriously affecting real hourly wages or the rate of profits per unit of output, the warnings of the anti-expansionists need cause us less anxiety (1939, p. 41).

This does not mean that Keynes had no explanations for qualifying the assumption of diminishing returns. In his 1939 article, he suggests two. First, short-run marginal cost curves are likely to rise "eventually." But under conditions of severe unemployment and excess capacity, as in the 1930s, many firms may reasonably be expected to be operating to the left of the minimum points of their marginal cost curves. In such circumstances, "marginal real cost may be expected to decline with increasing output, or, at the worst, remain constant" (1939, p. 44). Second, as a practical matter, business firms, reinforced by the "practical assumption" that they are "normally operating subject to decreasing average cost, even though marginal cost is rising," typically set prices by adding a mark-up to long run average cost, rather by adhering strictly to the profit-maximizing marginalist calculations. Under such practices, firms are resistive to price cuts when output and marginal costs fall (because average costs may be rising, or falling less than marginal costs) and tend to raise prices by less than increases in marginal cost (because average costs may be falling, or rising less than marginal costs) (1939, p. 46). Under such circumstances, real wages need not fall (or fall significantly) as output and employment rise.

Keynes' discussion in *GT* provides an additional explanation of why real wages need not fall (or fall significantly) as output and employment increases. In the Appendix to chapter 19, Keynes observes that Pigou's theory of unemployment tacitly assumes an equality between marginal wage cost and marginal prime cost. But this supposes that all inputs other than labor remain constant as output increases because of expanded employment of labor, which thereby precludes combining "any additional entrepreneurship or working capital or anything else other than labour" with the additional labor. It even precludes "allowing the additional labour to wear out the equipment any faster than the smaller labour force would have done" (*GT*, p. 273n). Analysis based on such a tacit assumption, however, has "almost no application" because businessmen, as a practical matter, do not

> refuse to associate with additional labour appropriate additions of other factors, in so far as they are available, and the assumption of equality between marginal wage cost and marginal prime cost will, therefore, only apply if we assume that all the factors, other than labour, are already being employed to the utmost (*GT*, p. 273n).

From a neoclassical perspective, the "tacit assumption" of full employment of resources other than labor, despite recessionary unemployment of labor, has a certain rationale. If one supposes that costs of entrepreneurship and both fixed and working capital are sunk, and that, consequently, these costs have to be met regardless of utilization, then (assuming input substitutability) it would be inconsistent with the profit-maximization assumption to fail to fully utilize such resources even under conditions of unemployment of labor and reduced output, resulting from a decrease in aggregate demand. Under these circumstances, diminishing returns to labor (and hence reductions in real-wages) are a plausible corollary to expansion in the employment of labor as aggregate demand increases.

According to Keynes, by contrast, costs of entrepreneurship and nonlabor inputs include both factor cost and "user cost." User cost is defined as:

> the reduction in the value of the equipment due to using it as compared with not using it, after allowing for the cost of the maintenance and improvements which it would be worth while to undertake and for purchases from other entrepreneurs (*GT*, p. 70).

Determination of user cost thus requires calculation of those costs (for example, those parts of depreciation) which occur only if physical capital is used. It also requires calculation of "the discounted value of the additional prospective yield which would be obtained at some later date if it were not used now," as well as the present value of the "opportunity to postpone replacement" (*GT*, p. 70). Application of the profit-maximization rule requires that entrepreneurs minimize factor cost plus user cost, not factor cost alone. Although it is "occasionally convenient" (*GT*, p. 67) to ignore user cost in discussing overall output, it is inadmissible to do so at the level of the individual firm and the determination of its supply price. Thus, ironically, neoclassical neglect of user cost has a certain intuitive, simplifying appeal in aggregate discussion, but is discordant with Keynes' profit-maximizing microeconomic foundations!

If user costs—and such actions as postponement of replacement of equipment—are recognized, then employment of labor is likely to be accompanied by underutilization of plant capacity and entrepreneurship, and reductions in purchases of nonlabor inputs from other firms. In this event (especially when supplementary factor costs are high relative to user cost), diminishing returns can be largely, if not entirely, circumvented over a certain range of output, and real wages can remain constant or fall slowly as unemployment falls in response to a resurgence of aggregate demand.

Whatever sense of descriptive realism motivated Keynes to resist abandoning diminishing returns to labor as a general assumption largely vanishes when we turn to the other components of the "first postulate," notably the assumption of competitive markets. It is true that in his mature writings, Keynes refrains from the clear identification (and tacit indictment) of monopoly presented earlier, for example, in *The End of Laissez Faire* (1926/1963). In chapter 24 of *GT*, Keynes states that if 90 percent of the labor force is employed, there is no reason to believe that the economic system "seriously misemploys" that fraction of the working population. But if 10 percent of the labor force has no employment at all, it is clear, by contrast, that the system has "broken down" (*GT*, p. 379). It is plain, however, that these comments stem from an assessment of the relative welfare costs of mass unemployment versus market monopoly power per se rather than from a perceived descriptive realism of the assumption of pure competition.

For Keynes, neither the theory nor the practice of imperfect competition raises problems comparable with those of mass unemployment and received theory's failure to comprehend the true bases for unemployment. For example, in *GT*, Keynes opines:

> if we have dealt otherwise with the problem of thrift, there is no objection to be raised against the modern classical theory as to the degree of consilience between private and public advantage in conditions of perfect and imperfect competition respectively. Thus, apart from the necessity of central controls to bring about an adjustment between the propensity to consume and the

inducement to invest, there is no more reason to socialize economic life than there was before (*GT*, p. 379).

Moreover, Keynes' acceptance of the descriptive realism of imperfect competition does not constitute an analytical basis for his theory of the causes of unemployment. Thus, in his 1939 *Economic Journal* article, Keynes characterizes full, average-cost pricing practices as "rightly ordered competition," as opposed to "dangerous and anti-social" monopoly, and attributes such practices to the "right and reasonable policy" of setting prices by references to long-run overhead, as well as current, cost. The business proclivity to reduce (and raise) prices by less than decreases (increase) in marginal costs when output and money wages fall (and rise) is "merely an example of the stickiness of prices arising out of the imperfection of competition intrinsic to the market conditions" (1939, p. 47).

Such price "stickiness," however, it not an assumption. Nor is it based on monopoly power per se. It is an endogenous conclusion derived from "practical" dimensions of market processes. Moreover, imperfect competition, for Keynes, does not negate the general argument that it is aggregate demand that drives output and employment and thereby real wages (rather than the other way around). Market imperfections are not incorporated into the argument to explain the origins of unemployment, but merely as a possible explanation of why, under the "practical workings of the laws of imperfect competition in the modern quasi-competitive system" (1939, p. 46), real wages may move in the same, rather than the opposite, direction to changes in money wages as output and employment change.

In conclusion, to return briefly to the theme of section 2, descriptive realism provides an unpersuasive explanation of Keynes' acceptance of classical theory's "first postulate." As argued earlier, there was a stronger motivation. When the "first postulate" is unpacked, it consists of the fundamental motivational (profit-maximization), institutional (purely competitive markets), and resource-technological (diminishing returns to variable proportions) assumptions of the central tradition in economic thought. By working within these assumptions, at least as a point of departure and "for purposes of discussion," Keynes challenges neoclassical perspectives on their own grounds, guarding against the counterargument— common in the contemporary new classical critique of Keynesian thought—that he has merely substituted alternative assumptions, and leaves to later discussion the demonstration that adoption of more descriptively realistic assumptions does not modify the core of his theoretical analysis. If this interpretation is correct, then, as already noted, Keynes' challenge to neoclassicism pertains as much, if not more, to its theory than to its assumptions. This brings us to Keynes' critique of the neoclassical theory of the efficacy of wage (and price) cutting as an antidepressionary strategy, in chapters 2 and 19 of *GT*.

## IV.  KEYNES' CRITIQUE OF THE EFFICACY OF WAGE CUTTING

Keynes begins his critique of the efficacy of wage cutting as antidepressionary in chapter 2 of *GT* and continues his argument in chapter 19, after presenting his own, alternative theory in the intervening chapters. The discussion in chapter 2 centers around what Keynes calls classical theory's "second postulate," summarized as follows:

> the utility of the wage when a given volume of labour is employed is equal to the marginal disutility of that amount of employment (*GT*, p. 5).

Just as the "first postulate"

> gives us the [neoclassical] demand schedule for employment, the second gives us the [neoclassical] supply schedule; and the amount of employment is fixed at the point where the utility of the marginal product balances the disutility of the marginal employment (*GT*, p. 6).

In contrast to his acceptance, at least for purposes of discussion in chapter 2, of the "first postulate," Keynes presents two objections to the second, as well as to the neoclassical labor supply schedule based on it. One objection, less fundamental, will be examined in the next section of this paper. The other, "fundamental," objection pertains to the powerlessness of labor to bring about the real-wage reductions necessary according to neoclassical theory to stimulate increases in employment merely by accepting money wage cuts.

The "classical theory," Keynes states:

> assumes that it is always open to labour to reduce its real-wage by accepting a reduction in its money-wage, that is, that wage bargains between the entrepreneurs and the workers determine the real-wage (*GT*, p. 11).

Now this claim, Keynes continues, is "not obviously true" (*GT*, p. 12). As noted earlier, Keynes holds that neoclassicism tends to identify marginal prime cost with marginal wage cost, ignoring both user cost (*GT*, p. 67) and nonlabor factor cost (*GT*, p. 272) in short-run enterprise adjustments. Consequently, if money wages were to decrease, neoclassical analysis would lead one to suppose that, with lower marginal costs, prices would fall "in almost the same proportion, leaving the real-wage and the level of unemployment practically the same as before" (*GT*, p. 12). In this event, there may exist "no expedient by which labour as a whole can reduce its real wages to a given figure by making revised money bargains with the entrepreneurs" (*GT*, p. 13).

Two conclusions follow. First, the "second postulate" that the $W/P$ tends to come into equality with the $MDUL$—and the corollary principle that interactions between the labor supply function, based on the "second postulate," and the labor demand function, yield full employment, market-clearing solutions—"clearly presumes that labour itself is in a position to decide the real wage..." (*GT*, p. 11). If labor is powerless to determine its own real-wage through money wage bargains, the tendency to equate the $MDUL$ with the $W/P$ (and thereby with the $MPL$ at full employment) is circumvented, and both the "second postulate" and the presumed self-adjusting market-clearing process are invalidated. Second, if it is decreases in real wages which elicit reductions in unemployment, and reductions in money wages are roughly matched by decreased money prices, reductions in money wages may well leave real wages, aggregate demand, and the level of unemployment unchanged.

In his critique of Pigou's *Theory of Unemployment*, in the Appendix to chapter 19 of *GT*, Keynes returns to the question of the relationship between money wages and real wages in a broader context. In contrast to Pigou's belief that "in the long run unemployment can be cured by wage adjustments," Keynes contends that although such adjustments "may have repercussions," real wages are "primarily determined" by "other forces," notably the marginal efficiency of capital and the rate of interest. Pigou's neoclassical argument of a proclivity toward full employment equilibrium is tantamount to an assertion that "labour is always in a position to determine its own real wage" and vice versa. For example, if the supply of labor function were to shift up, downward adjustments in money wages are expected to elicit decreases in real wages, and thereby higher employment and output. But this presupposes that the

> demand for the output of the nonwage-goods industries is such that employment in these industries is bound to increase by just the amount which will preserve equality between (the supply of labor and the demand for labor) (*GT*, pp. 274, 278).

And this, in turn, supposes that "the rate of interest always adjusts itself to the schedule of the marginal efficiency of capital in such a way as to preserve full employment" (*GT*, pp. 274-75). In short, to question whether adjustments in money wages yield full employment-equilibrating adjustments in real wages challenges not only tacit neoclassical assumptions concerning the institutional organization of the labor market, but neoclassical analysis of relationships among aggregate demand, output, and employment as well.

In the general body of chapter 19 of *GT*, Keynes extends his critique of the neoclassical theory of the prospective efficacy of wage cuts as an antidepressionary strategy by examining the effects of reductions in money wages on aggregate demand and thereby employment. This extended critique contains two related, but distinguishable, parts. The first pertains to the validity of transferring the neoclassical conceptions of the demand for labor from the realm of the individual firm and industry to the entire economy. The supposition that the neoclassical demand for labor function can be so transferred, Keynes contends, is "surely fallacious":

> For the demand schedules for particular industries can only be constructed on some fixed assumption as to the nature of the demand and supply schedules of other industries and as to the amount of the aggregate effective demand. It is invalid, therefore, to transfer the argument to industry as a whole unless we also transfer our assumption that the aggregate effective demand is fixed (*GT*, p. 259).

But this, Keynes concludes, is an *ignorachio ellenchi*. Far from being a mere affectation, this obscure Latin expression neatly summarizes a central aspect of Keynes' critical commentary. To engage in an *ignorachio ellenchi* is

> to ignore the argument, that is, to refute an argument which is slightly different from that which one pretends to refute; hence to reason fallaciously (Carroll, 1973, p. 78).

Under "certain circumstances," Keynes claims, money wage cuts are "quite capable" of "affording a stimulus to output, as the classical theory supposes" (*GT*, p. 257). Under what circumstances? Clearly, the most obvious such circumstances are those of the analysis of the individual firm or industry, where the overall level of demand is presupposed to be fixed. Here, lower costs accompanying money wage cuts plausibly would stimulate expanded employment and output, given aggregate demand. "No one," Keynes says,

> would wish to deny the proposition that a reduction in money-wages accompanied by the same aggregate effective demand as before will be associated with an increase in employment (*GT*, p. 259).

But the "precise question" under debate is whether, for the economy as a whole, where it is inappropriate to suppose that the level of demand is fixed, money wage cuts

> will or will not be accompanied by the same aggregate effective demand as before as measured in money, or, at any rate, by an aggregate effective demand which is not reduced in full proportion to the reduction in money-wages..."
> (*GT*, pp. 259-60).

As this quotation implies, it is quite possible, on the face of it, for a rightward shift in the aggregate supply schedule, because of lower costs, to be offset by an equivalent downward shift in the aggregate demand schedule, because of lower wage income, leaving the overall level of output, employment, and real wages unchanged. Because the neoclassical analysis extends, by improper analogy:

> its conclusions in respect of a particular industry to industry as a whole, it is wholly unable to answer the question what effect on employment a reduction in money-wages will have (*GT*, p. 260).

The second component of Keynes' critique of the efficacy of wages cuts as antidepressionary strategy presented in chapter 19 is rooted in the analysis of the intervening chapters (3-18). In chapter 18, Keynes summarizes that exposition by stating that underlying forces determining potential aggregate supply are taken as given (for short-run analysis), and that income and employment, therefore, are mainly determined by aggregate demand. Aggregate demand, in turn, depends partly on the level of income and employment and partly on "independent variables," designated, "in the first instance," as the propensity to consume, the marginal efficiency of capital, and the rate of interest, and in a more "ultimate" sense as the first two, the state of liquidity, preference, the money supply, and the level of money wages (*GT*, pp. 245, 247).

Money wages affect aggregate supply through their influence on costs. In assessing the neoclassical theory of wage (and price) cutting, Keynes takes the "most favourable" version of that argument by supposing that employers, concentrating on lower costs and ignoring potentially negative effects on income and demand, expect money wage cuts to have an expansionary impact on employment and act on this expectation.

In this event, the crucial question would be whether the increase in aggregate supply would be matched by an equivalent increase in aggregate demand. To answer this question, Keynes distinguishes between "direct" and "indirect" effects of money wage cuts on demand. Direct effects are those emanating from higher employment and real income, given the propensity to consume, the marginal efficiency of capital, and the rate of interest. Indirect effects are those caused by the proclivity (insofar as it exists) of money-wage cuts to stimulate upward shifts in the propensity to consume or the marginal efficiency of capital, or reductions in interest rates.

Beginning with direct effects, expanded employment presumably would stimulate increased consumption. But, asks Keynes, would this increase in consumer demand, by itself, be sufficient to offset the originating increases in potential supply? In response, Keynes claims that, in the plausible circumstances where society's marginal propensity to consume is greater than zero but less than one, the increase in consumption presumably would be less than that in real income. Consequently, in the absence of additional (indirect) effects of reduction in money wages (and prices), revenue from the sale of expanded output would be insufficient to match the costs and normal profits of that output, and entrepreneurs would reduce output and employment to their earlier levels. Therefore, in the absence of a marginal propensity to consume equal to unity, money-wage cuts can have a "lasting" favorable effect on output and employment only through their repercussions on the propensity to consume, marginal efficiencies of capital, or rate of interest (*GT*, p. 262). Keynes assesses these repercussions through identification of a rich congeries of favorable and adverse consequences, summarized in Table 1. In the

*Table 1.*   The Efficacy of Wage Cuts

| *Favorable Effects* | *Adverse Effects* |
|---|---|
| **A. Propensity to Consume** | |
| 1. $\downarrow W \to \downarrow MC \to \downarrow P \to \uparrow$ Money Wealth$/P$ | 1. $\downarrow W \to \downarrow MC \to \downarrow P \to$ Redistribution $Y \to$ $\uparrow Ynw/Yw, \uparrow Yr/Ye$ |
| 2. $\downarrow W \to \downarrow MC \to \downarrow P \to \downarrow I$ (see section D) $\uparrow$Money Wealth$/i$ | 2. $\downarrow W \to \downarrow MC \to \downarrow P \to$ expectations $\downarrow Pp/Pf$ |
| 3. $\downarrow W \to \downarrow MC \to \downarrow P \to$ expectations $\downarrow Pp/Pf$ | 3. $\downarrow W \to \downarrow MEC$ (see section C) $\to \downarrow$Asset Price |

| **B. Foreign Trade** | |
|---|---|
| 4. $\downarrow W \to \downarrow Wd/Wf \to \downarrow MCd/MCf \to$ $\downarrow Pd/Pf \to \uparrow(EX - IM)$ | 4. But may be offset by tariffs, quotas. |
| | 5. $\downarrow W \to \downarrow MC \to \downarrow Pd/Pf \to \downarrow$Yr. |

| **C. Marginal Efficiency of Capital** | |
|---|---|
| $\uparrow MEC$ | $\downarrow MEC$ |
| 5. $\downarrow W \to$ expectations $\downarrow Wp/Wf$ (But $\downarrow$ long run $MEC$) | 6. $\downarrow W \to$ expectations $\downarrow Wf/Wp$ (But $\to \uparrow$ long run $MEC$) |
| 6. $\downarrow W \to \uparrow$business optimism | 7. $\downarrow W \to \uparrow$labor troubles, $\downarrow$political confidence $\to \downarrow$business optimism |
| | 8. $\downarrow W \to \downarrow MC \to \downarrow P \to \uparrow$Debt$/P \to \downarrow$business optimism |
| | 9. $\downarrow W \to \downarrow MC \to \downarrow P \to \uparrow$National Debt$/P \to$ $\uparrow$Taxes |
| | 10. $\downarrow W \to \downarrow MC \to \downarrow P \to \uparrow$Insolvency $\to$ Severe $\downarrow I$ |

| **D. Rate of Interest** | |
|---|---|
| $\downarrow$Rate of Interest | $\uparrow$Rate of Interest |
| 7. $\downarrow W \to \downarrow MC \to \downarrow P, \downarrow Ym \to \downarrow Lt \to \uparrow Ms \to \downarrow$ $\to \uparrow I$ | 11. $\downarrow W \to \downarrow MC \to \downarrow P \to \downarrow Ms \to \uparrow i \to \downarrow I$ |
| | 12. Moderate $\downarrow W$ (via $\downarrow MC \to \downarrow P \to \downarrow Lt \to$ $\uparrow Ms) \to$ inadequate $\downarrow i$ |
| | Immoderate $\downarrow W$ (via $\downarrow MC \to \downarrow P \to \downarrow Lt \to$ $\uparrow Ms) \to \uparrow La$ |
| | 13. Slips Twixt Cup and Lip: $\uparrow La$ can offset $\downarrow Lt$ $\downarrow MEC$ can offset $\downarrow i$ $\downarrow P$ to $C$ can offset $\uparrow I$ |

| **E. Stock of Capital, Aggregate Supply** | |
|---|---|
| $\uparrow K, Z$ | $\downarrow K, Z$ |
| | 14. $\downarrow I \to \downarrow K \to \downarrow O/L \to \downarrow Z \to \downarrow C$ |
| | 15. $\uparrow$Insolvency $\to$ Severe $\downarrow I \to \downarrow Z \to$ Severe $\downarrow C$ |

interest of brevity, reference to the table will be selective and organized around only the elements most pertinent to subsequent exegesis of Keynesian and neoclassical debate. (For ease of reference, the seven propositions stating favorable effects shall be designated as F1-F7, the references to adverse effects as A1-A15.)

The first thing to note about Keynes' discussion of wage (and price) cutting in chapter 19 of *GT* is that he recognizes both favorable and adverse effects. These various effects operate at different (for example, comparative static and dynamic) levels of abstraction and presumably exhibit different empirical significance (which, moreover, also presumably vary in different circumstances). Consequently, an overall assessment is problematic. But this, for Keynes' purposes, is enough. Because effects may be adverse as well as favorable and the empirical magnitudes of some of the favorable consequences may be negligible, the overall impact of wage cutting may well be inefficacious. Aggregate demand may stay the same, or even fall, as wage and prices are cut. Demand may at first rise, but not sufficiently to establish full employment, and then fall. It all depends on the net result of uncertain and problematic opposing forces.

In any event, it would be a grievous misrepresentation of Keynes' argument in chapter 19 to concentrate on favorable, to the exclusion of adverse, effects of wage cuts. It would be especially misleading to focus on only one of the favorable effects. Ironically, this is precisely what is done in most "Keynesian" modelings, particularly in the textbook literature, where a potential upward shift in the *LM* curve is predicated on the impact of price reductions on the transactionary demand for money. This single possibility, selected in isolation from the much broader and more comprehensive set of Keynes' desiderata, has been strangely christened the "Keynes effect," as if this exhausted Keynes' intellectual arsenal.

It is certainty true that Keynes incorporated what has come to be called the "Keynes effect" into his analysis of the favorable effects of wage cutting (see Table 1, F7 ). He concedes that lower money wages (and thereby prices) would decrease the "need for cash for income and business purposes." This would decrease the overall demand for money, *ceteris paribus*, and thereby tend to decrease the rate of interest, increase investment, and reduce unemployment. Because Keynes is highly sceptical of the other favorable effects of wage cutting (and because of its adverse effects), he concludes that supporters of the theory of the optimally self-adjusting market "must rest the weight of their argument" on the "Keynes effect" and the hope that if the money supply is fixed, "its quantity in terms of wage units ($Ms/W$) can be indefinitely increased by a sufficient reduction in money-wages" (*GT*, p. 266). In effect, wage and price cutting is a theoretical analog to expansionary monetary policy.

Keynes identifies serious limitations to this optimistic scenario. First, if, as Keynes perceives to be likely, the "quantity of money (by the banking system) is itself a function of the wage-and price-level," the money supply (*Ms*) will fall along with, and thus quite possibly nullify the potentially expansionary consequences of, the decrease in the demand for money resulting from wage and price cuts, and "there is indeed nothing to hope in this direction" (*GT*, p. 266 A11).

Second, even if wage and price cuts were to result in a net decrease in the demand for money (and thereby a rise in the portion of a fixed *Ms* available for speculative purposes), this strategy is subject to the "same limitations" (*GT*, p. 266) as (as well as being more convoluted and time-consuming than) a simple increase in the money supply. On the one hand, there are the famous "slips between the cup and the lip" (*GT*, p. 173), adapted to the discussion of chapter 19 (A13). An upward shift in the speculative demand for money (*Ls*) can offset the favorable effects of price cuts upon reductions in the transactional demands for money (*Lt*), and thus prevent or constrain reductions in the interest rate. Downward shifts in marginal efficiencies of capital, generated by the several adverse effects of wage cuts, can offset reductions in the interest rate. Downward shifts in the propensity to consume, brought on by redistributions in income and wealth typically associated with wage and price reductions, can offset whatever increases in investment do occur. On the other hand, there is Keynes' famous minimum magnitude threshold argument (A12):

> Just as a moderate increase in the quantity of money may exert an inadequate influence over the long-term rate of interest, whilst an immoderate increase may offset its other advantages by its disturbing effect on confidence; so a moderate reduction in money-wages may prove inadequate, whilst an immoderate reduction might shatter confidence even if it were practicable (*GT*, pp. 266-67).

Indeed, sagging wages and prices (the most likely form of wage and price cutting according to Keynes) may well generate deflationary instability "so violent perhaps as to make business calculations futile in an economic society functioning after the manner of that in which we live" (*GT*, p. 269). Hence, an antidepressionary strategy based on wage reductions is suitable only for highly authoritarian societies. In a liberal democratic society, it is a recipe for social conflict and political disorder, perhaps revolution. Consequently, Keynes concludes, there is no more basis for supposing that a "flexible wage policy is capable of maintaining a state of continuous full employment" than for believing that expansionary monetary policy "is capable, unaided, of achieving this result. The economic system cannot be made optimally self-adjusting along these lines" (*GT*, p. 267).

Keynes' critique of what is now called the "Keynes effect" differs significantly from "textbook Keynesianism." The standard Keynesian modeling, like neoclassical theory, presupposes that the money supply is exogenous and fixed, not endogenous and variable, with wage and price cuts. Moreover, the positions of consumption and investment functions are typically presented as remaining given when the demand for money changes because of wage and/or price changes. Consequently, explanation of the persistence of unemployment rests on the shapes of the various functions.

This is shown pointedly by models incorporating a "liquidity trap," illustrated by a horizontal *LM* curve. In this classic textbook case, as long as the *IS* curve intersects the horizontal *LM* curve at a position below full employment, no amount of wage and price cutting (or expansionary monetary policy) can be expected to dislodge the economy from its depressed position. Keynes, by contrast, while believing that the practical efficacy of wage cuts varied inversely with the elasticity of the demand for money and that liquidity preference "may become virtually absolute" at low interest rates, states that he knows of "no example" in practice of this "limiting case" (*GT*, p. 207). In any event, Keynes' insertion of the word "virtually" as a modifier leaves open, at the strictly theoretical level, the possibility of some role for the "Keynes effect," however empirically small, at low interest rates. Clearly, Keynes' own, broader, argument does not depend on a literal "liquidity trap."

Neoclassicists criticize both Keynes' analysis in chapter 19 and standard Keynesian models based on the liquidity trap through incorporation of some version of a real balance effect. The simplest example is specification that aggregate consumption varies positively with real income and inversely with interest rates. This provides a direct and simple response to liquidity trap models: price reductions raise $Ms/P$, shift upward the propensity to consume (and, thereby, the $IS$ curve), and, in principle, eventually eliminate unemployment.

Sophisticated commentators recognize, however, that this is not a sufficient answer to Keynes' own more complex arguments. Thus, economists who desire to accommodate Keynes' ideas with neoclassicism often remain agnostic or accede to his conclusions on dynamic and practical grounds, but not on static, theoretical ones. Several of the adverse effects of wage and price cuts which Keynes identifies are, indeed, dynamic and expectational in character (for example, A2, A3, A5, A6). Because of these factors, "the stimulating real-balance effect of a price decline may be more than offset by its depressing expectations effects" (Patinkin, 1965, p. 337; DeLong and Summers, 1986, p. 1034). Moreover, several of the favorable effects (for example, F1, F2, F7) may well be very small in magnitude and may require substantial time, *ceteris paribus*, to do their stimulative work. The economy's adjustment processes, based on wage and price flexibility, Tobin states, "remedy very slowly if at all." They "may be too weak to eliminate persistent unemployment" (Tobin, 1975, p. 200). Insofar as this is true, there is the "very real possibility" that a wage-cutting strategy, like a pure monetary policy,

> would necessitate subjecting the economy to an intolerably long period of dynamic adjustment: a period during which wages, prices, and interest would continue to fall, and...varying numbers of workers would continue to suffer from involuntary unemployment (Patinkin, p. 339).

By contrast, on purely static, theoretical grounds, supporters of this perspective argue, Keynes' critique cannot be sustained. If prices, wages, and interest rates are flexible downward (albeit imperfectly), and dynamic processes and problems of magnitude and time are set aside, then favorable real-balance effects (notably F1, F2, F7) should ultimately triumph. This, it is held, compels the conclusion that there are:

> automatic market forces to push real income up from the unemployment level and that such forces not only exist, but even succeed eventually in raising income to the full employment level ... (Patinkin, 1965, p. 339).

Alternatively expressed in terms of an *LM*/IS formulation:

> ...the real balance effect, combining both the Pigou Effect (F1) and the
> Keynes Effect (F7), contends that falling wages and prices will shift both the
> *LM* and *IS* curves to the right until they intersect [at full employment output];
> even with a fairly elastic *LM* curve and a fairly inelastic *IS* curve, full
> employment equilibrium is in principle attainable. At the level of abstraction
> of the *General Theory*, [which] is essentially an exercise in comparative statics
> with some dynamic glosses, .... no effective reply can be given to this
> neoclassical argument (Blaug, 1978, p. 678).

Although now embedded into the conventional wisdom, this line
of argument diverges significantly from Keynes' own account:

1. Keynes draws no sharp contrast between "static" and
"dynamic" elements in his argument. Key relationships, which at first
may seem to be easily assimilable into a comparative static format,
appear elsewhere as precarious, uncertain, and interdependent (*GT*,
pp. 154, 158, 162, 172, 203, 316; Keynes, 1937). Consequently, to limit
criticism of Keynes' analysis to its "purely static" aspects is to have
already acceded to much, if not most, of it.

2. Moreover, "comparative static" elements shade into
"dynamic" ones, in Keynes' view, especially when the magnitude of
change is large. Thus, "immoderate" reductions in wages are likely
to cause an upward shift in liquidity preference schedules (A11).
Severe downward shifts in marginal efficiencies of capital are likely
to also trigger reductions in the propensity to consume (A3) and
upward shifts in the propensity to hoard (A12). Because large wage
reductions are more likely to engender adverse expectations than
small ones (A7), the adverse dynamic consequences of weak real
balance effects are more powerful than if those effects were stronger.

3. Hypotheses concerning real balance effects (F1, F2, F7) are
not clearly at a different level of methodological abstraction from
theorems concerning redistribution of income (A1), redistribution of
wealth and the increased burden of debt (A8, A10), or the
endogeneity of money supply by commercial banks (A11).
As for distribution effects:

> We cannot assume that the negative indebtedness of debtors are simply
> canceled by the positive effects of creditors. More specifically...a protracted

price decline will cause a wave of bankruptcies which will eliminate both the firms' liabilities and the households' assets, and leave only a seriously impaired state of business confidence (Patinkin, 1965, pp. 336-37).

As for endogeneity in the supply of money, if:

the money supply declines as prices decline, there is no necessary increase in monetary wealth, no real balance effect, and presumably no bounding mechanism [that is, no mechanism to keep the deflationary process within bounds] (Culbertson, 1968, p. 341).

Thus, it is not clear, a priori, that favorable real balance effects must invariably outweigh redistributive, bankruptcy, and money supply endogeneity effects of wage reductions.

The price-induced real balance effect has been insouciently described as the "knight that slays the imaginary (liquidity trap) dragon" (Culbertson, 1968, p. 341). In addition to the imaginary quality of the "dragon," in Keynes' view, the "knight" may well be methodologically tarnished. Economic practice does not display the kind of *ceteris paribus* wage and price reductions assumed by the theory:

In deflation, resources are idle, income declines, dis-saving may occur, rising debt burden leads to defaults and liquidation of businesses, values of capital assets commonly decline drastically.... If we consider the effect of deflation upon total demand, we must consider all of its effects, not include the ones that suit our story and leave out the ones that do not. This is an invalid use of *ceteris paribus* (Culbertson, 1968, pp. 341-42).

4.   Keynes' critique of wage (and price) cutting is intimately linked with his views on uncertainty. Two scenarios may be distinguished. In one, real income is rising, at or near full employment. Even if the propensity to consume, the marginal efficiency of capital, and the liquidity preference schedules were to remain at given positions, prosperity becomes increasingly vulnerable and difficult to sustain because of a rising average, and perhaps marginal, propensity to save, a tendency for interest rates to rise as income does, and a decline in the marginal efficiency on any given type of capital investment (*GT*, pp. 96-98, 127, 136, 199-201). Still, if these three schedules were all certain and stable, problems of ensuring sufficient aggregate demand to sustain full employment would be less than otherwise,

and the likelihood that the favorable effects of wage cuts—at least occasionally or for stretches of time—might outweigh adverse effects, would be enhanced.

For Keynes, this moderately pleasant scenario is ruled out because the propensities to hoard and invest are each infused with uncertainty. Because of uncertainty concerning future interest rates, liquidity preference "will not have a definite quantitative relation to a given rate of interest of *r*," for it depends not on "the *absolute* level of *r*, but the degree of its divergence from what is considered a fairly safe level of *r*... " Consequently, every decrease in *r* reduces both (1) the market rate relative to the "'safe' rate" by increasing the risk of liquidity and (2) current earnings from illiquidity, thereby creating "perhaps the chief obstacle to a fall in the rate of interest to a very low level" (*GT*, pp. 201-02). Uncertainty similarly surrounds expectations concerning future profits, thereby making marginal efficiencies of capital dependent to a large extent on "spontaneous optimism" rather than "strict mathematical expectations" (*GT*, pp. 161, 163). Uncertainty concerning expected profit rates leads business investors to rely heavily on the recent past and on conventional valuations, which are, thereby, subject to "sudden fluctuations" (*GT*, pp. 51, 154). Moreover, Keynes argued in his 1937b review article on *GT* in the *Quarterly Journal of Economics*:

> When a more pessimistic view is taken about future yields, there is no reason why there should be a diminished propensity to hoard. Indeed, the conditions which aggravate the one factor tend, as a rule, to aggravate the other (p. 218).

According to Shackle (1967, pp. 129, 133-34), Keynes' 1937 *QJE* article (with chapter 12 of *GT* serving as a kind of prospectus) reveals the "ultimate meaning" of Keynes' project. According to this interpretation of Keynes, the "ultimate ground" of massive unemployment is uncertainty. Rational expectation "being unattainable, we substitute for it first one and then another kind of irrational expectation." Thus, unemployment theory is "inescapably" a theory of "disorder."

Carried to an extreme, this "fundamentalist" version of Keynesianism, based on comprehensive and pervasive uncertainty, would reject the category of equilibrium and the use of any comparative static analysis as unwarranted. This approach, Coddington opines (1983, pp. 61-62), is "consistent but analytically nihilistic." A "root and branch" application of this extreme "subjectivism" to economics would be analogous to "an outbreak of Christian Science among the medical profession, or a passion for telekinesis among airline pilots." Whatever the merit of this criticism as applied to Shackle, it is misplaced as applied to Keynes himself, who takes an intermediate view. In chapter 12 of *GT*, after a playful romp with "animal spirits" and "the delicate balance of spontaneous optimism," Keynes warns:

> We should not conclude from this that everything depends on waves of irrational psychology. On the contrary, the state of long-term expectation is often steady, and, even when it is not, the other factors exert their compensating effects. We are merely reminding ourselves that human decisions affecting the future, whether personal or political or economic, cannot depend on strict mathematical expectation since the basis for making such calculations does not exist (*GT*, pp. 162-63).

In the 1937 *QJE* article, immediately following his discussion of the powerful role of uncertainty and fluctuation in the propensity to hoard and the marginal efficiency of capital, he proceeds to elucidate a second difference from the "traditional theory," namely a need to develop a theory of the demand and supply of output "*as a whole.*" This, in turn, is based on a distinction between investment and consumption, the latter resting on a relatively stable propensity to consume and the same "psychological law" stated in the *GT*. According to Keynes, the orthodox neglect of aggregative theory and of uncertainty are intimately connected. It is precisely because traditional economic theory focuses on the allocation of a given body of resources at a given level of overall income that it has tended to assume that "we have a knowledge of the future of a kind quite different from that which we actually possess" (Keynes, 1937b, pp. 320-23).

Thus, Keynes' argument operates at two related, but distinguishable, levels of abstraction. At a higher level of abstraction, uncertainty is the "ultimate" or "fundamental" source of unemployment and the sudden shifts, fluctuations, and disorder which stem from it. At this level of argument, wage cutting is rejected as inefficiencious because of the uncertainty of its effects (notably on the MEC and the rate of interest) at best and because of its own proclivity to enhance uncertainty and disorder at worst. At a lower level of abstraction, a partial commitment is made to comparative static analysis, based on a relatively stable propensity to consume and an accompanying "fundamental psychological law" concerning consumption, as noted earlier. However, even then, there is always the prospect that sustained propensity will be interrupted by downward shifts in marginal efficiencies of capital, typically combined with upward shifts in the propensity to hoard. When this occurs, the severity of contraction is likely to be greater, more pervasive, and more disorderly. In this event, the adverse effects of wage cutting are even more likely (than in the simpler case of inadequate aggregate demand with stable MEC and liquidity preference function schedules) to swamp the favorable ones, and the task facing wage cutting as an antidepressionary strategy plausibly becomes overwhelming, if not impossible.

Finally, Keynes' vigorous indictment of wage (and price) cutting as inefficacious, indeed detrimental, shows how far removed his own argument lies from neoclassical/Keynesian models based on the assumption of downward money wage rigidity. In a now-classic modeling, Modigliani (1944) combines elements from Keynes' analysis (propensities to consume, invest, and hoard) with neoclassical labor demand and supply functions. The unsurprising result is a proclivity toward full employment equilibrium. If, however, rigid money wages are incorporated into the model (at levels higher than labor market equilibrium), then unemployment and labor market disequilibrium result.

Keynes' analysis departs from this approach in two major ways. First, in chapter 19, Keynes unequivocally incorporates downward wage price flexibility into his own theoretical presentation. To ground unemployment in rigid money wages is clearly discordant with Keynes' argument. Second, in the first stage of his analysis in chapter 19, as in chapter 2 of *GT*, Keynes criticizes the neoclassical labor supply function by rejecting the view that reductions in money wages will necessarily elicit reductions in real wages and thereby an increase in employment as "fallacious" and "invalid" because of the presupposition that aggregate demand necessarily remains unchanged when money wages fall. "It is from this type of analysis (Keynes states) that I fundamentally differ" (*GT*, p. 258). In the second stage of his argument in chapter 19, he rejects the neoclassical labor demand function by explaining that potentially favorable effects of wage (and price) cutting may well be offset, nullified, or reversed by their adverse consequences.

Differentiation between Keynes' critique of the inefficacy of wage and price reductions and the reinterpretations of Keynes by Clower (1965) and Leijonhufvud (1968) is subtler. At various points in his exposition, Keynes states that wages and prices are "sticky" (though not fixed or rigid) in a downward direction. Similarly, in the Clower/Leijonhufvud analysis, wages and prices are presumed to be flexible downward, but not perfectly or instantaneously so. Consequently, transactors trade at nonequilibrium ("false") prices, information is inappropriate to guarantee market coordination, and, hence, full employment, general equilibrium, and aggregate demand falls, creating an excess supply of commodities or excess of ex ante saving above ex ante investment.

If price reductions were perfectly instantaneous, false trading would not occur and contraction in output and employment could be avoided. Because output does drop, however, prices must now fall below the levels required by the initial reduction in aggregate demand. Eventually, an "equilibrium" of sorts emerges, characterized by equality between a depressed level of aggregate demand and aggregate supply for commodities, but an excess supply of labor (Leijonhufvud, 1968, pp. 57, 86). In short, Clower/Leijonhufvud accept the neoclassical choice-theoretic analysis of the incentives structure of individual economizing-agents—but claim that the misinformation provided by disequilibrated market processes may well be such that, at least for a while, self-amplifying processes of further departure from full employment equilibrium outweigh self-correcting and equilibrating processes, especially when departure from equilibrium is large, abrupt, or widespread.

This interpretation of rising unemployment as a disequilibrium process, initiated by a downward shift in aggregate demand and extended by the excess of self-amplifying above self-correcting forces, certainly captures leading elements in Keynes' argument. Moreover, it seems a reasonable inference from Keynes' analysis that in an unreal world of instantaneous price flexibility and perfect foresight, such disequilibrium processes might well be avoided. However, once imperfect price flexibility is substituted for either instantaneous price (and wage) flexibility or price (and wage) rigidity, the explication of the efficacy of wage and price cutting becomes less clearly focused.

According to Clower/Leijonhufvud, because price flexibility is imperfect, prices must ultimately fall by more than they would have had to under a regime of instantaneous price adjustments. Thus, at least implicitly, if the degree of imperfection were smaller, the extent of output contraction and unemployment would also be smaller. And, eventually, when output and employment stop falling, price (and wage) reductions, imperfect though they may be, presumably contribute to upward shifts in aggregate demand and an eventual restoration of full employment.[2]

It is not at all clear that this benign view of price (and wage) cuts is concordant with Keynes' own position. Chapter 19 of *GT* suggests that price (and wage) reductions, either during an initial process of economic contraction or after the force of an initial reduction in demand has been spent, may not only fail to restore full employment equilibrium, if it is disrupted, but by an excess of adverse effects, may plunge the economy into even deeper depression. Once the assumption of instantaneity has been abandoned, Keynes' exposition implies that price and wage cuts may as easily be "too large" as "too small." As a recent study aptly puts it, starting from conditions of imperfect wage and price flexibility, increasing flexibility may well have destabilizing effects on output and employment (DeLong and Summers, 1986, p. 1042).

## V.   STICKY WAGES, MONEY-WAGE ILLUSION, AND KEYNES' SECOND OBJECTION TO THE SECOND POSTULATE OF CLASSICAL THEORY

As noted in the preceding section, Keynes describes money wages as being relatively "sticky" or resistive to reduction, though by no means rigid. However, he does not use sticky wages as a means to explain the origins or sustenance of unemployment. On the one hand, Keynes makes no claim, anywhere throughout the presentation of his own theory, in chapters 3 through 18 of *GT*, that unemployment is grounded in sticky wages. On the other hand, in chapter 19, as just summarized, he explains that wage (and price) reductions may well not be successful as automatic and spontaneous guarantors of the sustenance or restoration of full employment.

Sticky wages (and prices), however, do enter into Keynes' exposition, at three different levels of discussion. At the lowest level of abstraction, Keynes, like many of his critics, approaches the phenomenon of sticky wages as an assumption. For example, in his critique of Piqou, in the Appendix to chapter 19 of *GT*, Keynes suggests that, strictly as a "provisional assumption," rigid money wages "would bring our theory nearest to the facts," and cites experience in Great Britain in the decade ending in 1934 as an illustration. He immediately provides, however, a clear methodological rationale for such an assumption. To validate a theory's claim to be a "general theory," it must be applicable both to instances of fixed and flexible money wages. Whereas politicians can afford the luxury of contending that money wages "ought to be highly flexible," theorists "must be prepared to deal indifferently with either state of affairs. A scientific theory cannot require the facts to conform to its own assumptions" (*GT*, p. 176).

Similarly, in his overview of the theory of employment in chapter 3, Keynes states he is going to "assume that the money-wage and other factor costs are constant per unit of labour employed" (*GT*, p. 27). Again, however, an immediate caveat follows:

> But this simplification, with which we shall dispense later, is introduced solely to facilitate the exposition. The essential character of the argument is precisely the same whether or not money-wages, etc., are liable to change (*GT*, p. 27).

At a higher level of abstraction, Keynes examines "sticky" wages, that is, wages which are free to move, but are resistive to change, notable in a downward direction. Sticky wages, however, have a different foundation from the condition of fixed wages noted above, because they constitute "not an assumption but a prediction of Keynes' theory..." And because Keynes' theory "rejects the Classical theory of the labour market and its denial of sustained involuntary unemployment" (Chick, 1983, p. 132), sticky wages have different consequences and perform a significantly different function as well.

If one begins with an analysis—whether neoclassical or neo-Keynesian—founded on standard labor-market demand and supply functions and perfect flexibility of all prices, "unemployment can result only as a consequence of rigidities in some prices." Conversely, once one accepts an assumption that the money wage is exogenously given, "unemployment follows as a straightforward consequence" (Magnani, 1983, p. 257). The only alternative, within a modified neoclassical framework, is to change some other assumption. For example, by assuming monopoly power by firms and unions instead of atomistic competition, it is possible to predict (rather than merely to assume) wage and price rigidities per se (Grandmont and Laroque, 1976).

Because Keynes assumes atomistic competition, his prediction of sticky wages is derived differently. First, according to Keynes, money "comes into existence along with debts, which are contracts for deferred payments, and Price-lists, which are offers of contracts for sale or purchase" (1930, 1, p. 3; Davidson, 1977, pp. 280-83). To serve efficaciously as the generally accepted means of discharging debts and contracts, money's value must be perceived as remaining reasonably stable. This is facilitated if wages are "relatively more sticky in terms of money" (*GT*, p. 237) than in terms of other commodities. Wages would be relatively more stable in terms of another commodity than money if the excess of liquidity premium over carrying cost of such a commodity exceeded that for money. Because of money's negligible elasticities of production and substitutability, however, this is unlikely. In short:

> the experience of a relative stickiness of wages in terms of money is a corollary of the excess of liquidity-premium over carrying costs being greater for money than for any other asset (*GT*, p. 238).

Second, Keynes derives sticky wages from his characterization of the supply of labor. One of his claims is that the neoclassical theory of full employment labor market equilibrium requires that workers behave in accord with a neoclassical specification of the supply of labor's "second postulate." To satisfy this condition, workers must adjust the amount of labor offered to the point where $W/P = MDUL$. This, in turn, presupposes that the supply of labor is solely a function of real wages. Moreover, symmetry in workers' behavior requires equivalent accommodation to alterations in real wages caused by changes in money prices as to changes in money wages. For example, workers must respond equally to a five per cent decrease in real wages, whether it occurs through a reduction in money wages or an increase in the cost of living. By contrast, Keynes holds:

> within a certain range the demand of labor is for a minimum money-wage and not for a minimum real wage...Whilst workers will usually resist a reduction of money-wages, it is not their practice to withdraw their labour whenever there is a rise in the price of wage-goods (*GT*, pp. 8, 9).

Labor's stipulation, "within limits" for a money wage, and its stronger resistance to money wage cuts than to "a gradual and automatic lowering of real wages as a result of rising prices" (*GT*, pp. 264, 276), raises additional objections to neoclassical theory beyond the "fundamental" objection of impediments to reducing real wages by money wage cuts (and raising aggregate demand and employment thereby). If the supply of labor is not exclusively a function of real wages, the neoclassical argument "breaks down entirely" and yields a "quite indeterminate" answer to the question of the actual level of employment, because the neoclassical labor supply curve (or labor demand curve, depending on how one constructs the argument) "will shift bodily with every movement of prices" (*GT*, pp. 8, 9). The neoclassical system is "one equation short" (*GT*, p. 276). If workers behave asymmetrically in response to changes in real wages depending on whether such changes are initiated by alterations in money wages or prices, then a "reduction in the existing money-wage would lead to a withdrawal of labour," whereas a "fall in real wages due to a rise in prices, with money-wages unaltered," typically would not (*GT*, pp. 8, 13). If workers are resistive to reductions in money wags, then:

> more labour than is at present employed is usually available at the existing money-wage, even though the price of wage-goods is rising and, consequently, the real-wage falling [and] more labour would, as a rule, be forthcoming at the existing money-wage if it were demanded (*GT*, pp. 7, 10).

Under these circumstances, $W/P$ and $MDUL$ diverge, and "the second postulate does not hold good" (*GT*, p. 10). Conversely, the claim that the second postulate is correct despite these alternative specifications of labor market behavior requires the implausible supposition that unemployed workers, though willing to work at the "current money wage will withdraw the offer of their labour in the event of even a small rise in the cost of living" (*GT*, p. 13; also 277).

Keynes' explanation of labor market sources of sticky money wages serves to correct certain popular misconceptions of his theory. One common view (other than a mere assumption of downward money wage rigidity) is labor unions' market power under collective bargaining. But Keynes rejects union monopoly as an explanation of involuntary unemployment. Insofar as "open or tacit agreement amongst workers not to work for less" keeps wages up and employment lower than it would be otherwise, such unemployment:

though apparently involuntary, is not strictly so and ought to be included under the above category of voluntary unemployment due to the effects of collective bargaining, etc. (*GT*, p. 8).

The second postulate is perfectly compatible, he continues:

> with "voluntary" unemployment due to the refusal or inability of a unit of labour, as a result of legislation or social practices or of combination for collective bargaining or of slow response to change or of mere human obstinacy, to accept a real reward corresponding to the value of the product attributable to its marginal productivity (*GI*, p. 6).

Another answer commonly attributed to Keynes in various "neo-Keynesian" models is workers' "money illusion" (Tobin, 1952). In its straightforward meaning, this is a form of irrational, nonoptimizing behavior in which workers oppose reductions in money wages because they (perhaps incorrectly) presume such reductions constitute decreases in real wages, but gullibly fail to oppose reductions in real wages brought about by increases in prices because they are under the illusion (misapprehension) that their incomes are unchanged as long as their money wages do not alter. On this interpretation, Keynes' explanation of labor supply behavior is made to appear to be the result of irrational, nonoptimizing behavior.

Whatever may be true for "neo-Keynesian" models (see, for example, Crouch, 1972, p. 235 ff.), Keynes himself expressly rejects the notion that "it would be illogical for labour to resist a reduction of money-wages but not to resist a reduction of real wages" (brought about by higher prices of commodities purchased by workers) (*GT*, p. 9). To the contrary, it was essential for Keynes to demonstrate that labor's relative resistance to money wage cuts (and acceptance, within limits, of real-wage reductions through higher prices)—and thereby the existence of involuntary unemployment—is eminently "logical," that is, is consistent with unconstrained, optimizing behavior if he was to challenge neoclassical theory on its own terms. Keynes sought to accomplish this in part by distinguishing between distributive and aggregative aspects of wage determination. The "general level of real wages" depends not on "the struggle about money wages," he claims, but, as already discussed, on "other forces" in the economy (*GT*, p. 14). Collective bargaining over money wages primarily affects the distribution of the aggregate real-wage between different labour-groups, and not its average amount per unit of employment...The effect of combinations on the part of a group of workers is to protect their relative real-wage (*GT*, p. 14).

Insofar as this is true, workers should be expected to rationally resist money-wage cuts because they perceive that their status and income relative to other workers or groups of workers would deteriorate as a consequence:

Since there is imperfect mobility of labour, and wages do not tend to an exact equality of net advantage in different occupations, any individual or group of individuals who consent to a reduction of money wages relatively to others, will suffer a relative reduction in real wages, which is sufficient justification for them to resist it (*GT*, p. 14).

On the other hand, within a certain range, workers do not oppose lower real wages caused by increased prices:

it would be impracticable to resist every reduction of real wages, due to a change in the purchasing-power of money which affects *all workers alike* (*GT*, p. 14; italics added).

Thus, Keynes' claim, in chapter 2 of *GT*, that the supply of labor, within a certain range, is dependent on money wages rather than real wages contains two interdependent arguments: practicability and justification. It is "impracticable" (and presumably lacking in clear "justification") to resist all reductions in real wages, notably reductions which affect "all workers alike." Certainly, "no trade union would dream of striking on every occasion of a rise in the cost of living." But there is ample "justification" as well as practicability for resisting relative reductions in money wages because they constitute reductions in relative real wages, and thereby do not affect "all workers alike." "Every trade union will put up some resistance to a cut in money-wage, however small" (*GT*, p. 15).

In effect, workers intuitively have a sense of "justification" and "practicability" which parallels Keynes' own critique of downward wage flexibility. It is as if workers have a sense of fairness which elicits rational behavior concordant with both Keynes' economic analysis and value judgments (Elliott and Clark, 1987):

> Thus, it is fortunate that the workers, though unconsciously, are instinctively more reasonable economists than the classical school, inasmuch as they (generally) resist reductions of money-wages, which are seldom or never of an all-round character...whereas they (generally) do not resist reductions of real wages, which are associated with increases in aggregate employment and leave relative money-wages unchanged (*GT*, p. 14).

In short, according to Keynes, for good reasons embedded in the institutional and behavioral qualities of monetary and capitalist economies, money wages tend to be relatively sticky in a downward direction. Insofar as this is so, Keynes thereby provides a second part of his internal critique of the classical theory's "second postulate". Even if (1) money wage cuts did invariably elicit real-wage reductions which (2) did invariably cause changes in aggregate demand in the right direction, of sufficient magnitude, and in proper time, to sustain or reestablish full employment, (3) downward sticky wages would make the implementation of the first two propositions problematic in any event, within the framework of neoclassical theory itself.

This problematical quality of downward sticky wages arises, however, within the context of Keynes' internal critique of neoclassical theory. That theory rests the "supposedly self-adjusting character of the economic system on an assumed fluidity of money-wages; and, when there is rigidity,...lays on this rigidity the blame of maladjustment" (*GT*, p. 257). In Keynes' own theory, by contrast, sticky wages have quite different, and salutary, consequences (Milgate and Eatwell, 1983, pp. 268-71). As Keynes summarizes the stylized facts of capitalist experience, the relative stickiness of money wages (though asymmetrical, since workers are more likely to welcome higher wage rates than to resist lower ones) conduces to relatively stable prices (*GT*, pp. 251, 253):

> In fact we must have some factor, the value of which in terms of money is, if not fixed, as least sticky, to give us any stability of values in a monetary system...(*GT*, p. 304).

Indeed, Keynes holds, if money wages changed more or less proportionately with changes in aggregate demand, prices would be much lass stable than, in fact, they are. If, for example, an attempt were made to fix real wages, the effect "could only be to cause a violent oscillation of money-prices." Every small fluctuation in aggregate demand would cause prices "to rush violently between zero and infinity" (*GT*, p. 239). If, on the other hand,

> competition between unemployed workers always led to a very great reduction of the money-wage level, there would be a violent instability in the price level [for] there would be no resting-place below full employment until either the rate of interest was incapable of falling further or wages were zero (*GT*, pp. 253, 303-04).

Thus, in Keynes' theory, unemployment is not based on sticky wages. It begins as a "provisional assumption" or "simplification" to "facilitate the exposition." It becomes a prediction. As such, it is then used, first negatively, as a part of a critique of the neoclassical theory, then positively, as an explanation of relative price level stability. Finally, it ends as a policy recommendation:

> I am now of the opinion that the maintenance of a stable general level of money-wages is, on a balance of considerations, the most advisable policy...This policy will result in a fair degree of stability in the price level;— greater stability, at least, than with a flexible wage policy (*GT*, p. 270).

## VI.  SUMMARY AND CONCLUSIONS

To sum up: (1) Keynes accepts the "first postulate" of the neoclassical theory, but largely as a means of providing a critique of that theory on its own grounds and underlying assumptions. (2) He does not, however, accept all of neoclassicism's assumptions or methodological perspective—notably, certainty, perfect foresight, and instantaneous wage and price flexibility. He recognizes various institutional and psychological properties of market capitalism underemphasized by neoclassical theory insofar as those properties are consistent with the assumption of atomistic competition, and emends his own argument so that it does not necessarily depend on such dimensions of the "first postulate" as diminishing returns. (3) He criticizes both the neoclassical theory of the demand for labor and neoclassicism's "second postulate" concerning the supply of labor, thereby rejecting wage cutting as inefficacious as an antidepressionary strategy. (4) He then criticizes a second aspect of the neoclassical theory's second postulate concerning the supply of labor, and contends that workers, in effect, intuitively—and rationally—behave so as to make expansionary policy (wage flexibility) both practicable and justified (impracticable and unjustified).

Although the intent of this essay has been to provide a textual explication, not an evaluation, three points may be noted in conclusion. First, Keynes' critique of neoclassical views concerning the supply of and demand for labor—in contrast to textbook "Keynesianism"—provides a richer heritage of thinking about unemployment and depression than such "ad hoc" propositions as wage and price rigidity, money illusion, liquidity traps, or inelasticity of investment relative to changes in the rate of interest. Second, attempts to recapture Keynes' elusive insights in any kind of modeling—"neoclassical" or "neo-Keynesian"—based on standard labor demand and supply functions are at least problematic. Third, as noted at the beginning of this paper, by constructing a critical analysis of adverse as well as favorable effects of wage and price reductions, Keynes provides, in effect, anticipatory responses to at least some aspects of the "new classical economics" (Begg, 1982, p. 154 ff.) and its criticisms of "Keynesian" theories of unemployment.

## NOTES

1. In chapter 1 of *GT*, Keynes rather ideosyncratically uses the term "classical" economists to refer to "followers" of Ricardo, who "adopted and perfected the theory of the Ricardian economics, including (for example) J.S. Mill, Marshall, Edgeworth and Professor Pigou" (*GT*, n.1). Thus, Keynes' use of the term "classical" corresponds roughly to at least one prominent interpretation of the phrase "neoclassical". For present purposes, the two terms shall be used interchangeably.

2. Leijonhufvud places heavy emphasis on Keynes' discussion of real balance effects (*GT*, pp. 92-94, 178, 232, 319), notably the potentially expansionary impact on consumption caused by "a rise in asset values due entirely to a fall in interest rates" which he dubs "Keynes' Second Psychological Law of Consumption" (Leijonhufvud, 1968, p. 193). (Compare F1 to F2 in Table 1.)

## REFERENCES

Ackley, Gardner. 1961. *Macroeconomic Theory*. New York: Macmillan.
Begg, David K.H. 1982. *The Rational Expectations Revolution in Economics*. Baltimore: John Hopkins.
Blaug, Marc. 1978. *Economic Theory in Retrospect*. New York: Cambridge University Press.

Carroll, David. 1973. *The Dictionary of Foreign Terms in the English Language.* New York: Hawthorne.

Chick, Victoria. 1983. *Macro Economics After Keynes: A Reconsideration of the General Theory.* Cambridge: The MIT Press.

Clower, Robert W. 1965. "The Keynesian Counterrevolution: A Theoretical Appraisal." In *The Theory of Interest Rates,* edited by F.H. Hahn and F.P.R. Breeching. London: Macmillan.

Coddington, Alan. 1983. *Keynesian Economics: The Search for First Principles.* London: George Allen and Unwin.

Crouch, Robert L. 1972. *Macroeconomics.* New York: Harcourt, Brace.

Culbertson, John M. 1968. *Macroeconomic Theory and Stabilization Policy.* New York: McGraw-Hill.

Davidson, Paul. 1967. "A Keynesian View of Patinkin's Theory of Employment." *Economic Journal* 77(September): 559-78.

———. 1977. "Post-Keynesian Monetary Theory and Inflation." In *Modern Economic Thought,* edited by Sidney Weintraub. Philadelphia: University of Pennsylvania Press.

———. 1983a. "The Dubious Labor Market Analysis in Meltzer's Restatement of Keynes' Theory." *Journal of Economic Literature.* XX(1, March): 52-56.

———. 1983b. "The Marginal Product Curve is not the Demand Curve for Labor in the Real World." *Journal of Post Keynesian Economics* VI(1, Fall): 105-17.

Davidson, Paul, and Smolensky, Eugene. 1964. *Aggregate Supply and Demand Analysis.* New York: Harper and Row.

DeLong, J. Bradford, and Lawrence H. Summers. 1986. "Is Increased Price Flexibility Stabilizing?" *American Economic Review* 76(5, December): 1031-44.

Dunlop, John T. 1938. "The Movement of Real and Money Wages." *Economic Journal* XLVIII(September).

Elliott, John E., and Barry S. Clark. 1987. "Keynes' General Theory and Social Justice." *Journal of Post Keynesian Economics,* Forthcoming.

Grandmont, J.M., and G. Leroque. 1976. "On Temporary Keynesian Equilibrium." *Review of Economic Studies.*

Keynes, John M. 1926/1963. "The End of Laissez Faire." In *Essays in Persuasion.* New York: W.W. Norton.

———. 1930. *Treatise on Money,* 2 vols. London: Macmillan.

———. 1936. *The General Theory of Employment, Interest, and Money.* New York: Harcourt Brace.

———. 1937a. "The Theory of Rate of Interest." In *The Lessons of Monetary Experience: Essays in Honor of Irving Fisher.* New York: Farrar and Rinehart.

———. 1937b. "The General Theory of Employment." *Quarterly Journal of Economics.* (February): 212-23.

———. 1939. "Relative Movements of Real Wages and Output." *Economic Journal* XLIX(March): 34-51.

Leijonhufvud, Axel. 1968. *On Keynesian Economics and the Economics of Keynes: A Study in Monetary Theory.* New York: Oxford University Press.

Magnani, M. 1983. "Keynesian Fundamentalism: A Critique." In *Keynes' Economics and the Theory of Value and Distribution*, edited by John Eatwell and Murray Milgate. New York: Oxford University Press.

Meltzer, Allan H. 1981. Keynes' General Theory: A Different Perspective. *Journal of Economic Literature* XIX(1, March): 34-64.

————. 1983. "Interpreting Keynes." *Journal of Economic Literature* XXI(1, March): 66-78.

Milgate, Murray, and John Eatwell. 1983. "Unemployment and the Market Mechanism". In *Keynes' Economics and the Theory of Value and Distribution*, edited by John Eatwell and Murray Milgate. New York: Oxford University Press.

Modigliani, Franco. 1944. "Liquidity Preference and the Theory of Interest and Money." *Econometrica* 12(January): 45-88.

Patinkin, Don. 1965. *Money, Interest, and Prices*. New York: Harper and Row.

Samuelson, Paul A. 1952. "The General Theory." In *The New Economics*, edited by Seymour E. Harris. New York: Knopf.

————. 1967. *Economics*. New York: McGraw-Hill.

Shackle, G.L.S. 1967. *The Years of High Theory: Invention and Tradition in Economic Thought, 1926-1939*. New York: Cambridge University Press.

Tarshis, Lorie. 1939. "Changes in Real and Money Wages." *Economic Journal* XLIX(March).

Thirwall, A.P. 1981. "Keynesian Employment Theory is not Defunct." *Three Banks Review* 131: 14-29.

Tobin, James. 1952. "Money Wage Rates and Employment." In *The New Economics*, edited by Symour E. Harris. New York: Knopf.

————. 1975. "Keynesian Models of Recession and Depression." *American Economic Review Proceedings* 65(2, May): 195-202.

Tuchscherer, Thomas. 1979. "Keynes' Model and the Keynesian." *Journal of Post Keynesian Economics* 1(4, Summer): 96-109.

Weintraub, Sidney. 1958. *An Approach to the Theory of Income Distribution*. Philadelphia: Chilton.

# FERNANDEZ FLOREZ'S
# *LAS SIETE COLUMNAS:*
## MANDEVILLE REHEARSED

Susan Pozo and Warren J. Samuels

> *The Seven Deadly Sins were the seven pillars on which rested our society; civilisation, progress; our customs, our laws, our work, our well-being, even our emotions, rested their enormous and age-long weight on them. The seven strong pillars fell, and everything fell. Humanity is now wandering amongst ruins.*
>
> —Wenceslao Fernandez Florez
> *Las siete columnas*

In 1926, 212 years after the publication by Bernard Mandeville of his *Fable of the Bees: or, Private Vices, Publick Benefits*, the Spanish novelist and journalist, Wenceslao Fernandez Florez published *Las siete columnas*. The central argument of the two books is substantially identical: that practices deemed vice by traditional

Research in the History of Economic Thought and Methodology, Volume 9, pages 171-197.
Copyright © 1992 by JAI Press Inc.
All rights of reproduction in any form reserved.
ISBN: 1-55938-428-X

morality are in fact the basis of modern prosperity, that the seven deadly sins are the pillars on which rest modern culture and civilization. As remarkable and surprising as it may be to historians of economic thought, it is not clear that Fernandez Florez knew of Mandeville's celebrated treatise.[1] Indeed, Sir Peter Chalmers Mitchell, who in 1934 translated *Las siete columnas* as *The Seven Pillars*, while referring in his Introductory Note to the irony of Anatole France and the bitter pathology of Octave Mirabeau, does not take notice of Mandeville. Moreover, it appears that no connection has yet been drawn between the two works in either language.[2] This article will report on and interpret Fernandez Florez's novel, apparently hitherto unacknowledged in both the English- and Spanish-language literature of the history of economic thought.

## I. THE AUTHOR AND HIS TRANSLATOR

Wenceslau Fernandez Florez (1879-1964) produced thousands of newspaper articles on all facets of Spanish life, the most important of which were his political journalism collected as *Acotaciones de un oyente* (2 vols., 1916-1918). He published at least a dozen major works of fiction; his *Obras completas* (7 vols., 1945-1961) are not complete, omitting several novels and at least one short story. Several novels other than *Las siete columnas* also were satires. While a prolific and somewhat popular writer during his lifetime, Fernandez Florez is reasonably well known but not considered a major Spanish author.

Fernandez Florez was born in 1879 in La Coruna, the largest city in Galicia in the Northeast corner of Spain.[3] The death of his father when the son was only 15, forcing him to earn his own livelihood, prevented him from studying medicine as he had hoped. It became his responsibility, as eldest son, to support his mother and siblings. Recognizing that the one skill he had acquired by that age was writing, Fernandez Florez began his career by reporting for the local newspaper, *La Manana*.[4] In 1903 Fernandez Florez became editor of another local newspaper, *Tierra Gallega*, and director of *Diario Ferrolano*. From these respectable positions he began contributing to newspapers and magazines in Madrid. These writings allowed him to move to the capital in 1905.

Despite contributing to several dailies and other periodicals, it was necessary for Fernandez Florez to supplement his earnings (as he had in Galicia) with a job at the customs office. It was not until his third novel, *Volvorete* (1917) that it was possible for him to rely exclusively on writing for a living. From the publication of *Volvorete* until his election to the Spanish Royal Academy in 1934, Fernandez Florez published his best work.[6] Fernandez Florez died in April 1964.

Overall, Fernandez Florez is considered a controversial figure in Spanish literary circles, with a handful of critics arguing that he deserves more recognition for his works than he has received (Nora, 1968, p. 8; Lopez, 1985, p. 14; Ward, 1978, p. 208). Several reasons have been suggested to explain why Fernandez Florez had few supporters in the Spanish literary world. Mainer (1967, p. 1) suggests that many critics mistrusted him because successful political journalists were viewed as "serving the oligarchy." Nora (1968, p. 9) argues that both the left- and the right-leaning politically minded considered his sympathies to be elsewhere. Mature (1968, pp. 5-6) cites three reasons for Fernandez Florez's unpopularity with the critics: His writing techniques were considered out of date. He was pegged as a humorist and, therefore, not a serious writer. He isolated himself from the literary circles of the day.

Although Fernandez Florez has by no means been ignored by Spanish-language literary critics and historians, and although he was not a writer of the first rank, he nonetheless may have been given less attention and credit that he would otherwise have received but for three factors: his career as a journalist, his immense popularity, and his apparent acceptance of the anti-communist ideology of Franco after the Civil War—manifest in *Una isla en el mar rojo* (1939).

Fernandez Florez attributed his reluctance to attend literary conferences and other similar gatherings to having become disillusioned by them as a young man. "...the literary gatherings are backbiting contests. I heard it being said in such gatherings that Cervantes was silly; that Dickens never learned to write correctly.... I lost all respect for those persons I recognized at the gatherings that made such statements" (Gomez-Santos, 1958, p. 12).

Despite not being recognized as a "serious" novelist, Fernandez Florez was very highly acclaimed as a political journalist, author of *Acotaciones de un oyente*, a series of parliamentary sketches that were first published in the daily Catholic newspaper *ABC*.[7] He was also very successful as a popular writer, the "'best read' of the contemporary narrators; 'one of the most popular and best paid'" (Mature, 1968, p. 5). Success in this arena, however, only increased disdain by critics.[8] Lopez (1985, p. 14) finds it necessary to defend Fernandez Florez as "not only the festive humorist for ladies that are bored on Sunday afternoon."

Fernandez Florez was frustrated by the lack of recognition as a novelist. In the prologue to an anthology of humorous works he edited, he defends humor in literature. "Humor appears in a nation's literature when the country has already lived much, and when in its literature there is much drama, much tragedy, much lyricism, and when discontent has genuinely become exteriorized in anger and tears, in satire and reproachful diatribes" (Fernandez Florez 1957, p. xiii).

Maturity in its literature is not the only requirement for the creation of humorous works, according to Fernandez Florez. The author himself needs to be mature. When a young man, he confesses, he only wrote "serious" works. "At the time, to provoke a smile seemed to me dishonorable" (1957, p. xiii). Despite defending humor, Fernandez Florez rejects the notion that it was his intention to make readers laugh when he wrote his most famous novels, including *Las siete columnas*. Instead he had hoped to "battle ideas I thought were wrong" (1957, p. viii).

It is unclear why Sir Peter Chalmers Mitchell undertook the project of translating *Las siete columnas*. Indeed, it is puzzling that he chose to translate novels at all, as he was a distinguished British zoologist, writer of numerous scientific books and articles, elected in 1906 as Fellow of the Royal Society (Debus). His interest in Spanish literature was perhaps the result of his residence in Spain, perhaps something to occupy his leisure time. Mitchell had planned to spend the winters of his retirement years in a small villa he bought in Malaga, Spain.[9] Despite the unpleasantness he faced during the civil war, Mitchell remained in Malaga. He angered the Republican coalition by helping a Nationalist neighbor, whose life was endangered, escape with his family from Spain. Mitchell compromised himself to a much greater extent with the Nationalists, however, by providing supplies to a Republican hospital and by sending his own accounts of the war to the foreign press. These reports contradicted much of what had been supplied to the foreign press by others. In 1937, Franco's troops recaptured Malaga and

Mitchell was arrested. Diplomatic negotiations between the British and the Spanish resulted in his release, but also his expulsion from Spain.

Mitchell's translation of works such as Ramon Sender's (1935) *Seven Red Sundays* can be understood as due to Mitchell's wish to understand the Spanish Civil War. Sender's account of the historical background for the war could provide some clues. But why a zoologist should undertake to translate a novel such as *Las siete columnas* is less obvious. One hypothesis is that Mitchell considered Fernandez Florez's novel to be a statement or viewpoint about the political, social and economic changes that were being contemplated and implemented. In the Introductory Note to the translation, Mitchell suggests that a best seller such as *Las siete columnas* "must tell something of what Spanish readers and writers are thinking" (Fernandez Florez, 1936, p. vii).

Mitchell's translation of the novel was published by Macmillan in 1934, a few years after Mitchell had decided to spend his winters in Spain and just about the time remodeling of the villa he had purchased for that purpose was completed. However, in *My House in Malaga*, Mitchell's account of his experiences for the period 1932-1937, he never mentioned the translation of *Las siete columnas*. Perhaps the translation was not so personally important to him after all. Perhaps, however, his silence was because of Fernandez Florez's association with Franco.[10] Mitchell's translation is a close rendering of the original Spanish, not a paraphrase.

## II. THE STORY

The book commences with a "Prologue. In Which Satan Acts with Results Apparent Only in the Second Part of this Book." In the Prologue a hermit, Acracio,[11] preoccupied with extirpating vanity from his actions and thoughts,[12] has an encounter with the Devil. The Devil is apparently sincerely distressed due to the fact that in the present world no one fears him because no one believes in him.[13] The present world is hell for the Devil: he feels unimportant and lacks stimulation. Because of his desperate need for conversation with someone who will take him seriously,[15] which the hermit agrees to pursue only upon the following condition, the Devil is convinced to do away with the Seven Deadly Sins: to repudiate not the sinful status

of certain actions but both the actions themselves and the motives
which lead to them. Part I is comprised of seven chapters in which
a dozen and a half or so central characters are introduced and we
learn, through a series of stories and substories, of their beliefs,
actions and lifestyles, all manifesting various of the Seven Deadly
Sins. The title of chapter one is representative of Fernandez Florez's
style: "In which Humanity begins to file before us."

One story tells of the philanthropist, Archibaldo Granmont and
his successful recruitment of the ambitious but heretofore virginal
actress, Adriana Sander as his mistress. Granmont's charity is clearly
in the service of his egoistic self-interest: the asylum which he endows
must have the most grotesque occupants.[16] Adriana exchanges her
soul for "success and happiness" (p. 23), for stardom on "the first
stage in the country" (p. 18), to the dismay of Florio Olivan, producer
of foie gras, friend from early youth, and secret lover of Adriana.

Another story concerns the late Baron de la Cetea who was literally
forever seeking the distinguishing marks of status.[17] In life, he sought,
among other things, the positions and garments of status. At death,
"Our hero arranged for himself a sensational funeral. He contrived
to give trouble to more people at his death than most men give during
their whole lives" (p. 31).[18] In death, the baron was no less concerned
with the trappings of distinction:

> ...I am afraid of meeting undesirable persons; I am not very fond of the
> rabble.... What distinguishes us in life is the way in which we came into it,
> and I don't see why the same should not apply to our death. I came into life
> in a cradle with a coat of arms. That was enough. And I came into the cemetery
> in a state coach. Very good, you are not going to tell me that it would have
> been all the same if I had come here third class (p. 35).

"Breaking the simple manners of the dead, the Baron soon
succeeded," we are told, "in dividing them into castes" (p. 36). As
for the lineage of the Baron himself, upon learning that the original
baron, whom he had understood to have been the captain of a royal
vessel, had been a murderous pirate whom the king had rewarded
for attacking his enemies, the Baron abets the theft of his ancestor's
bones to be made into buttons, lest he have to introduce this bandit
to his friends (p. 40).

Other stories tell of the invention of an aerial stabilizer motivated
by the desire to impress and win a woman;[19] the extreme repression

of present consumption in order to accumulate wealth to be enjoyed during old age; the morbid quest for the notoriety and fame of heroism; the surrender of the paradisaical life of a woodcutter in order to enjoy the higher income but miserable life of a miner; war calculated to maximize military promotions and decorations; the praise of obesity in defense of gluttony; the loss of Azucena's virginity, carefully maintained during life, to a worm; God's reproach to the Abbess of Capuchines for considering the world "a vale of tears, a land of sorrows, a home of strife, a cell of mortification" (p. 115);[20] and the quest by Granmont for further honor through the invention of a word (stymied temporarily because "the trouble is that I don't know what it means" [p. 96]). All tell of one pursuit or another of the Seven Deadly Sins: pride, covetousness, lust, anger, gluttony, envy and sloth. Behavior is conducted in their pursuit; beliefs are functional as rationalizations on their behalf.

At the end of Part I the narrative returns to the meeting of Acracio and Satan. The hermit explains the origin of Satan's frustration thus: "God leads men by the good that is in them; you by their evil. The poor human soul was about to go mad under the rival influences when it took refuge in the sordid and shameful indifference which is such a shock to your pride" (pp. 169-170). Upon Acracio's return to prayer, Satan pleads, "Acracio, this won't do. Have you made up your mind never again to listen to me? Don't carry things too far, confound it. You know quite well that you are the only one with whom I can discuss theology, and that I can't get on without talking about that" (p. 171). Their dialogue subsequently continues:

"What do you ask?"

"Stop all your temptations."

"Oh! Acracio!"

"Remove from amongst men, the Seven Deadly Sins, so that the hearts of God's creatures be pure and clean, and the lost peace of Paradise reign again on earth. Allow humanity to renew itself in a life of well-doing in which suffering and sin will never again be known."

"Well-doing? No; to create virtue is out of my power."

"But you can destroy Sin."

"I am only to destroy Sin? Is that your wish?"

"Yes."

Lucifer cast an ironical glance at the hermit and kept looking at him for a minute as if he were thinking over the audacious demand of the servant of God.[21]

"I had never thought of that," he murmured at last. "I shall oblige you" (pp. 172-173).

The five chapters of Part II for the most part describe a world that in five years became transformed from wealth, prosperity and splendor to poverty, economic depression and squalor. The shame of eating has replaced the Sin of gluttony. Saving is now seen as avarice[22] whose decline has brought a resigned passing of the fetish of wealth; progress, seen as the product of avarice, is not missed, except by Olivan. The old passions no longer stir the heart; actions formerly done and sanctioned are no longer pursued. What had been done for prestige now lacks rationale and is not pursued. The King himself unsuccessfully seeks to give his crown to another, attributing the former value of kingship to pride, whereas he now prefers his collection of spurs. The fall of pride leads to disincentive effects; industrial decay is ironically attributed to the disappearance of sloth which formerly motivated effort to facilitate idleness; unemployment and blight result.[23] Anger and pride, as well as the other sins, disappear. There is now serenity and indifference to the values hitherto esteemed. Population declines due to the low birth rate, threatening species extinction. Intercourse is seen as a ridiculous act, due to lust, and, with love, is now passe. War, newly seen to be due to greed rather than anger, whose real significance was hid behind "a mask of flowery words of which the poets and the politicians made pretty nosegays" (p. 256), is now a thing of the past, as is conspicuous consumption in the service of envy. The delights of life have vanished "for Sin has ceased" (p. 271). Paradoxically, idleness has increased at the same time that the people "have ceased to covet idleness" (p. 236); and "there is no need to have a caretaker on the property. There is nothing there of any great value, and even if there were, there are no thieves" (p. 264).

Not all are indifferent, however. Some are calm but others worry: "What is going to happen after this universal collapse? No one knows and it seems as if no one cared" (p. 197). In the final chapter, which carries the name of the book, Acracio is eventually confronted by Olivan, unofficially representing those who are disturbed with the new order of things. Contrary to Mandeville's *Fable of the Bees*, there is not much extended philosophizing or social analysis in *The Seven Pillars*. Much of the argument qua argument derives from the structure of the story plus occasional statements, sometimes but not always in the form of dialogue. The final chapter of Part II, however, is largely an exception. Though the form remains the same, the concentration of analysis is heavier.

The chapter begins by noting that "As the years went on, all the evils increased that arose when Temptation was removed. Property had almost ceased to exist.... Authority had vanished, as it no longer was upheld by violent means, and men moved about the wide world like animals in fear" (p. 272). Moreover, "With the violence of a spiritual plague, a debilitating mysticism spread over mankind. The most deeply rooted of all the superstitions was a belief in the end of the world" (p. 273).

Olivan confronts Acracio without reproach but in a voice "dulled by long-standing resignation, of one talking about what could not be helped":

"You have destroyed the happiness of mankind," said Olivan.

"I have freed men from Evil."

"I don't know if it was Evil, but I do know that now they are living in misery."

"It was Evil, and all creation breathed in its damnable slavery. The world was ruled by the Seven Deadly Sins. Few were the souls who were free from that leprosy of hell."

"Yes, the infernal leprosy had reached everyone, but all the same, life was pleasanter then. The removal of Pride broke the spring of many good actions. Charity and Philanthropy were often the fruits of that Sin.... A large part of human organisation rested on Pride. And, in ultimate analysis, what was the proud man? The truth is that he was dependent on others, in perpetual anxiety, more concerned with shocks to his vanity than is the miser with the depredations of thieves.... There is a minor kind of Envy, a jealousy rather unimportant which causes small individual tragedies and which passes with us as the official Sin, but there is another Envy to which we pay respect, and which disguises itself under the name of stimulus, of emulation, and which we encourage, as if it were something really useful. And it was so. Envy prevented idleness, stimulated the will, and was a spur for those who used it, and a restraint for those who feared it. Envy kept awake, always alert, the indispensable critical faculty. Like reins, it guided and restrained the ambitious."

"Envy was the broth of Hatred and of Anger."

"Do you know what we owed to Anger, Acracio? The whole of our social organisation. Violence set the boundaries of the peoples; violence had to stand behind even the most just laws to secure obedience to them; violence brought property into existence, watched over it, disciplined mankind, made order possible among the hordes of humanity, sometimes came to the support of reason, but more often took its place, was the chief agent in bringing about human inequality, and without it hierarchies would not have existed nor the ordered layers of humanity.... We might almost say that our society had Anger as its father and Fear as its mother . . . Even to submit ourselves to

God, we have to speak of His Anger, and we cannot imagine laws without punishments. . . . Only fear makes man a domesticated animal.... Fear of those above keeps those below in subjection, enduring their comforts and controlling their restlessness; fear of those below compels those above to make concessions, overcoming the selfishness of their luck. And now there are no leaders, no authority, no respect for law, and the world is like an arena filled with a purposeless crowd, brooding in confusion and despair. There is no stern, angry hand, enforcing its will. There is no fear and no obedience."

"But the awful sin of Cain no longer occurs amongst men."

"That is true. But am I trying to deny that good has been produced? I am only placing alongside the mountain of benefits the heap of ruins of the disintegration that has befallen us. The influence of Covetousness has also disappeared. And what has followed? It has been like a paralysis of the social body. No human mind can grasp all the ramifications of that Sin. Its roots spread so widely through modern life that it could not be plucked without dragging with it, in a solid mass, progress and much of civilisation. If Pride is at the root of all evil, Covetousness is the most widespread, the most powerful, and the most dynamic of forces. . . . Any enterprise, however difficult, will find heroes prepared for it, if only there is treasure at its end. There is no human need, no pleasure, no human emotion that is not exploited by Covetousness.... and we had reached a stage when it was not gold which brought pleasure, but pleasures were invented to attract gold. . . . tell me if there is anything not marked with the stamp of Covetousness.... It ceased, and all it supported has collapsed."

"Riches are a deceitful illusion."

"By all means; but the thirst for them worked miracles" (pp. 274-279).

It is later in this conversation that Olivan makes the statement comprising the epigraph of this article:

"The Seven Deadly Sins were the seven pillars on which rested our society; civilisation, progress; our customs, our laws, our work, our well-being, even our emotions, rested their enormous and age-long weight on them. The seven strong pillars feel, and everything fell. Humanity is now wandering amongst ruins" (p. 284).

Acracio makes one final defence of the new status quo: The present age is "but a slight and fugitive fragment of eternity.... But humanity is still young and is still in its childhood." Whereas the humanity of the past and the present relied on Sin, Cruelty, Covetousness and Envy:

"In the mysterious future yet to come, perhaps better men will arise who shall know how to found their happiness and their progress on God.... and what has broken down now will seem a primitive barbarism. And even if it should never come, if we are always to be as we are now, we must continue hoping for its coming, as an only alleviation for those who realise and endure the evil, and the error, the injustice and the sinful desires of men. Believe in this future, and your hope will bring you a joy, the pure unselfish joy of what we shall never taste.... All that has happened to mankind was first an aspiration of mankind" (p. 285).

But the crusade of stricken people implore, "Sin, give us Sin.... Satan! Satan! Give us back Sin! Satan!" And in the end Acracio succumbs. Thus closes the book:

"The last stragglers were then passing Acracio's hut. Erect in the shadow the holy man watched the halting progress of the wretched creatures, and pity and sorrow flooded his gentle heart.

Suddenly, perturbed but resolved, he joined the stragglers and marched out of the city with them" (pp. 288, 289).

## III. COMMENTARY:
## HISTORY OF ECONOMIC THOUGHT

Mandeville's *Fable of the Bees* is a significant work but, although deep, pregnant and controversial, not the equal of the more celebrated works of Smith, Montesquieu, Hobbes, Locke, Rousseau and others, including Hume. Fernandez Florez's *The Seven Pillars* is neither as deep nor as significant as Mandeville's *Fable*; and, certainly outside of Spain and related literary circles, it is so far from being celebrated that, until now, it does not seem to have been noticed at all in the literature of political economy and political theory.[24] For one thing, *The Seven Pillars* is complete fiction. Its author never appended to it, as Mandeville did to "The Grumbling Hive," his original fable, a series of extended theoretical and quasi-empirical remarks and other essays (whose total length was many times that of the original), generally in defense of his original venture. But all this is not to say that Fernandez Florez's *Las siete columnas* is not without interest, indeed, even significance.

First, we have, as with the *Fable*, a conflict between two moralities, one representing a pre-modernist way of life, almost ascetic and spiritual; the other, a modernist set of values. Each has consequences (costs and benefits) in regard to economic performance and, what is equally if not more important, each evaluates its own performance on its own terms; that is to say, the objective statements or indicia of performance are variously evaluated. Evaluation is moral-system specific.

Evaluation of actions and their consequences generally, but obviously by no means necessarily, is made on the basis of received moral rules, rules which channel and limit the evaluation. For each book, acts have consequences which appear differently depending upon the criteria used to identify and evaluate them. In each of the two works, there is the uncomfortable situation that certain benefits are the product of certain behaviors and values deemed negative by a particular moral code but deemed positive by another moral code. In each of the two works a society possessed of all of the traditional virtues falls into apathy and economic paralysis. The absence of self-love, of the seven deadly sins, is the death of progress. But it is progress as defined in a modernist valuational system which conflicts with the pre-modernist moral view.[25]

Second, it is clear that Fernandez Florez effectively follows the lead of Mandeville (as well as John Locke, Francis Hutcheson, Adam Smith, David Hume, and others) in focusing upon individual psychology as the locus of the variables explaining socioeconomic performance. Granted that moral rules and theological systems are methodologically collectivist phenomena, his focus is on the motivations and behavior of individuals and their consequences.

Third, it also seems clear that Fernandez Florez joins Mandeville (and many others, of course) in affirming modernist materialism in the sense of preoccupation with material prosperity and well-being. That, like Smith, Fernandez Florez acknowledges, if not stresses, certain reservations, only underscores his general, or final, position affirming the superior moral status of materialism. We shall return to this matter in the concluding section.

Fourth, it is clear that for both writers once the ruling system of moral values has been selected, the function of social control (for which the Devil is the metaphor in *Las siete columnas*) is to channel behavior in accordance with the criteria and desired performance consequences established by the chosen moral system. The same is true of Smith's *Wealth of Nations* (1937), in which the system of natural liberty, as understood by him, would reinforce those propensities of man promotive of the growth of the wealth of nations and inhibit or constrain those propensities antagonistic to that growth. The economy requires social control, one form of which is moral rules (for example, those identifying certain motivations and relevant behavior as sinful); but, given recognition of that requirement, there remains the necessity to determine what form and, especially, what content the moral rules are to have.[26]

Fifth, it is no more clear that Fernandez Florez knew Smith's *Theory of Moral Sentiments* (1976) than that he knew Mandeville's *Fable of the Bees*—nor, for that matter, apropos of status emulation, Thorstein Veblen's *Theory of the Leisure Class*. It may well be that Fernandez Florez's principal, if not sole, exposure to economic thought was the work of Henry George,[27]—which is striking, inasmuch as George's *Progress and Poverty* (1879), as well as Edward Bellamy's *Looking Backward* (1887), had a profound impact on opening people's minds to the opportunity for social reform. Be that as it may, as the foregoing account of the story of *Las siete columnas* should have made clear, the basic argument adopted by Fernandez Florez is the operation of what Smith considered to be the great deception,[28] that wealth is important. Moreover, Fernandez Florez also makes it abundantly clear, again as does Smith, that it is the pursuit of status emulation—to look and indeed to be successful in one's own eyes and in the eyes of others—that drives the economic system, including its institutions, such as private property (Smith, 1976, pp. 50ff and passim). Vanity given substance and direction by status emulation is central to Mandeville, Smith and Fernandez Florez.

Sixth, again not unlike Smith but much more pronounced and, we think, more important than for Smith (but that is another story), Fernandez Florez understands, or seems to believe that he understands, that hierarchy is the key to social order. Indeed, Fernandez Florez's account (pp. 276ff) seems to resonate much more with the sentiments we perceive emanating from an aristocratic temperament than a pluralistic, upward-mobility emphasizing, free market mentality.[29] In this regard as well as with respect to status emulation, Envy, as "the brother of Hatred and of Anger" (p. 276), is the operative force.

Seventh, one finds in *Las siete columnas*, in addition to the ideas of status emulation and conspicuous consumption, both the division of labor and the idea of unintended consequences, concepts also important to Mandeville as well as to Smith. Obviously, Fernandez Florez not only calls attention to (as did Smith) but underscores the adverse consequences of the division of labor, which are ultimately reckoned in terms of the pre-modernist system of values which by book's end is compromised in favor of the modernist. The idea of the division of labor is more conspicuous than that of unintended consequences, which is latent throughout the book but fundamental to its central argument—albeit in a complex manner, given the clash of moral systems in which the consequences are considered and assessed.[30] That social order is a product of anger and fear, and that the driving force of economy and society is covetousness, are neither applauded by pre-modernist morality nor (in the novel) extolled by modernist morality, except in terms of their unintended consequences.

Eighth, whereas Mandeville's work is subject to a variety of conflicting interpretations and assessments as social science theory,[31] in part because his argument is more complexly developed, Fernandez Florez's book seems relatively simple in comparison and thus not so likely to be so variously interpreted (but see below).

Ninth, the present discussion is relevant to Hispanists interested in the origins of Fernandez Florez's ideas. Two alternative interpretations arise, once the parallel between Mandeville and Fernandez Florez is recognised. First, one can consider that their respective works and ideas are too homologous for *Las siete columnas* not to be based on *The Fable of the Bees*. The structural parallels are too compelling to give pause in drawing that conclusion. From this perspective, Fernandez Florez evidently simply borrowed from Mandeville. Second, one can feel that both works are manifestations of the same enduring circumstance, that the link is not one of influence but of comparable interpretations or ideas arising within and indeed deriving from similar situations. The historical parallels between England and Scotland in the eighteenth and Spain in the early nineteenth century, centering on the processes and stresses of transformation from post-feudal to bourgeois culture, are too compelling to give pause in drawing that conclusion. From this point of view, Fernandez Florez rediscovered the analytical problem (the conflict between moral systems) about which Mandeville had also written in comparable times in a different society two centuries earlier; and having written *Las siete columnas* indicates Fernandez Florez's ability to theorize (in fiction) about the situation of Spain in the 1920's.[32] In either respect, the historical presence of Mandeville may help explain the phenomenon of *Las siete columnas* from the Hispanist interest, a presence which historically has not been brought to bear, it appears, on Fernandez Florez. Nonetheless, as will be discussed below, the precise relevance of Mandeville to the understanding of Fernandez Florez depends also in part on the interpretation given *Las siete columnas.*

## IV.  FURTHER INTERPRETATION AND CONCLUSION

Fernandez Florez's *Las siete columnas (The Seven Pillars)* is an interesting, even remarkable book. Given Sir Peter Chalmers Mitchell's status in English meritocratic society, we can perhaps sense his attraction to it—though still uncertain and perplexed why he neglected in his Introductory Note to relate the work to Mandeville's *Fable of the Bees.* The story itself is an ingenious one and the moral and economic philosophizing or theorizing ensconced within it is straightforward; considered for what it is, a literary work, a novel, neither its humor nor its seriousness is overdone. That is not to say, however, that *Las siete columnas* is a monumental or even great work, or that Fernandez Florez is an author of the first rank.

One can surmise from the fact of *Las siete columnas* having been written that the paradox, or conflict, of "Private Vices, Publick Benefits" continues, two-and-three-quarter centuries after Mandeville, to bedevil the moral sense of mankind. This is no less plausible for *Las siete columnas* having been written in a Catholic country; indeed, that may help explain its national origin. But the conflict between materialist and nonmaterialist values, between a Judeo-Christian ethos of love and that of egoism, between the two cities of St. Augustine, remains, if typically only beneath the surface, in moral philosophy as well as in welfare economics and economics as a whole.[33]

To this point the discussion has proceeded upon the understanding that the gravamen of *Las siete columnas* is the affirmation of the modernist system of morality of a commercial society. It is not out of the question, however, to interpret *Las siete columnas* as affirming not modernist morality but the lost world of true virtue surrendered in consequence of the Mephistophelean bargain in pursuit of wealth. Such an interpretation would be consistent with an emphasis on the novel's apparent irony and satire and, for example, with the passages in which Fernandez Florez has Acracio call for a wait of some half-century in order to appreciate the new order of things based upon the old morality. It would affirm not the restoration of the seven pillars as the foundation of society and economy but the price incurred thereby. The world, in the interlude provided by Acracio's arrangement with the Devil, would have learned how to shrug, and, in the aftermath of that desolate period, would have learned the meaning of "alas."

An alternative, centrist interpretation is that while Fernandez Florez is advocating continuing modernization, he prefers nonextremist or middle-of-the-road reforms rather than the putatively more extreme reforms of the time, in part to avoid the social conflict that was, in the view of many, destroying the fabric of Spanish society.[34] This interpretation can be grounded as follows— although elements of what follows can also support either of the other two interpretations.

Around the time that Fernandez Florez wrote *Las siete columnas*, the conflicts in Spanish society that eventually resulted in the Spanish Civil War were brewing. One area of controversy centered on the role of the military. Many Spaniards objected to military activity in Africa, especially after the disastrous Moroccan compaign of 1921. Nonetheless, the military continued to flex its muscle, imposing martial law in Barcelona from 1919-1923, terminating industrial strikes with violence, and suppressing the results of parliamentary investigations into its activities (Jackson, 1974, pp. 12-13). In addition, King Alfonso XIII apparently had the support of but few of his subjects, though not all whom he displeased were anti-monarchists. The king and the military joined forces in 1923, as public sentiment against the two grew, and replaced the parliamentary monarchy with a military dictatorship headed by Primo de Rivera.

Though the Catholic Church (partly out of self-preservation) was closely aligned with the Nationalist forces during the Civil War, it is not correct to say that the Church had been highly regarded by all parties in the coalition. For decades prior to the War the Church's influence and power had declined rapidly (Jackson, 1974, p. 163), and many Nationalists were clearly anti-clerical, favoring the separation of Church and State. Overall, there was a wide range of sentiment about the appropriate role for the Church in Spanish society and government throughout the pre-Civil War years, including debate over the obsolescence of Christian ethics, carried on by both the Nietzschean right and the Marxist left. Spain was then still suffering reactions to the loss of its colonies, most notably in 1898. The period between the loss of empire and the Civil War was a period of both hiatus and profound crisis.[35]

Thus during the time Fernandez Florez was writing, Spain was suffering the pains of what is conventionally called modernization. Institutions were evolving to undertake, or be given, new roles. Moreover, Spain was suffering from the effects of the cyclical booms and busts to which any modern capitalist economy is subject.[36] The current situation was flawed, according to Fernandez Florez, but radical alternatives were flawed as well. That Spain needs to continue on a path of nonextremist modernization is one interpretation of Fernandez Florez's novel.

In *Las siete columnas*, Fernandez Florez appears to condemn the existing condition of Spain. Though many benefit from Granmont's philanthropy, the reader is induced to be repulsed by his motives. But the world without sin, without greed, the "perfect" world, is, aside from being unattainable or inconsistent (the absence of lust results in depopulation), undesirable. Even if a world without sin could be attained, the starving masses evoke emotions of pity that parallel the reader's disgust at Granmont's motives.

Fernandez Florez admits that 1918-1931 was "a point in time at which it was necessary to apply large reforms to Humanity's political, economic, social, moral, and sentimental structure..." (Mature 1968, p. 60). Fernandez Florez is not satisfied with the current order. But given certain situations in his other novels, it could be hypothesized that he advocates not a return to premodernist times, but rather a constrained push for further reform. He appears to advocate family planning in *La familia Gomar* ([1915] 1922) with family size chosen according to a family's means. In *Las aventuras del caballero Rogelio de Amaral* (1933), though he does not condone abortion outright, he censures the state's hypocrisy in its code of laws. Beatriz, victim of a violent rape, is unsuccessful in her bid to get a doctor to abort the fetus she is carrying. As she sees it, "It is necessary to jealously respect children in their mother's womb in order to kill them in battlefields" (Mature, 1968, p. 102). In *Relato immoral* (1927, p. 217) the author sees Spanish courting practices as causing love to be "a constant tragedy and women—a nest of displeasures." These episodes do not suggest that Fernandez Florez sees a better world resulting from turning back. Nor does he accept the visions urged by the radical revolutionaries of his day.[37]

A further, quite different interpretation of *Las siete columnas* is possible, however. It may very well be that Fernandez Florez was affirming not the superior moral standing of either the old or the new moral system but the greater compatibility of materialist morality with human nature. If so, then the argument of the book is more descriptive and interpretive than evaluative.[38] Whatever Fernandez Florez's intentions, moreover, this is another possible interpretation which a reader can give to the book. One can affirm this interpretation—or any other interpretation, for that matter— quite independent of what its author may have intended.[39]

Historians of economic thought (as well as literary critics, Hispanists among them) now seem increasingly sensitive to the distinction between the intentions of the author and the meaning of a text as discerned by a variety of readers. It is not possible, it would seem, to ascertain the intentions of Fernandez Florez in *Las siete columnas*; we are severely limited by the absence of additional elaborative and legitimizing essays, such as one finds in Mandeville's work (though that has not prevented diversity of interpretation of the meaning of his work). Whatever the intention of its author, the book clearly can be read and interpreted differently by different readers and, moreover, can have diverse moral meaning for its readers.[40]

One reasonably clear lesson from the volume, however, is that the focus of economics on wealth is moral-system specific. This is a lesson from Mandeville and Smith only echoed and rehearsed by Fernandez Florez.[41] In this respect, at least, economics reflects the modern world and its Mephistophelean bargain, whatever one thinks of its costs and benefits.

## ACKNOWLEDGMENT

The authors are indebted to Jeff Biddle, Steven Medema, and Stephen Woodbury for comments on an earlier draft of this article; Mary Randsdell, Jane Rossetti, and the staff of Servicio de Informacion Bibliografica of Biblioteca Nacional, Madrid, for bibliographical and other research assistance; and Pedro Schwartz Giron, Dr. Fernando Mendez, and Malcolm Compitello, for invaluable advice and assistance.

# NOTES

1.   It appears that The *Fable of the Bees* was never translated into Spanish, although a French translation published in London dates from 1740 (though possibly at a fictitious location in order to protect the anonymity of a French publisher from the censor; this was the case with works of the group centering on Vincent de Gournay in the 1750s; see the report on a paper by Antoin Murphy in *History of Economic Thought Newsletter*, no. 32, Spring 1984, p. 5). It also appears that there is no significant interpretive literature on the *Fable* in Spanish, only brief expositions in dictionaries and encyclopedias. On the other hand, Fernandez Florez was very proficient in English and the Spanish had been very interested in English literature, including English political economy. It may not be unreasonable to suggest that Fernandez Florez had either read or heard of Mandeville's book, or his ideas, but the fact remains that Mandeville does not enter even in a minor way into the Spanish critical literature.

2.   Fernando Mendez (unpublished letter to Warren Samuels, undated [July 1988], p. 1, translated by Susan Pozo and Warren Samuels), after research in the Biblioteca Nacional and elsewhere, supports the finding that "there does not exist any reference in the Spanish literature about the parallel... between the works of Bernard Mandeville and W. Fernandez Florez.... The studies about WFF that have been published in Spain allude only to literary and social aspects making a *few brief* references about the works and novels containing economic themes, but never going in this direction in any depth and, of course, never analyzing the similarities with Mandeville." The same point is made by Pedro Schwartz (unpublished letter to Warren Samuels, May 9, 1988, p. 1). The important interpretive works of Mainer and Mature make no mention of Mandeville.

3.   The biographical material in the following two paragraphs is from Mature, 1968, pp. 11-21.

4.   Fernandez Florez's strong background in writing and in literature was acquired from his father. He notes in an interview with Gomez-Santos (1958, p. 13) that his father "had very good taste in literature."

5.   The success of *Volvorete* was partly due to Fernandez Florez's recent recognition as a clever political journalist.

6.   It was not until 1945, however, that he was able to accept the position in the Academy, because of the Spanish Civil War.

7.   Fernandez Florez became a household name within eight days of beginning this series in *ABC*. His columns were originally unsigned, but King Alfonso XIII insisted on knowing the author (Mature, 1968, p. 14). From then on, Fernandez Florez, it seems, never needed to worry about making a living. *Acotaciones de un oyente* was published in *ABC* from October 1916 through October 1918.

8.   Fernando Mendez suggests (unpublished letter to Susan Pozo and Warren J. Samuels, 20 June 1989, p. 2; translated by Susan Pozo) that this disdain can be attributed "to what in Spain we consider a national sport: envy" and that "the more satirical is a writer in exposing the defects of his compatriots, the greater is the disdain with which he is treated, *perhaps* because more envy is produced." Mendez cites the chapter on envy in Spanish literature in Diaz-Plaja, 1967).

9. The following information on Mitchell is derived from his account of his experiences in Spain during 1932-1937, published as *My House in Malaga* (Mitchell, 1938).

10. Mature (1968, p. 123) claims that Fernandez Florez was a member of the Nationalist Party and recounts that it was necessary for him to take refuge in the Dutch embassy in 1936 when Madrid was in the control of the Republicans.

11. Fernando Mendez (letter to Susan Pozo and Warren J. Samuels, 20 June 1989, p. 4) notes that the name Acracio is related to anarchist. Mendez equates *acracia* with anarchy; it may be defined as opposition to authority.

12. Acracio longs for a meeting with God but, after interpreting the appearance one day of a dove during his prayers as a sign from heaven, "meditated on his illusion, and saw that it was vanity" (p. 2). He also interprets a thought that "the Evil One had come to conquer him by terror" as another vanity, a lapse from humility "although in truth they came from a longing for perfection and a holy impatience for putting his faith to the proof." Although the "fame of the good hermit grew day by day" and "notwithstanding his edifying steadfastness, never had there been launched against him, to conquer him, the hellish devices of temptation which had been lavished on other saints..." (pp. 2-3). It seems that Acracio was tempted by the prospect of temptation itself as a demonstration of his own importance. At this same point the author tells of Acracio's thoughts concerning "those infernal women who dance in the moonlight at the doors of hermits, their shifts wantonly opened to display their softly lighted bodies, their arms inviting, their breasts aflower, the fire of hell in their eyes, their skins with the lovely golden tint that comes from eternal flames" (p. 4)—thoughts which one can readily imagine Vilfredo Pareto designating as preaching virtue so that the mind can linger on matters of sex (Samuels, 1974, p. 75).

13. Not only Satan but God as well: "HE and I divided the earth, and no living creature refrained from enlisting on one side or on the other." But now they "have turned disdainful backs on Us, and seem to have forgotten that We ever existed. If anyone does concern himself with HIM, it is to try to analyse HIM scientifically in the cold language of reason and the petulance of logic.... As for me,...I was the Adversary—and now, I am ashamed to own it, I am hardly even an oath; if men didn't require to interlard their words with interjections, would my name ever be mentioned?... Unhappy fate; no one loves me, no one fears me, no one believes in me"(pp. 8-9). Speaking of those whom he has possessed "by the classical methods," Satan says, "But it was no good. The medical profession pronounced them cases of epilepsy" (p. 11).

Perhaps it is not inapposite to take cognizance of a letter from Harold Laski to Justice Oliver Wendell Holmes in the seventh year of their marvelous correspondence: "*My dear Justice*: First of all, and above all, the happiest of New Years to you both. I hope it will bring me a sight of you; at least I would give two years of life for a real talk. In the middle ages the devil would have appeared and taken me at my word. We, being sophisticated, have abolished the devil with the result that my appearance depends upon the liking of Cambridge undergraduates for political theory" (Howe, 1953, p. 466).

14. Says Satan to Acracio: "...you, alone in the world, keep up the fine old traditions, the customs of the good days, even faith itself" (p. 10).

15.   "Never shall I try you with my temptations. Never shall I disturb your prayers. You alone of mortals remind me of what I was, and what I could do. I'll do nothing to hinder the salvation of your soul; I am asking nothing from you. Only let me come to see you now and again, and talk about HIM.... For many long years I've found no one to discuss that topic...my only subject" (p. 12) (ellipses in original).

16.   "...No other asylum in the world owned a pair of children like the one with the gigantic head and the other with the minute head" (p. 26).

17.   "...He had fifteen or twenty different uniforms, the wearing of each of which carried a distinct privilege, even if it had become no more than the right to meet other wearers of the same uniform" (p. 30). "You must understand that I only had it [the position of "private chamberlain of the cape and sword of His Holiness"] to put on my death certificate. It is well known that there are many offices and many distinctions that have no other object except to be put on the death certificate" (p. 36).

18.   "To see that dignitary [the representative of the king] behind the coach was the chief pleasure the defunct owed to his new estate. But soon he found other reasons to be glad that he was dead, enjoying himself more than he had thought possible. To pass through the streets in a sumptuous coach, holding up the traffic, with hundreds of well-dressed people on foot following behind, is a deep joy; but to be saluted by all the world, to obtain from old and young, from rich and poor, a solemn courtesy in which for a space bared heads showed bald skulls, curly hair, white or ruddy locks, is a pleasure granted to very few whilst they are alive. The baron received these salutes with the reserved gravity that came from conscious merit" (pp. 32-33).

19.   "I must get a great deal of money—a very great deal of money, the wealth of Midas. Very likely on that depends whether my life is to be happy or miserable" (p. 49). "You realise that all these people here are not really interested in the stabiliser, but in the dividends that the Company will pay. And all that I really care about is Celia.... The secret motive of nearly all the efforts men make is a woman" (p. 50). "I can almost say that Celia invented the stabilisers. At least the longing to win her inspired my efforts" (p. 49).

20.   "Unhappy woman, how dare you condemn what is My work? You have made yourself find on the earth only blackness and sin, and sorrows and tears. Always tears, streams, lakes, oceans of tears. You have wilfully shut your eyes to what was good, what was beautiful, what was pleasing to the senses, and what was lovely, because you imagined that beauty and pleasantness were sinful. How can you condemn My creation without condemning Me? Return again to the world. Know it!" (pp. 116-117).

21.   Pedro Schwartz considers that "This shows that Lucifer knew what he was about when he conceded the hermit's wish" (Letter from Pedro Schartz to Samuels, July 26, 1988).

22.   "...my prudence was only a secret Avarice," "the prudence of saving is only a mask for the sinful pleasure of Avarice" (pp. 192, 193).

23.   The crisis has been "turning the chief industrial centre of the kingdom into a graveyard of dead activities" (p. 227). "There is no work to be had anywhere. The countryside is full of poor devils ready to work for nothing but bread enough to keep them from starving" (p. 182). "As factory after factory closed its doors, it sent

hundreds, thousands, of families into beggary.... All over the world, millions and millions of beings had given up any hope of food except from charity. There seemed to be no remedy for the increasing evil" (p. 203). Skilled cultivation under scientific horticulture "had vanished and everything gave the impression of tillage abandoned to the careless production of Nature" (p. 185). "...it is impossible to have joy at the table. We human beings are ashamed of all our natural necessities. The act of eating has become purely physiological, and it revolts us, as it is an expression of our weakness; it has become a mere animal function and we eat like animals" (p. 189); the support which gluttony gave to "the improvement of agriculture, to an increase in the quality and quantity of the fruit-harvest, and to the labours of the aviculturalist and the breeder in making fowl and flesh more succulent" (p. 188) has now been lost. Granmont, who had "long since...abandoned his charity," "could not understand why he had ever thought of giving a home, teaching, and food, to a set of children who were of no interest to him and whose parents he didn't know" (p. 213). Armies have often been disbanded: "Almost all the nations have taken that step. We have kept up our armies out of respect to our statutes and to vested interests. But in the present state of society, armed force is useless...never again will Anger make men raise their hands. Let us disband our armies and nothing will happen except that we shall increase the numbers of the unemployed" (pp. 225-226).

24. Neither Fernandez Florez nor *Las siete columnas* is cited in Lyman's (1978) analysis of the concept of the seven deadly sins as found in the literature of philosophy, religion, and the social sciences. For a history of the concept of the seven deadly sins with special reference to the medieval English literature, see Bloomfield (1952).

25. Teichgraeber (1986), among others, in his discussion of Frances Hutcheson in relation to Mandeville, indicates that the relation of wealth to virtue can be altered by changing the definition of virtue and thereby the relationship between private vices and public benefits (see also Tribe, 1988, pp. 344, 345).

26. We may note in passing that apropos of Granmont's charity school, Mandeville's longest addition to "The Grumbling Hive" is "An Essay on Charity, and Charity-Schools." This may be either coincidence or an indication of prior knowledge.

27. Mainer (1975b, pp. 223, 241 and passim) suggests that among the sources of Fernandez Florez's thought were Gustave Flaubert, Henry George, Eca de Queiroz, and H. G. Wells. Mainer suggests that George's ideas may have induced in Fernandez Florez a hope for a post-industrial society with the virtues but without the vices of capitalism. (Letter from Pedro Schwartz to Warren Samuels, July 26, 1988.) Fernandez Florez himself explicitly cited Eca de Queiroz, among others, saying further, "After these I have been influenced by all the great Spanish writers and by those outside of Spain, as I was an insatiable reader" (quoted by Fernando Mendez in Gomez-Santos, 1958, p. 41; letter from Mendez to Samuels, July 1988, p. 2; Mendez also repeats that "we remain unclear whether or not FF read Mandeville." Mendez notes that "The legend that is described in *Las siete columnas* has as a literary precedent the work from the middle of the 19th century of Gustave Flaubert, *Les Temtations de Saint Antonie*, a work that was translated into Spanish and published in 1911; it doesn't seem that WFF knew of it. Rather, FF appears to have been inspired by the flaubertian Lendas dos Santos, by the Portuguese writer

Eca de Queiroz" (Gomez-Santos, 1958, p. 2, citing Mainer 1975a, p. 225). Mandeville appears in none of the cited interpretive literature. Mainer (1975b, pp. 237-238) also cites the Georgist writings of Baldomero Argente and the translation in 1921 of the *Principios de reconstruccion* of Bertrand Russell. Apropos of George, Mendez writes: "It is very probable that the major part of the readings of economics by WFF, as with his ideas in this area, come from Henry George. This affirmation is only an hypothesis, as I have no written confirmation." Mendez quotes Lucas Beltran (in de Urquia et al., 1988, pp. 83-101) thus: "...for reasons that I still do not clearly understand, in the second half of the 19th century, Spanish economic science entered into decadence. . . . I think that in the year 1927 there weren't 20 persons in Spain with the knowledge that today a graduate in economic science has. These persons were the Economics professors on the Faculty of Law and in some special schools and a few researchers and politicians who were interested in some economic problems and had studied on their own.... [Although the works of Smith, Ricardo, the historicists, the marginalists, and most other writers were not readily if at all available in Spanish before World War Two,] On the other hand, as if it were a joke, in this scientific desert there was a Georgian Library. Henry George, an anecdotal figure in the history of economic thought [sic], had captured the interest of a group primarily of Spanish politicians, and a few dozen books of the author and his disciples and successors had been translated into Spanish" (p. 4).

28.   Fernandez Florez (1934, p. 279): "Riches are a deceitful illusion." Smith (1976, p. 183): "It is this deception which rouses and deep in continual motion the industry of mankind." (For Smith's negative statements, see Smith, 1976, pp. 61-62 and passim.)

29.   In this respect at least Fernandez Florez parallels Ferguson 1980 (1767); see, for example, Sher 1985, chapter Five, especially p. 199 and passim. Ferguson's argument in favor of the individual pursuit of virtue within the existing hierarchical status quo is implicitly shown to be quite systemically relative by Fernandez Florez's tale: virtue, and the pursuit of virtue, depend upon the existing moral system which defines virtue—and in Fernandez Florez's novel, while virtue is generally identified with premodernist morality, modernist morality would make virtues of the Seven Pillars. As Sher (1985, p. 195) avers, Ferguson had in mind "a *universal* theory of political conservatism that would provide a sociological justification for supporting virtually every existing government." The work of Mandeville, Smith and Fernandez Florez went beyond that position, inquiring somewhat more discriminatingly into the problem of the desirable system. Ferguson, however, did affirm hierarchism per se. Fernando Mendez suggests (letter to Susan Pozo and Warren J. Samuels, 20 June 1989, p. 2) that Fernandez Florez's ideology was very close to elitism, and akin to democratic despotism.

30.   Regarding Mandeville, see Schneider 1987, pp. 168ff; and also pp. 194ff in re paradox, irony, and satire.

31.   See, for example, Horne (1978) and Schneider (1987); see also Bryson (1968, 1945), Hont and Ignatieff (1983), Pocock (1985), Goldsmith (1985), and Teichgraeber (1986).

32.   Fernando Mendez (letter to Susan Pozo and Warren J. Samuels, 20 June 1989, p. 2) notes that while the dictatorship of Primo de Rivera was, in comparison with the Franco regime, relatively permissive in matters of the freedom of the press

and expression, pressure nonetheless existed, leading writers to either express themselves in a circumspect way or not at all; and that this may account for the lack of extended philosophizing or social analysis in *Las siete columnas*.

33.   Fernando Diaz-Plaja's (1967) interpretation of Spanish culture, *The Spaniard and the Seven Deadly Sins*, lists Fernandez Florez and several of his writings, including *Las siete columnas*, in the bibliography. Apropos of this study of Fernandez Florez's story in *Las siete columnas* about the abdication-minded king, Diaz-Plaja begins his chapter on Pride (the first chapter in the book) with the short paragraph: "It may be that pride is the key to the Spanish attitude toward society. The pride which allows the humble man to say, 'I don't have the royal wish'" (p. 13). Diaz-Plaja's argument is, generally, that pride is the primary vice of the Spaniard. It serves to motivate other sins, such as anger, envy, and sloth, while encouraging the exaggeration of lust. On the other hand, pride stifles avarice; leads the Spaniard, through fear of ridicule, to limit socially unacceptable behavior, such as drunkenness; and, through the openness of lust and anger, contributes to the diminution of sexual and other violent crimes. Also attributable to pride are the dignity and generosity characteristic of the Spaniard. Positive values also are derived from other sins. The bravery associated with anger and the satisfaction associated with gluttony and sloth are two examples. Although the Spaniard may be characterized as self-centered, cruel, and indolent, the sins from which these characteristics are derived (pride, anger, and sloth, respectively) also contribute positively to Spanish society. Again, this is a general summary of Diaz-Plaja.

34.   As already indicated, Mainer (1975b, pp. 223, 241 and passim; noted by Schwartz, letter to Samuels, July 26, 1988) explores the theme that Fernandez Florez was not a cynic, hoping for a post-industrial society with the virtues but without the vices of capitalism. Mendez (letter to Samuels, July 1988, p. 2, referring to Mainer 1975a, and 1975b, p. 222), writes that whereas in *El secreto de Barba Azul* (1954/ 1926) the protagonist "attempts to penetrate the reasons that sustain the meaning of human life" but "concludes with universal skepticism," in *Las siete columnas* "Florio Olivan starts from the contrary point: If the seven deadly sins disappear, the comfortable structure of the world will collapse due to lack of incentives, so he urges the finding of new moral bases for the necessary activity."

35.   It was also the "silver age" of Spanish literary culture, centering on the work of such writers as Pio Baroja, Antonio Machado, Miguel de Unamuno, and Ramon del Valle Inclan, often referred to collectively as the "generation of 98."

36.   Carr (1966, p. 509) in particular dwells on labor strife in Spain as employers and unions attempted to hold onto World Ware I wages and profits in the post-war period.

37.   Mendez (letter to Samuels, July 1988, p. 3) notes that several themes presented in *Las siete columnas* are repeated in other writings by Fernandez Florez, for example, his aversion for the industrial world and toward the banking world (seen as the cause of poverty in private economies), and the obstruction of industrial and economic prosperity by the actions of government officials.

38.   Interestingly, Diaz-Plaja (1967, p. 7) says in his Preface of his own approach, "The writer, then, is not a judge; he is rather a witness, and sometimes an accomplice."

39.   Fernando Mendez (letter to Susan Pozo and Warren J. Samuels, 20 June 1989, pp. 3-4) suggests that it is possible that Fernandez Florez "was trying to comply

with or appear in agreement with...the social norms of those who had power and ruled in Spanish society (clerics, aristocrats, large bourgeois...)." Alternatively, Mendez suggests that "perhaps what is happening is not that WFF is intending to comply with certain powerful groups, in reality WFF had his own convictions and moral beliefs (that he received and that he was educated in) and some parts of his work could be—possibly—an intent to save his moral ideas or to not reject them without something else." Also, recognizing that it may be an exaggeration to interpret Fernandez Florez's work using a cost-benefit framework, Mendez also poses the possibility that the author perceived the modernist morality of the seven deadly sins "as having fewer costs and more benefits than the morality" of the premodernist "saints and hermits.") As a further alternative, Mendez suggests the possibility that the author "is trying to tell us that we don't know how to appreciate the benefits of each of these moral orders through its repercussions on *the growth of wealth* (GNP), that is, on production." Mendez also suggests that perhaps "behind all of this is a belief that the market should limit itself to certain norms or moral rules," perhaps in the manner in which Smith may have intended to presume the philosophy of the *Theory of Moral Sentiments* (1976) in the economic system considered in the *Wealth of Nations*, or in its idealized form. Apropos of the problem of authorial intentions, see the next paragraph in the text.

40.   This is true of particular episodes in the novel as well as of the argument of the novel as a whole. For example, Fernandez Florez's story of the king endeavoring to surrender his crown can be interpreted as an effort to make kingship appear like any other occupation or, alternatively, as a satire on (pointing to) the actual king's personal affectation as king and his sense of hierarchical superiority.

41.   The problem of the moral evaluation and reconciliation of conflicting moral positions (in which each denies the moral standing of the other) is of course complex. Sher (1985, p. 205) thus notes that "[Adam] Ferguson was willing to concede that a certain amount of luxury and economic self- or group interest was unavoidable in a free, commercial society, and that the liberty and prosperity of modern civilization justified that much of a sacrifice. Yet the main thrust of his work was to exalt virtue as the only possible solution to the serious problems posed by modernization. Unless a way were found to limit selfish desires to maximize personal wealth and pleasure at the expense of virtue, the progress of civilization would prove to be an illusion.... The *Essay*... [showed] that the road from savagery to civil society could all too easily lead to decadence and doom. In each case the point was to demonstrate the close correlations between modernization and moral corruption on the one hand, moral corruption and social and political decline on the other. For Ferguson, political economy was literally a division of *moral* philosophy." The absence of textual elaboration in *Las siete columnas*, contrary to the case of Mandeville's Fable, prevents more direct analysis of the former.

# REFERENCES

Bloomfield, Morton W. 1952. *The Seven Deadly Sins*. East Lansing: Michigan State College Press.

Bryson, Gladys. 1968. *Man and Society*. New York: Kelley. Originally published 1945.

Carr, Raymond. 1966. *Spain: 1808-1939*. Oxford: Oxford University Press.

Debus, Allen G., ed. 1968. *World Who's Who in Science from Antiquity to the Present*. Chicago: Marquis Who's Who.

de Urquia, Rafael Rubio, et al. 1988. *La herencia de Keynes* [The Inheritance from Keynes]. Madrid: Alianza. Editorial.

Diaz-Plaja, Fernando. 1967. *The Spaniard and the Seven Deadly Sins*. Translated by John Inderwick Palmer. New York: Charles Scribner's Sons. (Originally published 1986 as *El Espanol y Los Siete Pecados Capitales*. Madrid: Alianza Editorial.)

Ferguson, Adam. 1980. *An Essay on the History of Civil Society*. Edited by Louis Schneider. New Brunswick: Transaction Books. Originally published in 1767.

Fernandez Florez, Wenceslao. (1915)1922. *a Familia Gomar* [The Gomar Family]. Madrid: Prensa Grafica. Reprinted in *La Casa de la Lluvia* (The House of the Lluvia). Barcelona and Madrid: Sociedad general de publicaciones, 1925).

———. 1927. *Relato Immoral* [Immoral Relation]. Madrid: Ediciones Atlantida.

———. 1933. *Las aventuras del Caballero Rogelio de Amaral* [The adventures of the gentleman Rogelio de Amaral]. Madrid: Editorial Paego.

———. 1934. *The Seven Pillars*. Sir Peter Chalmers Mitchell, trans. London: Macmillan.

———. 1939. *Una Isla en el Mar Rojo* [An Island in the Red Sea]. Madrid: Ediciones Espanoles.

———. 1954. *Las siete columnas* [The Seven Pillars]. Barcelona: Editorial Planeta. Originally published in 1926 by Libreria Ameller, Barcelona.

———. 1957. *Antologia del Humorismo en la Literatura Universal* [Anthology of the Humorous in World Literature]. Barcelona: Editorial Labor, S.A.

Goldsmith, M. M. 1985. *Private Vices, Public Benefits*. New York: Cambridge University Press.

Gomez-Santos, Marino. 1958. *Wenceslao Fernandez Florez*. Barcelona: Ediciones Cliper.

*History of Economic Thought Newsletter*. 1984. No. 32 (spring).

Hont, Istvan, and Michael Ignatieff, eds. 1983. *Wealth and Virtue*. New York: Cambridge University Press.

Horne, Thomas A. 1978. *The Social Thought of Bernard Mandeville*. New York: Columbia University Press.

Howe, Mark DeWolfe, ed. 1953. *Holmes-Laski Letters*, Vol. 1. Cambridge: Harvard University Press.

Jackson, Gabriel. 1974. *A Concise History of the Spanish Civil War*. London: Thames and Hudson.

Lopez, Francisco. 1985. "Acotaciones sobre una novelistica olvidada" [Notes about a forgotten novelist]. *INSULA Revista de Letras y Ciencias Humanas* 466(September): 14ff.

Lyman, Stanford M. 1978. *The Seven Deadly Sins: Society and Evil*. New York: St. Martin's Press.

Mandeville, Bernard. 1970. *The Fable of the Bees*. Edited by Phillip Harth. Baltimore: Penguin Books.

Mainer, Jose Carlos. 1967. "Una Revision: Wenceslao Fernandez Florez" [A Revision: Wenceslao Fernandez Florez]. *INSULA Revista de Letras y Ciencias Humanas* 243(February): 1ff.

————. 1975a. *Las novelas de Wenceslao Fernandez Florez* [The novels of Wenceslao Fernandez Florez]. Unpublished doctoral Thesis, University of Barcelona.

————. 1975b. *Analisis de una insatisfaccion: las novelas de W. Fernandez Florez* [Analysis of an unhappy person: The novels of W. Fernandez Florez]. Madrid: Editorial Castalia.

Mature, Albert Phillip. 1968. *Wenceslao Fernandez Florez y su novela* [Wenceslao Fernandez Florez and his novel]. Mexico: Ediciones de Andrea Edison.

Mitchell, Sir Peter Chalmers. 1938. *My House in Malga.* London: Faber and Faber.

Nora, Eugenio G. De. 1968. *La Novela Espanola Contemporanea (1927-1939)* [The Contemporary Spanish Novel, 1927-1939]. Tomo 2. Madrid: Editorial Gredos, S.A. segunda edicion ampliada, 1968.

Pocock, J. G. A. 1985. *Virtue, Commerce, and History.* New York: Cambridge University Press.

Samuels, Warren J. 1976. *Pareto on Policy.* New York: Elsevier.

Schneider, Louis. 1987. *Paradox and Society.* New Brunswick: Transaction Books.

Sender, Ramon Jose. 1936. *Seven Red Sundays.* Translated by Sir Peter Chalmers Mitchell. London: Faber and Faber.

Sher, Richard B. 1985. *Church and University in the Scottish Enlightenment.* Princeton: Princeton University Press.

Smith, Adam. 1937. *The Wealth of Nations.* New York: Modern Library.

————. 1976a. *The Theory of Moral Sentiments.* New York: Oxford University Press.

Teichgraeber, Richard E. 1986. *"Free Trade"and Moral Philosophy.* Durham: Duke University Press.

Tribe, Keith. 1988. Review of Teichgraeber. *Economics and Philosophy.* Vol. 4 (October): 342-349.

Ward, Philip, ed. 1978. *The Oxford Companion to Spanish Literature.* Oxford: Oxford University Press.

# REVIEW ESSAYS

# MacINTYRE'S
# *WHOSE JUSTICE?*
# *WHICH RATIONALITY?*
## A REVIEW ESSAY

S. Todd Lowry

---

**Whose Justice? Which Rationality?**
**By Alasdair MacIntyre**
**Notre Dame, IN: Notre Dame Press, 1988. 432 pages.**
**ISBN 0-268-01942-8. $22.95 Cloth.**

For the intellectual historian, this book offers a thematic survey from Homeric to modern times. For the economist and jurisprudent, it offers a stimulating and provocative examination of some of our most important methodological premises and processes. It is the kind of book that is becoming increasingly necessary in a scholarly world where intensive specialization and narrowly prescribed inquiry is the

Research in the History of Economic Thought and Methodology, Volume 9, pages 201-207.
Copyright © 1992 by JAI Press Inc.
All rights of reproduction in any form reserved.
ISBN: 1-55938-428-X

smoothest path to success. By the same token, such surveys are increasingly difficult to write because they require a comprehensive grasp of more and more detailed information. The only hope is for the author to strive for a particular level of abstraction or generalization that can put a vast panorama of time or space into a common focus. In such an operation, the sharpness of the focus on any particular aspect of the material is almost always at the price of fuzziness in dealing with other parts of the vista. Nevertheless, the value of the overview transcends the problem of questionable parallelisms. Although sometimes irritating to specialists, it should always be kept in mind that those who attempt to keep specialized inquiry in touch with the broader context should be encouraged in their missions. Their wounds should be treated with sympathy when they return bloodied from critical encounters with those who detail the uniqueness of their specialized periods or areas of thought. For these reasons, there should be a greater appreciation of the importance of extensive auxiliary support in refining and correlating the material in such a work, if not at the prepublication level, then by sympathetic reviewers.

One of the most conspicuous characteristics of this book is the somewhat self-contained nature of various chapters or sets of chapters. This suggests its genesis in separate lectures and it adds a particular value to the work for those primarily interested in specific periods. Many economists will be drawn to chapters XII and XIII on the foundations of the Scottish Enlightenment, chapter XIV on Hutcheson, and chapters XV and XVI on Hume. Economists interested in institutionalist considerations will find some suggestive insights in MacIntyre's analysis of Hume's somewhat naturalistic emphasis upon "the passions" as the starting point for human conduct and his distancing maneuvers from the moralistic premises with which Hutcheson undergirded the Scottish cultural and intellectual tradition. The resulting dichotomy between the Humean branch of Scottish thought on the one hand and the Aristotelian branch on the other, represented by Reid and Dugald Stewart, raises many methodological issues. This Aristotelian methodological tradition can be pursued to advantage in Pietro Corsi's recent article "The Heritage of Dugald Stewart" (1987).

The culmination of the historical analysis of justice and rationality in their social contexts is found in chapter XVII, "Liberalism Transformed into a Tradition." This chapter is well worth reading on its own for the clarity with which it presents the dilemma of the apparent paralysis of intellectual individualism where the social and political system must contend with a hodge-podge of basically different values. The conclusion is that effective systems of justice and practical reasoning function in terms of clearly defined intellectual traditions and that liberalism has devolved into a system where the only cohesive perspective is the rules for formal procedure under a nominal egalitarianism. Such a system can hardly cope with major social challenges or offer coherent leadership for the society.

Chapters XVIII and XIX develop MacIntyre's theory of "intellectual traditions" that give structure and coherence to perceptions of justice and practical rationality. This analysis seems to grow out of the issues developed in the preceding chapter on liberalism, but it can be read separately. Those interested in the interaction between various schools of thought and in what has come to be called "scientific revolutions" will find these chapters of independent interest. However, those familiar with contemporary work in the history of science will immediately recognize that MacIntyre, who is working in his own isolated tradition of moral philosophy, is dealing with many ideas popularized by Thomas Kuhn two decades ago. While MacIntyre innocently walks in Kuhn's path, paraphrasing "paradigms" and "normal science," he does add some interesting ideas in his discussion of "languages" and "translation," meaning idiom rather than tongue. MacIntyre's unacknowledged debt to Kuhn, however, is no less egregious than Kuhn's naïve extrapolation from his initial study of the Copernican Revolution, innocently paraphrasing the basic schema of a Marxist dialectical analysis of history with its these or paradigms confronting conditions that generated antitheses and new syntheses. Or is this Hegelian, Aristotelian or Platonist?

As we proceed with our discussion of this book from back to front, we must comment on a major skip from the thirteenth to the seventeenth century, which many may question. However, the analysis of the Scottish Enlightenment is tied to its Scholastic heritage and in chapters X and XI, on Thomas Aquinas, we find an interesting methodological thesis regarding his role as a synthesizer of the Augustinian legacy and the Averroist version of Aristotelianism brought into Europe from the Moslem world. MacIntyre's conclusion is that Aquinas compromised the conflicting theological traditions by developing a concept of an Aristotelian dialectic which served as a process for investigating competing theologies. This dynamic approach to rational process would seem to be relevant to the discussion of liberalism in chapter XVII, but the idea of a dialectical search for particular justice within the context of competing premises is not generalized. This lack of integration only adds to the sense that this book evolved from a series of lectures, each prepared as independent presentations, and each successively contributing to the maturation of the author's ideas. The clarity and precision that emerges toward the end of the book was not used as a reference base for revision of the interpretations in the earlier chapters.

Chapter IX provides a useful outline of Augustinian thought and explains the premise of free will in the service of God and his acceptance of such service through grace. Just as Aquinas was prepared to deduce particular justice by rational processes from the universals of Natural Law, Augustine was prepared to adapt individual action to the City of God through God's grace. I have trouble, however, with the Platonism of this perspective, and the apparently contrasting development in the preceding chapters in which Aristotle is characterized as Plato's heir. The intellectual elitist and authoritarian aspects of Plato's theory of justice as efficient order in achieving an ideal city tends to coincide with the Judaic and Egyptian traditions of duty and gratitude for acceptance. This is epitomized in the Book of Job in the *Old Testament* and its Egyptian heritage is developed by James Breasted in his *The Dawn of Conscience*. Secondarily, Plato developed an individualistic theory of personal order, the justice or inner peace of one's own rational administration of the tripartite self, the soul, needs and passions. This elitist individualism and Plato's endorsement of anarchistic democracy as an acceptable arena for elitist activity in his *Statesman* would have provided an interesting reference point for MacIntyre's discussion of liberalism in Chapter XVII. My own treatment of Plato's theory of justice (Lowry, 1987, pp. 103-16) differs considerably from MacIntyre's.

The broader problem is the premise in chapters VI, VII and VIII that Aristotle was Plato's heir, pure and simple. While this may be true in part, it fails to allow for the methodological divergence in Aristotle from Plato which can be attributed to sophist and atomist influences. While Aristotle deduced the purposes of political and economic life from the teleological ideal of a stable polis, he also carefully built the polis from a multilayered sequence of material interactions bonding atomic entities—husband and wife, master and servant, parent and child—into a family unit. Mutually interacting families comprise the village, and interdependent villages make up the polis. A glance at David Furley's *Two Studies in the Greek Atomists*, would have contributed something here and broadened the author's insight into the influence of the sophist tradition in the Scottish Enlightenment. Adam Smith's emphasis on human sympathy in his *Theory of Moral Sentiments* sounds a great deal like Protagoras's theory of justice and aidos, or fellow feeling.

The treatment of Book V of Aristotle's Nicomachean Ethics which deals with justice, leaves much to be desired. The analysis of universal and particular justice and distributive and corrective justice is presented in the material on Aquinas, but the mutuality implicit in "justice in exchange" is not treated in a scholarly way. Polanyi's status analysis of this material from 1957 is the latest citation while R. A. Gauthier and J. Y. Jolif's classic French commentary and translation *L'Ethique à Nicomaque*, which supports the analysis of cumulative interaction bonding the populace into a polis, is not consulted. The analysis of the third proportion representing reciprocal justice or justice in exchange would have added an extra dimension to the lightly treated topics of individualism, naturalism and, ultimately, liberalism.

The real problem is that Aristotle worked with two different paradigms from which to rationalize social process or justice, the Platonist ideal type and the sophistic participative dialectic. We get hints of the sophist tradition that was so clearly appreciated by the nineteenth century economist, Sidgwick, but the recent classics in the literature on ancient Greek justice are not cited or reflected in MacIntyre's presentation: for example, Hartvig Frisch's *Might and Right in Antiquity*, E. R. Dodds' *The Greeks and the Irrational*, Hugh Lloyd-Jones' *The Justice of Zeus*, and Eric A. Havelock's *The Greek Concept of Justice*.

It is further to be deplored that in his development of the distinction between the success ethic and the concept of excellence as a social value in the earlier chapters on Greek thought, MacIntyre does not take account of A. W. H. Adkins's well-known classic *Merit and Responsibility*. This work deals specifically with the development of "the quiet virtues"—cooperative social attitudes that supported the evolution of the polis and community commitment in contrast to the aristocratic success ethic. This material could have enriched MacIntyre's development of the subject considerably.

Such criticism raises two fundamental problems. First, it is much easier and, in modern circumstances, almost necessary to develop one's own ideas without trying to splice in discussions of the vast array of tangential material available in contemporary research libraries. While granting this consideration, good scholarship, nevertheless, requires researchers to tie their work into existing contributions in the field so that we can participate in a cumulative process instead of a chaos of idiosyncratic expositions, each with its own vocabulary, paradigms and clichés. The second problem is that disciplinary specialization has led to the development of schools of thought and discussion circles with their own private terminology so that philosophers, classicists, political scientists, jurisprudents, sociologists and economists all have separate analytic frameworks and vocabularies so that they develop their ideas in relative isolation. It is this dilemma that makes this kind of book so difficult to write and, at the same time, so important to the broader synthesis of contemporary scholarly activities.

It is in this spirit that I would commend the author for offering this broad survey of what are essentially core concepts in social theory and relevant to all social science disciplines. At the same time, I must re-enforce the caveat that such efforts require the support of thorough and committed friends, readers and editors. The responsibility for scholarly care in their preparation and presentation is particularly heavy. One would have wished that a friend or editor would have marked what are frequently referred to as "run on sentences." Eight to ten lines is too long! Long, involved chains of abstractions lose cogency and readers. In addition, since the role of a university press should be to promote the publication of scholarly books, one would think that the editors of Notre Dame Press would have not permitted this long and complex work to go to press without a subject index and a bibliography. A simple index of names cited does not suffice to make this book of maximum value to interdisciplinary scholars who are browsing certain chapters and looking for discussions of specific ideas or topics.

While many scholars may have the commitment to read through this entire book, if they are discouraged by the somewhat obscure prose at times, I would urge them to skip to the parts in which they are particularly interested. I must repeat that each chapter is introduced in such a way that it keys the reader into its place in history and stands as a more or less self-sufficient essay. This will add immensely to the usefulness of the book as a source of stimulating ideas, although it cannot be relied upon as a survey of the literature on any given topic or period.

## REFERENCES

Adkins, A.W.H. 1960. *Merit and Responsibility: A Study in Greek Values*. Oxford: Clarendon Press.

Breasted, James. 1933. *The Dawn of Conscience*. New York: Scribner's.

Corsi, Pietro. 1987. "The Heritage of Dugald Stewart: Oxford Philosophy and the Method of Political Economy." *Nincius. Annali Di Storia Della Scienza* II(2): 89-114.

Dodds, E.R. 1957. *The Greeks and the Irrational*. Boston: Beacon Press Paperback.

Frisch, Hartvig. 1949. *Might and Right in Antiquity*. Trans. C.C. Martindale. Copenhagen: Glydendalske Boghandel..

Furley, David. 1967. *Two Studies in the Greek Atomists*. Princeton: Princeton University Press.

Gauthier, R.A., and J.Y. Joliff. 1970. *L'Ethique à Nicomaque*, 2nd edition, 2 vols. Louvain: Publications Universitaires.

Havelock, Eric A. 1978. *The Greek Concept of Justice: From Its Shadow in Homer to Its Substance in Plato*. Cambridge, MA: Harvard University Press.

Lloyd-Jones, Hugh. 1971. *The Justice of Zeus*. Berkeley: University of California Press.

Lowry, S. Todd. 1987. *The Archaelogy of Economic Ideas*, pp. 103-116. Durham, NC: Duke University Press.

Polanyi, Karl. 1957. "Aristotle Discovers the Economy." In *Trade and Market in the Early Empires: Economies in History and Theory*, edited by Karl Polanyi, Conrad M. Arensberg, and Harry W. Pearson, pp. 64-94. New York: Free Press.

Smith, Adam. 1937. *Theory of Moral Sentiments*. (1776), ed. Edwin Cannan. New York: Modern Library.

# PROFESSOR VAGGI AND THE PHYSIOCRATS:

## NEW EXPLORATIONS IN THE CLASSICAL THEORY OF VALUE AND DISTRIBUTION: A REVIEW ESSAY

Peter Groenewegen

---

*The Economics of François Quesnay*
**By Giani Vaggi**
**Durham, NC: Duke University Press, 1987. Pp. xv + 149.**
**Price $37.50.**

Although neglected for considerable periods over the last two hundred years as important contributors to economics, sometimes even being reduced "to an embarrassed footnote ... [or] ... a vast mystification" (Gray, 1948(1931), p. 106), the Physiocrats more recently have experienced a strong resurgence of interest in their work. Prior to the twentieth century, only Adam Smith and Karl

---

Research in the History of Economic Thought and Methodology, Volume 9, pages 209-219.
Copyright © 1992 by JAI Press Inc.
ISBN: 1-55938-428-X

Marx seem to have fully appreciated their profound analytical contributions (particularly those made by their undisputed master, Quesnay) if contemporary French appreciations of their work such as that by Turgot are ignored. This is not to say that their work was forgotten. During the nineteenth century McCulloch (1824, pp. 41-42) and following him, Alfred Marshall (1920(1890), pp. 756-7) praised the Physiocrats for founding the science of political economy for a variety of reasons. They were respectively described as the first investigators of the sources of wealth, and as the first to proclaim the freedom of trade and to give economics an aim in seeking to raise the quality of human life. However, if Marshall's notes on the Physiocrats, and particularly those on the *Tableau économique* (now preserved in the Marshall Library) are anything to go by, his study of their work was neither very serious, nor very profound. Schumpeter, particularly in the early *Epochen der Dogmen- und Methoden Geschichte* (Schumpeter, 1954(1912), pp. 42-43) also praised the Physiocrats strongly. In his view they, together with Adam Smith, created an economic science through their contributions to circular flow analysis and development of the general equilibrium concept. Finally Gide and Rist (1949(1909), chapter I) in their still very useful text on the history of economics, carefully placed Physiocracy in its broad political setting. Their account explains, as did James Mill's entry on "The Economists" for the 1824 Supplement of the *Encyclopaedia Britannica* almost a century before, that Physiocracy above all, was a political and legal system designed to achieve social order. Nevertheless, only after the second world war did renewed interest in the work of the Physiocrats produce clear and significant interpretations of their economic theory on a par with the understanding of Smith and Marx.

Vaggi starts his book by reviewing this literature, particularly that following the Tableau bicentenary publication of Quesnay's collected economic writings (Quesnay, 1958). In this review he draws attention to its almost universal deficiency with respect to one aspect of Quesnay's work. Physiocratic interpretative literature has emphasised far too much the material or physical aspects of their economics, and has ignored its value-and-price contribution. In fact, the thrust of Vaggi's argument in this book is to redress this imbalance in interpretation and demonstrate once and for all the crucial influence of Quesnay's value and price interrelationships for his theory of reproduction, accumulation, progress and growth. This non-value perspective in Quesnay interpretation derived in part from Marx's vision of physiocracy. Brilliant though Marx's general appreciation of Quesnay's work was, his wrong material (non-value) interpretation of their surplus analysis is only really understandable from his restricted access to their work by what had been reprinted by Daire (1846) combined with his fascination with the dynamic aspects of their growth theory. In this, he was substantially followed by Meek (1962) and by a stream of subsequent writers as Vaggi (1983, pp. 1, 5-8) clearly documents. More recently, and therefore not mentioned by Vaggi, are misleading if not erroneous accounts of Physiocracy in this and other respects by Hollander (1987, chapter 3) and Hutchison (1988, chapter 16). Hollander's consequently wrong perspective on French developments in economics of the 1750s and 1760s strongly influences his misguided approach to classical political economy, particularly in Smith; Hutchison's treatment claims to be informed by Vaggi's new work (by citing it among his references (Hutchinson, 1988, p. 435) but no impact from its contents is visible in Hutchison's treatment of Physiocracy. As is well known in economics, sins of misinterpretation die hard, even among historians of economics who ought to know better.

Vaggi's objectives are clearly explained in the opening pages of this important book. It presents "a different interpretation of Physiocratic economics, starting from an analysis of what Quesnay and his disciples wrote about the theory of value and of prices" (p.2). More fully, Vaggi's reinterpretation involves three major propositions. First, and contrary to common belief, "the Physiocrats put forward a detailed analysis of the laws of market exchange, from which they derived interesting, and complexly interrelated notions of price." Second, these price concepts were indispensable to the Physiocratic analysis of production and distribution because their value treatment of wealth and revenue has connotations going well beyond analysis of these categories solely in physical terms. While unravelling this part of his story, Vaggi focuses on solutions as well as on unresolved contradictions in Quesnay's analysis to facilitate more precise identification of his analytical legacy to classical economics. An important aim of the book is to throw "further light on the historical and analytical features of the development of economic ideas from Sir William Petty to Adam Smith" (pp. 2-3). Third, there is therefore a broad historical purpose in Vaggi's book which makes his work of crucial importance to historians of economics interested in explaining evolution and development of classical economics.

In addition, Vaggi lists four other aims. One is his intention to demonstrate that Quesnay's peculiar method of devoting each of the articles he wrote to a single, well-defined topic, implies that none of his writings, not even the celebrated *Tableau économique*, can stand by itself as a summary of his doctrine. Secondly, in identifying *prix fondamental* as Quesnay's most important price concept, Vaggi shows this not only involves physical cost of production but also includes the net element of rent thereby linking the formation of prices to the process of reproduction in a manner resembling Smith's subsequent treatment of natural prices. This procedure gives Quesnay a prominent place in the development of classical price theory from Petty to Smith. Third, Vaggi demonstrates that Physiocratic free-trade doctrine was not based on Ricardian comparative advantage but needs to be viewed as policy designed to enhance effective demand for agricultural produce with additional price, profit and accumulation ramifications for the pace of agricultural development and economic growth in general. Fourth, and most heretical as compared with most current interpretation, Vaggi demonstrates the "essential role" of farmers' profits in the Physiocratic analysis of economic growth (p. 4).

Apart from setting out these aims, chapter 1 contains a number of other preliminaries. These include an account of where, in Vaggi's view, contemporary interpretations have been misleading, his emphasis on the importance of studying Quesnay's errors as well as insights for a proper historical understanding of the development of economics in this period, and an outline of the argument as it unfolds in subsequent chapters. Chapter 2 provides textual evidence to support his view that Quesnay and the Physiocrats treated wealth and revenue *both* as physical quantities of product and as value magnitudes. Chapter 3 introduces Quesnay's price concepts. Many of these were initially developed in "Hommes," an article intended for but not published in the *Encyclopédie*. Here, among other things, Quesnay carefully distinguished the price received by the producer (current price) from that paid by the consumer (retail price), distinguishing these in turn from the fundamental price already identified by Vaggi as Quesnay's most important price concept. Chapter 4 explains Quesnay's use of these concepts for the analysis of surplus, which decisively rebuts the view that Quesnay saw net product as a simple gift of nature. In addition, the chapter reviews the interrelationship between Quesnay's value categories and the distinction he made between productive and sterile labor. In chapter 5, Physiocratic price theory is used to investigate Quesnay's complex analysis of distribution of the surplus product thereby to clarify as well the meaning of farmer's profit. Vaggi depicts this profit as a "systematic share" of the net product indispensable for that investment of capital enabling reproduction of the product on an expanded scale. The concluding chapter 6, further illuminates the importance of Quesnay's work for the development of classical economics.

Before discussing the degree of success with which Vaggi achieves these objectives, it is necessary to draw attention to one further feature of his book. Although aptly titled "the economics of Quesnay," the book covers both the work of Quesnay *and* his disciples. This strategy permits focus on two matters partly obfuscated in Meek's (1962) study. First, Quesnay's economics was the major source of Physiocratic thought, both chronologically because it formed its beginning *and* in terms of analytical contents because it developed the basic form of the Physiocratic argument. Secondly, Quesnay's exposition sometimes lacked clarity because he tended in his writings to treat particular questions in isolation, hence writings by his followers sometimes explain aspects of the argument more clearly, because their explanations are set in a wider context. Where relevant, Vaggi therefore supplements his account of the Physiocratic system based on Quesnay's authoritative writings from writings of other Physiocrats, particularly Baudeau, Du Pont de Nemours, Le Trosne, Mirabeau and Mercier de la Rivière, the last the author of what for many of their contemporaries (including Adam Smith) was the most authoritative account of Physiocratic doctrine. While Meek's economics of Physiocracy is substantially the economics of Quesnay, Vaggi's economics of Quesnay is widened to include the necessary Physiocratic treatment of the problems with which he is concerned. Now that the preliminaries are out of the way, the major thrust of Vaggi's account can be more fully examined.

Chapter 2 of the book clearly demonstrates that certain categories of Physiocratic analysis are impossible to conceive without an appreciation of value, even though the Physiocrats were aware that quantities could be expressed in physical as well as in value terms. In their definitions of wealth and revenue, marketability, or vendibility at a reasonable price, is a crucial part of the framework for discussion (pp. 39-40). Prices are therefore basic to the determination of wealth. The relevant prices in this context are "prices at first hand," that is, the prices at which farmers sell, the source of their income and hence ability to reproduce their output. Reference to this price category emphasises the richness and variety of Quesnay's price theory. Prices "at first hand" are able to influence the wealth and revenue of society; other prices such as those charged by middlemen can only transfer incomes. The sterility of trade follows from this conception of price (pp. 41-5), without denying either usefulness or even necessity of trade. Conscious recognition of heterogeneity in inputs and the need to homogenise for aggregation purposes are further signs that value was essential for Physiocratic theorising and that a corn model simplification was never really contemplated by them as useful (pp. 46-52). Finally, by means of a simple set of equations, Vaggi demonstrates differences between the pure classical (Sraffian) price model and the pure Physiocratic one as contained in Quesnay's work (pp. 8, 55-7).

Chapter 3 develops these price notions further. It starts with their association with natural order (pp. 58-60), then distinguishes between use value and exchange value on grounds similar to those advanced by Adam Smith (p. 60) before turning to the more crucial distinction between current and retail price: *prix du vendeur* and *du acheteur* respectively (pp. 62-6). This distinction underlies Quesnay's analytical proposition that harvest fluctuations tend to produce a higher average price for consumers of grain relative to prices obtained by farmers. This incidentally, provides a basis for conflict in a class structure more diverse than the well known social division between proprietors, productive and sterile class which Quesnay used in his *Tableau économique* analysis. Quesnay introduces merchants as persons whose wealth enables them to keep stocks of the staple commodity, thereby profiting from what, in their perspective, is a dichotomy between their role as buyers (from farmers) and sellers (to consumers) in the market. Increased competition in trade (the activity of the merchant) allows a potential wedge between producer and consumer prices to be removed. Such equalisation of prices follows from competition by increasing the number of merchants, removing regulations on marketing and improving transport and communication between districts. This part of Physiocratic price theory explains that freeing the corn trade is in the interest of producers *and* consumers, because only the middlemen lose from this increased competition. Fundamental price is introduced as the bench mark for the current price—its point of gravitation as Smith was to put it, provided that there is adequate competition (pp. 76-77). Vaggi accepts that this type of price relationship goes back at least to Petty but that its analysis steadily improved through the eighteenth century. Analytical advance came from extending the natural price concept to cover not only the physical costs of production but also a necessary rate of return on the producer's investment, hence enabling its use as a variable explaining reproduction. Vaggi convincingly demonstrates that this wider concept of necessary price was not only used by Smith and Turgot, but had already between developed in Quesnay's concept of fundamental price (pp. 80-86, 88-93). For Quesnay, fundamental price included technical expenses of production (that is, wage costs, raw materials and depreciation, what Quesnay called the "annual reprises" or sum of annual advances and interest on the original advances), together with taille (taxation) and rent. Vaggi's explicit identification of the significance of this part of Quesnay's analysis is in itself one of the major contributions to understanding Physiocracy which arises from his new interpretation.

Vaggi's second major contribution is to highlight the complexities of the Physiocratic notion of surplus (net product) partly within his new interpretation of their price theory. This subject is interestingly, and indirectly, approached via Galiani's antiphysiocratic critique and the well known Physiocratic stress on capital accumulation in agriculture, a matter of vital concern to Quesnay from his first paper onwards. Galiani's critique of the exclusive surplus-producing characteristics of agriculture relied on two factors. The first concerned limitations to agricultural product when all the land is cultivated, which in turn limits its export as population grows. Such limitations to agricultural product are not shared by the manufacturing sector. Secondly, manufacturing output is more stable than agricultural output where production is exposed to the vagaries of the seasons (pp. 97-8). From the outset Quesnay had attempted to refute such objections to his explanation for the dominant role of agriculture in his system. In his view, capital investment and capital intensive techniques were able to raise agricultural productivity irrespective of the land/population ratio. This links surplus product directly to capital intensity in a dual way: the greater the capital intensity of farming, the greater the surplus product; the greater the surplus the easier it is for farmers to invest in agriculture (pp. 98-101). In addition, Quesnay distinguished the creation of surplus in the two sector by the differential effects of competition on price in them. In manufacturing, competition (more sellers) diminished surplus (a profit from alienation) by lowering selling price until it approaches costs; in agriculture strong aggregate demand can lift produce prices and raise the surplus of the primary sector. Hence raising the demand for agricultural produce is essential to enhance surplus. This required direction of upperclass (Church, State, nobility) demand to "luxe de subsistence" (agricultural products) rather than "luxe de décoration" (manufacturing products or imports), together with opening export markets to agricultural produce. Competition of buyers is the clue to raising agricultural value surplus to its highest extent and free trade is therefore not an end in itself. However, competition among sellers (producers) in agriculture is not adequately explained by Quesnay. He relies on the existence of institutional and seasonal frictions to prevent supply from rapidly rising to meet the effective demand for produce (pp. 115-6). As Vaggi puts it (pp. 117-8), this creates "a vicious circularity" in the argument: "landlords must spend their revenues on purchases of the products of agriculture and the government must encourage their exportation, *because* this is the only sector that yields a surplus to the country. But *only* if there is a large domestic and foreign consumption is there also a high effective demand for the products of French agriculture, thus securing the existence of a surplus over costs in this sector." In spite of this problem, Quesnay's theory of the surplus conceived in this way has four strengths: surplus is made a crucial variable in the system, it is not a datum; surplus is seen as both a physical and value magnitude; stress on capitalistic production methods and their productivity explains physical influences on surplus; the different nature of competition in the two sectors introduces the role of effective demand.

The implications of this view of surplus for the Physiocratic theory of distribution are explored in chapter 5. Vaggi's view of the nature of surplus in Physiocratic theory allows the inclusion of incomes other than rent, in particular farmers' profits, to share in the surplus of agriculture. Vaggi demonstrates this by using textual evidence (pp. 122-6) and by the proposition that the Physiocrats were fully aware of the role of profits and favourable prices (*bon prix*) as incentives for farmers to reproduce on an expanded scale. Profits of the farmers are an essential part of the explanation of agricultural productivity. How can this line of thought be reconciled with attempts (such as that in Meek, 1962) to show that Physiocratic profits could have no long-term existence because they were competed away through competition by farmers on the renewal of the leases?. Vaggi's argument in rebuttal of Meek is particularly fascinating. He points to the Physiocrats' strong support for extending agricultural leases beyond the customary maximum period of nine years in order to raise the stake of farmers in their leased land, and the unpopularity this gained for their writings (pp. 141-2, 161-4). In addition, he notes a dichotomy in Physiocratic attitudes to the subject; from 1763 onwards, they de-emphasised this importance of profits as a long term income share to farmers. This is explained, Vaggi argues (p. 143), by the visible caution in Physiocratic writing from that date so as not to give offence to nobility and the administration, a caution induced by the persecution Mirabeau experienced in 1760 from the publication of his *Théorie de l'impôt*. Most importantly, Vaggi relies on the crucial importance of farmers' profits for Physiocratic dynamic analysis of accumulation and growth, as against the static equilibrium analysis considerations which underly Meek's perspective on the disappearance of long-term profits (pp. 153-5). As Vaggi concludes his long chapter: "the Physiocratic analysis of profits and investment illuminates the close relationship which exists between the theory of distribution of output, especially surplus, and that of its expenditure... two pillars of the overall dynamic analysis of the transformation problem of the economy" (pp. 154-5).

The final chapter draws conclusions from the new interpretation to enhance the understanding of classical political economy's origins. Despite Quesnay's links with recent economic theory "from general equilibrium to input-output analysis," its real historical significance and "major merit is that [it] contributed to the foundation of the theories of surplus" (p. 165). Establishing this proposition requires assessment of both Quesnay's achievements and failures. On Vaggi's interpretation, Quesnay's major merit is his realisation that "to explain why and how wealth springs from production, *it is necessary* to analyse market forces and prices." Hence his legacy to classical economics consists of interrelating the theory of wealth with surplus, reproduction, prices and markets (pp. 189-90). In addition, Physiocracy embodied the first serious attempt to define social classes in terms of their economic functions (p. 169). Quesnay's analytical weaknesses, and those of Physiocracy in general, are well known and were clearly apparent to their more able contemporaries. They underplayed the rising importance of manufacturing and its high productivity potential, perhaps because appreciation of a manufacturing division of labor through subdivision of processes in commodity production was not within their vision. Quesnay, for example, more or less ignores the division of labor (an exception is Quesnay, 1958, p. 737). Likewise, their free trade advocacy and analysis of competition was slanted to favour agricultural productivity and assisted in explaining the exclusive surplus creating properties of primary production. The class analysis also has its contradictions. For example, freeing the grain trade initially benefits consumers and producers at the expense of middlemen but ultimately living standards of labor come into conflict with the profit requirements of farmers. Likewise, despite the focus on harmony in the natural order, conflict between farmers' profit and landlords' share in the surplus is inherent in Physiocratic analysis even though suppressed in some of their later work (pp. 171-82). Such problems in Physiocracy must be clearly recognised, Vaggi concludes, (pp. 191-2) if their contribution to classical political economy is to be properly appreciated.

Vaggi's careful interpretation of Physiocratic value and distribution theory, foreshadowed though it was in earlier journal contributions (especially Vaggi, 1983, 1985) is an important addition to and correction of our understanding of Physiocracy and classical economics in general. In this important book, only a few, minor "warts" can be noted. Murphy (1986) casts grave doubts on Vaggi's confident assessment that Cantillon's *Essai* (not *Essay sur la nature*, etc.) was "originally written in English" (p. 23). Another misprint (p. 49) has "awles" for "axles" in a quote from my translation of *Fermiers*. I have some reservations about Vaggi's argument (p. 182) on similarities between aspects of Smith's rent theory and that of Quesnay. These in my view reflect the demand considerations the Physiocrats stressed and not land scarcity problems as Vaggi implies. Also Marx (1963, p. 4) qualified his praise for Quesnay's contributions to capital theory by stressing it remained "within the bourgeois horizon," a qualification Vaggi (1983, pp. 717-2) seems to ignore. Finally, I am curious why some tables (pp. 64, 74) have French headings and those of another (p. 125) are in English. The nature of these criticisms shows how difficult it is find fault with this book.

As John Eatwell suggests in his foreword (p. xiii) Vaggi's work emphasizes once again the importance of that 1766 Paris trip for the development of Smithian theory because it clarifies the links between natural price and distribution which so considerably enhanced Smith's exposition of these subjects over the subsequent decade. Vaggi's book therefore not only assists understanding of the Physiocrats, it improves our grasp of Smith's economics and therefore of classical economics as a whole. The book is therefore even more outstanding because of the wide implications of its contents.

## REFERENCES

Daire, Eugene. 1846. *Physiocrates*. Paris: Guillaumin.

Gide, C., and C. Rist. 1949. *A History of Economic Doctrines*. London: George G. Harrap. (Originally published in 1909).

Gray, Alexander. 1948. *The Development of Economic Doctrine*. London: Longmans, Green and Company. (Originally published in 1931).

Hollander, Samuel. 1987. *Classical Economics*. Oxford: Blackwell.

Hutchison, Terence. 1988. *Before Adam Smith*. Oxford: Blackwell.

McCulloch, J.R. 1824. *A Discourse on the Rise, Progress, Peculiar Objects and Importance of Political Economy*. Edinburgh: n.p.

Marshall, Alfred. 1920. *Principles of Economics*. London: Macmillan.

Marx, Karl. 1963. *Theories of Surplus Value, Part I*. Moscow: Foreign Languages Publishing House.

Meek, R.L. 1962. *The Economics of Physiocracy*. London: Allen and Unwin.

Mill, James. 1824. "The Economists." In *Supplement to Encyclopaedia Britannica*, Vol. III. Fourth, fifth, sixth edition. Edinburgh: Constable.

Murphy, Antoin E. 1986. *Richard Cantillon: Entrepreneur and Economist*. Oxford: Clarendon Press.

Quesnay, Francois. 1958. *François Quesnay et la Physiocratie*. Paris: Institut National d'Etudes Demographiques.

Schumpeter, Joseph. (1954). *Economic Doctrine and Method*. London: Allen & Unwin. (Originally published in 1912).

Vaggi, G. 1983. "The Physiocratic Theory of Prices." In *Contributions to Political Economy*, No. 2, pp. 1-22.

————. 1985. "The Physiocratic Model of Relative Prices and Income Distribution." *Economic Journal* 95(380): 928-947.

# ISLAMIC ECONOMICS:
## A UTOPIAN-SCHOLASTIC-
## NEOCLASSICAL-KEYNESIAN SYNTHESIS!
## A REVIEW ESSAY

Sohrab Behdad

---

*Islamic Economics: Theory and Practice (Foundations of Islamic Economics)*, revised edition.
**By Muhammad Abdul, Mannan**
**Sevenoaks, Kent, UK: Hodder and Stoughton (U.S. distribution by Westview Press), 1986, Pp. xvi, 425, paper.**

Islam is explicitly concerned with worldly life and provides extensive guidelines for the conduct of economic affairs. The study of these guidelines, in an effort to adjudicate in Islamic societies which have been governed by Islamic law, or to answer the questions of believers on their economic affairs, have constituted a significant aspect of Islamic jurisprudence (*fiqh*). Abu Yusuf (731-798), Nasiruddin Tusi

Research in the History of Economic Thought and Methodology, Volume 9, pages 221-232.
Copyright © 1992 by JAI Press Inc.
All rights of reproduction in any form reserved.
ISBN: 1-55938-428-X

(1201-1274) and Ibn Khaldun (1332-1406) are among the Islamic scholars who have contributed to the analysis of economic conditions in Islamic societies.

The literature that has come to be known in the past three decades as Islamic economics attempts to draw a blueprint for an Islamic economic system in the Muslim countries of the third world. Islamic economics is clearly influenced by the ideological orientation of the Islamic political movements in their effort to disassociate themselves from the socialist-marxist movements, on the one side, and the oligarchic rule of the landlords and big business, on the other. Islamic economics seeks to prove the supremacy of the Islamic economic order to the two rival and existing systems, capitalism and socialism. It heralds a new order, a third pole or path, which it claims is more humane, harmonious and equitable than the other two systems. Thus, Islamic economics has a clear protagonist posture. Yet it is diverse, ideologically and methodologically. This diversity reflects the spectrum of ideological orientations in the Islamic political movements and the familiarity and affinity of different "Islamic economists" with contemporary economic paradigms.

Mannan's *Islamic Economics* is one of the pioneering attempts to construct a theoretical framework for Islamic economics. The first edition (1970) had become a standard reference in the English language to Islamic economics. The revised edition is in three parts (18 chapters), dealing with the methodology of Islamic economics, the general character of an Islamic economy, and the micro and macro setting of an Islamic economy.

Mannan maintains that "there is a unique Islamic economic system and science" (p. 4). Islamic economics, he asserts, explains the economic problems of "the Muslim community of today" (p. 4), or those of the "people imbued with the values of Islam" (p. 18). Mannan's contention about the uniqueness of Islamic economics sets him apart from the Islamic economists who see the uniqueness in the economic system of Islam and not in the analysis of it (e.g., Sadr, 1968) and maintain that Islamic *economics* is an extension of mainstream economics (e.g., Choudhury, 1986).

In the first three chapters Mannan lays out the methodological foundations of Islamic economics. He asserts that the underlying assumptions of the "neoclassical orthodox paradigm" or the "Marxist-radical paradigm" are "either inappropriate or inadequate or incapable of explaining the Muslim worldviews on economic matters" (p. 4). He does not elaborate on his objections to the "Marxist-radical paradigm" in these methodological chapters. He later (p. 88) criticizes Marx for his "belied prophecy" on the course of development of class conflict and for his labor theory of value ("because it is not possible to reduce all labourers to one grade," and because the theory "ignores the demand factor altogether and does not recognize the contribution of fixed capital in producing surplus value.") All this in eight lines. The same ideas are repeated almost verbatim (as many other ideas are in this book) on page 324 and alluded to repeatedly throughout the book. Mannan rejects Marx's materialist conception of history in his critique of communism as an economic system (pp. 322-326) and introduces an "Islamic concept of history" (pp. 330-333). Other Islamic economists (for example, Sadr, 1968) have criticized Marxism more rigorously along the traditional line of the mainstream literature.

Mannan's critique of mainstream economics is centered around its distinction between positive and normative analysis. The epistemological basis of Mannan's critique is Islamic scholasticism. Islamic economics, as Mannan asserts, rests upon the "timeless," "universal and fundamental" prescriptions of the Divine Law (*shari'a*) (pp. 11, 15, 124, and 146) and, as Mannan readily admits, "a number of issues in Islamic economics cannot be settled solely by an appeal to observation" (p. 12). Mannan fears that the positive-normative distinction "may perhaps backfire...[by giving] rise to the birth and growth of 'secularism' in Islamic economics" (p. 11), as "the positivists' pre-occupation with empirical tests and immediate results," contributed to the decline of Christianity (p. 12). "The tendency to test everything with limited human knowledge and bias may," according to Mannan, "destroy the basic foundations of Islamic economics" (p. 11). He sees, of course, no contradiction between this view and his criticism of communism as " a sort of a priori dogma...which rejects free criticism...believing itself to be eternal and unchanging" (p. 324). Mannan is not, however, completely liberated from "the intellectual stranglehold of the positivists" (p. 12). He accepts the "positive" and "normative" categories in economic analysis, but maintains that in Islamic economics these elements are inseparable (p. 9).

To Mannan, the *ceteris paribus* mode of analysis is the basis of economic theorizing, and an economic law is a natural law in the same sense that a law of chemistry is (p. 26). The only difference is that an economic law is a statement of tendency and as such, quoting (Edwin R.) Seligman (from "his *Principles of Economics*," full reference is not given), is "hypothetical," and therefore less exact than the laws of natural sciences (pp. 26-27). The acceptance of economics as a set of natural laws and the neoclassical human want-scarcity dilemma as the fundamental axiom of economics brings Mannan to formulate his scholastic-neoclassical-Keynesian synthesis.

Mannan states that "the fundamental economic problem of mankind...[is] that we have wants and ... [we have] limited resources of human energy and material equipment" (p. 18). As Mannan admits, there is little difference in substance between this statement and that of Lionel Robbins which he quotes on the same page (without source and citation, as is the case for most of the quotes in this book). Mannan, however, suggests "if there is any difference" between Islamic economics and "modern economics" on the issue of scarcity, it is in the way choices are made "in the eternal conflict between multiplicity of wants and the scarcity of means" (pp. 18-19). In an Islamic society, choices are to be made according to divine prescriptions. In this way, Islamic economics superimposes the divine prescriptions of Islam as "normative" constraints upon "the laws of economics" to explain and to regulate the working of the market in an Islamic society (pp. 5-8 and 26-39). For example, the Islamic prescriptions for moderation in consumption and profit-making are incorporated into the neoclassical analysis of consumer preference and the theory of the firm (pp. 8, 10-11, and passim); or Islamic taxes (*zakat*) and prohibition of interest are introduced into Keynesian macroanalysis and investment theory (pp. 126, 237, and passim).

Hence, Mannan's Islamic economics, in spite of his methodological contentions, is little more than an extension of mainstream economics. This methodological approach is feasible because an Islamic economy is clearly a market economy (see chapters 4-7). Muhammad's explicit emphasis on the proper functioning of the market makes any fundamental negation of the market heretical. Muhammad's Tradition (*sunna*) reflects also his preference for a cash, rather than a barter economy (see, for example, a statement by Rafi on page 57). Mannan does not therefore violate the Islamic precepts when he states that "Islamic economics deals mainly with problems involving money" (p. 18), although it is interesting that he feels compelled to quote Marshall to make his case (p. 27).

Islam's emphasis on social harmony and justice is also indisputable although the specific definitions of these concepts in the concrete social circumstances have been controversial. The adherence of individuals to the divine prescriptions of Islam in their worldly affairs, and in their conduct in the market, in particular, would materialize this harmony and justice. Since individuals may not act in complete compliance with the divine prescriptions, the state must intervene to assure this harmony and justice (pp. 356-357). Therefore, in my view, the basic epistemological difference between mainstream economics and Islamic economics is that one relies on man's nature "as is," and the other on what his character "ought to be." To one, state intervention is the last resort (a leviathan) for the resolution of social conflict, and to the other, the state is a necessary social guardian of the less-than-ideal man. In both cases, however, an idealized market is the nexus of social relations of production among individuals.

The Islamic notion of God's ultimate ownership (not unlike that of Christianity) is the basis of Islamic ideological collectivism and the source of legitimacy of state intervention in the market. According to Islam, man holds property as a trustee, responsible to God (p. 65). Hence God's ownership supersedes the right of the individual to property, and an Islamic state, representing the will of God, may impose limits on private property rights. The Islamic notion of God's ultimate ownership has been interpreted narrowly by some as no more than the eminent domain right of the state in capitalism. On the other end of the spectrum, however, it has also been relied upon to justify various forms of socialist collectivism. This spectrum of views closely corresponds to the ideological spectrum in the Islamic political movements extending from a position not unlike the post-Reformation (bourgeois), Christian paternalistic ethic (à la E. K. Hunt, 1986, pp. 108-110) to one not dissimilar to the radical versions of the Christian socialist and liberation theology movements. There is ample evidence in the Koran and Tradition to substantiate this wide spectrum of views. Islamic economists are, however, not only conscious but, one may also say, obsessed with making clear the lines of demarcation between their conception of the Islamic economic system and the fundamentals of capitalist and socialist (some prefer calling it communist) systems. Every treatise in Islamic economics begins and continues its analysis of the Islamic economic system with a critique of the other two systems.

Mannan criticizes the "unrestricted ownership of property in capitalism" and "collectivism or State ownership of everything" in "communism" (pp. 64-65). One is "responsible for the gross maldistribution of wealth and income" (p. 64). The other "has reduced man to a machine" and has "limitations of a serious character" about "incentives and...personal liberty" (p. 65). Islam, according to Mannan, "maintains a balance between [these] exaggerated opposites" (p. 65). "The uniqueness of the Islamic concept of private ownership," Mannan claims, "lies in the fact that in Islam the legitimacy of ownership depends on the moral sign attached to it" (p. 64). Property in an Islamic society, according to Mannan, must be used by the owner to "discharge his social responsibilities in a manner consistent with the injunctions of [Islam]" (p. 366), that is, by promoting social welfare (p. 312). If such a purpose is not served, the state can deprive the owner of his/her ownership rights (p. 366). Hence, private property in Islam "becomes very vulnerable" (p. 312). This "vulnerability" is reflected in the limitations imposed on the use of property and conduct of affairs in the market, and in the permissible domain of state intervention in the economy.

Islam prohibits usury (*riba*, meaning excessive gain), monopoly, hoarding, speculation and production and consumption of certain products such as pork and intoxicants, and requires payment of a wealth tax. The market in an Islamic economy would work within these constraints and with the Islamic "high standard of straightforwardness, reliability and honesty" (p. 285). The outcome is a "healthy competition" (p. 147) which, according to Mannan, unlike free competition provides "all aspects of basic needs with which an Islamic market is concerned" (p. 148).

Mannan's Islamic theory of the firm (chapter 8) is a utopian-mainstream theoretical muddle. He relies on the standard neoclassical analysis to justify the undesirability of noncompetitive (monopoly) markets to Islam. In this effort his analysis contains a number of errors and theoretically awkward statements. One may not quibble about a possible misprint on page 150 stating that the equilibrium for a firm in a perfectly competitive market is reached when "marginal revenue is equal to price" but it is amazing that the same "misprint" is seen on page 208 of the first edition of the book. On another occasion he states: "In a free economy, demand for and supply of commodities determines the normal price, *which measures the effective demand being determined by the degree of the scarcity of supply"* (p. 146, italics mine). Mannan also states that an altruistic, socially concerned Islamic firm which does not strive to maximize profit may not have a unique equilibrium. Then he adds: "Different theories may yield different predictions. For example, a sale maximizing theory which predicts larger output and lower prices than a profit-maximizing theory in a particular situation have *different implications for the elasticity of demand at the firm's market price"* (pp. 149-150, italics mine). These are, at best, awkward theoretical statements. Mannan never explains what he means when he says "in Islamic theory we are more inclined to accept the concept of 'average' rather than of 'margin'" (p. 147). Nor does he elaborate in this chapter, or elsewhere, the incorrect statement made earlier, that "in an Islamic framework it should be possible to conceive of a firm which may require to satisfy only the first order condition [for profit maximization]" (p. 11). Mannan either is confusing minimum acceptable profit for an entrepreneur who does not wish to maximize profit with minimum possible profit (i.e., maximum loss, which may be the case if the second order condition is not satisfied) or is unfamiliar with elements of calculus. (Although this sort of theoretical error and misstatement of the mainstream analysis is not rare in the works of other Islamic economists, it certainly is not typical of the Islamic economic literature. Some have formulated sophisticated neoclassical-Keynesian models for explaining the working of the market in an Islamic economy. See for example, Choudhury, 1986 and Kahf, 1980).

With these confusions in Mannan's Islamic-neoclassical synthesis of the theory of the firm, how are prices determined in a "healthy competitive" Islamic market? By "consensus of opinions" (whose opinion?) and "correct adjudication," says Mannan without explaining either (p. 147). "Proper co-operation between consumers and producers" is also necessary and may be achieved, according to Mannan, by "inject[ing]...the spirit of Islamic values and code of business conduct through systematic education" (p. 147) Meanwhile it is the responsibility of the state to maintain "fair" prices (p. 147).

Dealing with capital is a difficult task for Islamic economists. Interest is not permitted by Islam but profit is, and Islamic economists have to provide the theoretical justification for this fine line of separation between the capitalist heaven and the Islamic hell. Mannan's journey into the mainstream theory of capital (pp. 121-132) is no more rigorous than his neoclassical treatment of prices.

One example should suffice. He asserts that the mainstream theory of capital is inadequate because "it does not explain why a particular rate of interest is paid" (p. 121). He continues by saying "if interest is paid because of the productivity of capital, then it should be variable for productivity itself tends to vary from one industry to another" (p. 121)! Mannan relies on Keynes to argue that interest payment is not necessary for accumulation of saving (pp. 61, 121 and 126), and on Wesley Mitchel to suggest that rising interest rate may cause a depression (pp. 127-128). His principal objection to the payment of interest is, however, ethical. He maintains that "interest is a negation of the universal principle of brotherhood of man and co-operation... a naked exploitation of brother's needs... exploitation by the 'haves' of the 'have nots'" (pp. 130-131). Mannan proclaims "an interest-free economy, as advocated by Islam, is the only solution to mitigate the suffering of the degraded humanity of the capitalist economic system" (p. 126).

Mannan justifies a return on capital in the form of profit. He is "inclined not to consider capital as a a fundamental factor of production" but, in the words of Wicksel, as "a single coherent mass of saved-up labor and saved-up land" (p. 60). Whether a fundamental factor of production or not, "nobody can challenge that capital is productive," claims Mannan (p. 121). Because market activities involve risk for capital and "assumption of risk is a disutility, it is to be paid in the form of profit" (p. 132). Of course, Islam does not sanction "unrestricted and abnormal profit which a capitalist earns" (p. 131). Such profits are "generally the result of monopolies and cartels" and are "clear exploitation of society" (p. 131). This is as close as Mannan comes to defining the terms capitalist and exploitation. He does not, however, confine himself to this definition in his attacks on the capitalist class ("the existence of which is a threat to the basic economic ethics of Islam" [p. 81]) and in his condemnation of exploitation. It appears that to Mannan anyone who engages in "excessive" accumulation of capital is a capitalist and any "unfair" economic relation is exploitation.

When he comes to the consideration of capital-labor relations, Mannan, however, contends that "Islam...does not recognize the exploitation of labour by capital, nor does it approve of the elimination of the capitalist class" (p. 88). Recognizing the "eternal conflict of interest between classes in modern society" (p. 90) Mannan maintains that Islam will bring a "happy marriage between labour and capital" (p. 88) and "a happy relation between master and servant" (p. 90) by giving the problem "a moral bent" (p. 88). This moral bent is that "neither employee nor employer can exploit each other," (p. 59) that "the servant shall do his work faithfully... and the master shall pay him fully" (p. 88). Mannan believes that many issues in labor relations, such as strikes and lockouts, "would be relatively unimportant... if both workers and employers are imbued with the values of Islam" (p. 94). But this does not appear to provide much relief since only a few pages earlier one reads that in "modern society... it is difficult, or rather impossible, to imbue workers with [Islamic values, such as] a spirit of austerity of conduct and a high sense of dignity of labour" (p. 90). Employers do not seem to be as resistant to being "imbued" by these values.

Mannan's analysis of wage determination in an Islamic economy is also within the mainstream tradition in economics. Mannan does not appear to be content with the neoclassical model for wage determination when he says that "even if the Marginal Product Theory of wages, which has been subjected to various criticism [on what grounds and by whom?], is taken for granted, it will remain valid only under condition of perfect competition" (p. 116). But this implied criticism amounts to no more than saying that in imperfect competition in the labor market the workers may "get wages much lower than their marginal [revenue] product" (p. 116) Mannan calls this, which is itself a conclusion of the marginal productivity theory, capitalist exploitation of labor (pp. 92, 116). He declares it a phenomenon "foreign to the Islamic faith" (p. 116). Neither A. C. Pigou nor Joan Robinson receive any credit from Mannan, and he remains unclear about whether "fair wages" in Islam is anything but the marginal revenue product of labor.

The state must, according to Mannan, engage in regulation of the market and in economic "planning by inducement and direction" (p. 352 and chapter 18). More specifically, he suggests that the state may intervene to "change the composition of economic activities in different sectors" (p. 56), to "secure a balance of economic activities and to prevent wasteful use of property" (p. 66), and to prevent capital from being "used to the detriment of society" (p. 60). The state may "prevent undue concentration of wealth by progressive taxes" (p. 69), may use fiscal policy to the same end (p. 68), may "enforce decent wages" (p. 116), or may control "conspicuous waste" (p. 154). Punishment may await "dishonest activities," hoarding and "monopolizing" (p. 70). The state may "control and regulate monopoly price and profit" (p. 150), and "as an extreme step" may nationalize monopolies (p. 151) or deprive the owners of "speculative and anti-social businesses" of ownership (p. 154). Of course, the severity of the imposed limitations on property rights will depend on the operational definition of the above reasons for state intervention. But, in my view, the above causes for state intervention in an Islamic economy are categorically not different from those already accepted in the developed or underdeveloped, non-Islamic, capitalist economies.

Mannan contends that an Islamic economy is a "fusion of capitalism and socialism" (p. 168), "a social system which is capitalist in broad outline restricted very largely by socialist institutions and ideas" (p. 330). He sees the Islamic economic system as the point of historical convergence between the existing economic systems:

> Both the capitalist and communist systems are making great efforts in improving themselves in such a way that communism seems to have started to lose its rigidity towards the ownership of personal property and capitalism is finding more ways and means for the equitable distribution of natural wealth for the benefit of the common people. But Islam has already provided these fundamentals in its economic system where free enterprise and ownership of private property are allowed and accumulation of wealth in a few hands and exploitation of the poor by the rich are prohibited. This Islamic economic system is called Islamic socialism or social order (p. 346).

Whether or not a convergence hypothesis is plausible is not our concern here. The relevant question is the viability of the Islamic economic system, as an economic order distinct from the existing systems. The outline or the structure of the Islamic economy is capitalist, as Mannan states. The socialist character of such an idealized system rests upon the assimilation of the collectivist ideology of Islam and the regulatory function of the Islamic state. Both appear doubtful to me. The idealized injunctions of Islam have never been followed throughout history, except for a short period of time by Muhammad and his small circle of Companions. Mannan makes a qualifying admission to this effect in this book (p. 81). I doubt that such values can be "imbued" no matter how forcefully they are "injected" in the social context of the capitalist relations of production. Once this idealized world is put aside, what we are left with is an interventionist state regulating a capitalist economy. The extent and intensity of restriction imposed by the state is, of course, a reflection of the balance of powers in the society. In an Islamic state there is also a severe jurisprudential constraint. That is, each regulatory function of the state must be sanctioned by Islamic jurisprudence, a fourteen-century-old legal tradition which is within the exclusive domain of Muslim jurists (*mujtahids*). Mannan and other Islamic economists may pick and choose among various precepts of Islam, but the final say on what the teachings of Islam imply in modern times is with the Muslim jurists. Historically "the capitalist class" seems to have had the upper hand in "interpret[ing] the Qur'anic Law in a way that suited their interest and did not hamper the exploitation of poor people" (p. 81). If Mannan's concept of an Islamic economy is anything radically different from the existing economies of Saudi Arabia and Pakistan, he must be expecting a radical Islamic reformation which would entail major reinterpretations of the fundamentals of Islamic jurisprudence. I do not expect such a reformation. The protection of property and the propertied class is too explicit in the Islamic tradition to be challenged successfully by any reformist movement which claims its legitimacy in Islamic ideology (Rodinson, 1981; Behdad, 1989). The history of Islamic movements, including its last episode, the Iranian revolution, supports this claim.

I must, however, confess to my fascination with utopian thoughts, pure or eclectic, religious or secular. They offer the inquiring mind limitless horizons to search for boundaries of intellectual imagination. The similarity between the utopian thought of Islamic economists and that of the nineteenth century West is striking. It is strange that neither Mannan nor any other Islamic economist shows any awareness about this extraordinary achievement in intellectual imagination, or about its political fate. There is a great deal to be learned from both, I believe.

## REFERENCES

Behdad, Sohrab. 1989. "Property Rights in Contemporary Islamic Economic Thought: A Critical Perspective." *Review of Social Economy*, 47(2):185-211.

Choudhury, M.A. 1986. *Contributions to Islamic Economic Theory*. New York: St. Martin Press.

Hunt, E.K. 1986. *Property and Prophets; The Evolution of Economic Institutions and Ideologies*. New York: Harper & Row.

Kahf, Monzer. 1980. "A Contribution to the Theory of Consumer Behavior in an Islamic Society." In *Studies in Islamic Economics*, edited by K. Ahmad, pp. 19-36. Leicester, UK: Islamic Foundation.

Mannan, M.A. 1970. *Islamic Economics: Theory and Practice* [*A Comparative Study*]. Lahore: Sh. Muhammad Ashraf.

Rodinson, Maxime. 1981. *Islam and Capitalism*. Translated by Brian Pearce from *Islam et le capitalisme*. Austin, TX: University of Texas Press. (First English edition published 1973).

Sadr, Muhammad Baqir. 1968. *Iqtisaduna* [Our Economies]. Beirut: Dar al-Fikr. (First published 1961).

# WHY BOTHER WITH THE HISTORY OF ECONOMICS?

## A REVIEW ESSAY

Keith Tribe

*The Economics of John Stuart Mill. 2 vols.*
by Samuel Hollander
Toronto: University of Toronto Press, 1985. Pp.xx + 978 +
bibliography and index.

> *It has emerged from our investigation that the economics of Ricardo and J.S. Mill in fact comprises in its essentials an exchange system consistent with the neo-classical elaborations. In particular, their cost-price analysis is pre-eminently an analysis of the allocation of scarce resources, proceeding in terms of general equilibrium, with allowance for final demand, and the interdependence of factor and commodity markets.*
>
> —Samuel Hollander
> (1985, p. 931)

Research in the History of Economic Thought and Methodology, Volume 9, pages 233-245.
Copyright © 1992 by JAI Press Inc.
All rights of reproduction in any form reserved.
ISBN: 1-55938-428-X

Samuel Hollander's lengthy commentary on John Stuart Mill is the third in a series of texts which have as their object the relocation of classical economics in a grand tradition of economic analysis. The first two works in this series—*The Economics of Adam Smith* (1973) and *The Economics of David Ricardo* (1979)—gained a kind of notoriety for the relentless way in which these figures were made congruent with later economic argument. Now it is Mill's turn: but it is not entirely evident why Hollander should devote over 900 pages to "Millian economics." In however garbled a form, Smith and Ricardo live on in debate among today's economists—there is even a research institute in London named after Adam Smith, and every economics undergraduate knows that the names Ricardo, Heckscher and Ohlin belong together. But what of Mill? When Penguin Books issued a paperback of Mill's *Principles in* 1970, they chose to exclude the first three books (on production, distribution and exchange), sections of the text that embodied the theoretical foundations upon which the later books were built. Contrast this approach with that taken by the same publisher with respect to Smith's *Wealth of Nations*: here the focus was on the principles expounded in Books I and II, and the important critique of the mercantile system and Physiocracy contained in Book IV was excluded together with the fifth, and lengthiest, book on governmental revenue.

The reasoning behind this option is quite plain: Adam Smith is today the property of economists, and Mill that of social and political theorists. There seems to be little to detain the modern economist in the political economy of John Stuart Mill. Why then should a writer with Hollander's predilictions expend so much effort upon a figure whose direct contribution to the development of economic analysis is relatively negligible? There is an argument, which will be outlined below, to the effect that Mill's political economy retains great importance on account of the programmatic foundation it provided for later developments in economic theory and policy; Mill's "economics" was extremely important to Mill's contemporaries, and so to understand them we need to understand Mill. But I would not expect this line of thinking to cut much ice with Hollander. What then is his motive?

Hollander provides an explanation of sorts in the Preface—first Hicks is reported to have said that Mill is the "most undervalued economist of the nineteenth-century" (p.xi); then, on the next page, rows of eminent economists dismiss Mill's work as passé, while Stigler is then wheeled in talking up Mill's theoretical stock. In fact, aside from reporting this difference of estimation among famous names, Hollander does not himself offer any serious argument for his enterprise at this point—in comparing Mill to Everest (p. xii), he has perhaps at the back of his mind the explanation proffered by all who wish to scale a mighty peak—"because it's there." But then so is Sidgwick, or Bagehot, or Carey, or even of course J.B. Say—hardly a meaningless figure in the formation of international consensus on the principles of political economy. Once we embark on this line of reasoning, there are any number of nineteenth-century classical economists that big books could be written about.

It is a curious fact that Hollander has in effect produced a large book on the work of John Stuart Mill without offering the reader any serious reason for reading it. By and large, Mill has in the twentieth century been appropriated by political scientists, but Hollander is not writing for them. He writes for economists, he uses economic terminology and indeed his analytical stance is entirely that of a modern economist. But why should a modern economist interest herself in the "economics" of Mill?

The first thing that we notice about this book is that it is divided into two volumes: Volume One, "Theory & Method," Volume Two, "Political Economy'." There is, of course, ample justification for this approach—not only did Mill compose in the *A System of Logic* (1843) one of the most important methodological treatises of the nineteenth century, his article "On the Definition of Political Economy" (first published in 1836) was quickly recognised as a classical statement of the method of English political economy, its theses being developed by Cairnes in his *Character and Logical Method of Political Economy* which in turn was until the 1880s the major recommended text on method—that is, until the appearance of J.N. Keynes's *The Scope and Method of Political Economy* (1891). But this apparently justifiable division of the book into two broad sections turns out, on inspection of the chapter headings, to be entirely spurious: while Hollander does indeed begin with a discussion of methodology, by the midpoint of Volume One he is well stuck into economic exposition and he himself notes in the Preface that the division is dictated by the publisher, not by the structure of his argument (p. xv).

The manner in which Hollander then goes about constructing the "Methodological Heritage" in chapter One also has some curious features. Mill's essay on definition was in fact drafted in 1831, and at this time the significant "methodological" debate revolved around deduction, induction, the distinction of "science" and "art," and the question of moral sciences and human understanding. The names that are important here are, among others, Dugald Stewart, Herschel, Brougham, Bentham, Mackintosh, and Mill's own father James. Hollander, on the other hand, is more concerned to establish the relative merits of Smith, Ricardo, and James Mill as economists; his purpose is to demonstrate that, despite the role played by James Mill in the composition of Ricardo's *Principles*, the two differ sharply with respect to method. Hollander is thus able to represent John Stuart's "reaction" against his father in the 1830s as a return to Ricardo, and, additionally, as meaning that J.S. Mill did not, contrary to modern belief, originate a "new view" on method (p. 35).

Hollander's narrative strategies and presentation usually lack lucidity, and the example before us is no exception. In a bulky book on John Stuart Mill, the first chapter launches straight away into a convoluted assessment of his father, his father's friend, and everybody's mentor—put this way the nature of "heritage" becomes clearer, as does the reason for neglecting direct discussion of work by the person the book is meant to be about. But there is a problem here which Hollander seems to have overlooked: John Stuart is in fact the contemporary of his father and his father's friend, not simply their heir. This fact renders the process of intellectual inheritance at the very least confused. Ricardo the economist has a public life dating from 1810, while his pre-eminent authority dates from the publication of his *Principles* in 1817 (in Sraffa and Dobb, 1970); and although James Mill had published *Commerce Defended* in 1808 (in Winch 1966), as a political economist he, like Ricardo, came fully into prominence as a leading political economist during the 1820s. So in his way did John Stuart Mill; it was from his notes that his father composed *Elements of Political Economy* and, as I will outline below, this does in fact have important ramifications for both the composition and significance of J.S.Mill's *Principles*.

Striking evidence of the confusions to which Hollander's approach gives rise occurs in this first chapter; seeking to evaluate the novelty of Ricardian economics, reference is made to Malthus's 1824 *Quarterly Review* article criticising this "new school" (p. 37). No mention is made at this point that John Stuart Mill wrote a savage rebuttal of this very article and cleverly lampooned Malthus's use of the term "new school" in suggesting that Malthus thereby rejected all the advances of political economy since 1776 (*CW*, 4, p. 29). While John Stuart Mill was only 18 when this review appeared, the fact that the attack on Malthus took the form of a defence of the objects and methods of Political Economy surely warrants mention in Hollander's treatment of the critics of Ricardo. John Stuart Mill participated in the debates over the status of "Ricardian economics," he was not simply heir to their outcome. The fact that he happened to be a teenager at the time makes no difference.

The second chapter in Hollander's book does address questions of method more directly, basing its exposition primarily on Mill's *A System of Logic* (1843) but not, it must be said, placing this in relation to the work of Whewell (1837), which had both stimulated resumption of work on the book in 1837 and with which Mill was later to enter into debate. This then leads directly into discussion of the *Principles* of 1848, which for the remainder of the book remains the principal source for the evaluation of "Millian economics." The fourth chapter, the first in the series evaluating Mill's economics directly, concerns itself with "The Sources of Increased Efficiency," while the fifth deals with "Allocation, Trade and Distribution." Hollander's statement of intent here is self-explanatory:

> It would appear that Ricardianism and neoclassicism—while not sharing identical procedures and certainly not identical preoccupations—have in common a similar "central core" amounting to allocation theory based upon the mechanisms of supply and demand.

Likewise the succession of subheadings of this chapter speak for themselves:

II. Aspects of National Accounting
III. Derived Demand
IV. Consumer Behaviour
V. Short-Run Price Formation
VI. Cost Price and Profit Rate Equalisation
VII. Demand-Supply and Cost Price: The Adjustment Mechanism
VIII. Variable Cost Conditions
IX. Imperfect Competition

From this list we could be looking at a modern textbook of microeconomics—but if we were, it would be legitimate to ask why so much effort had been put by so many into the production of the shelves and shelves of economic textbooks written since 1848. Ironically enough, Mill does spell out in Book III, chapter 3, the elements of what the modern undergraduate would recognise as the conditions for the perfectly competitive firm (*CW*, 2, pp. 471 ff.). In noting this, we come no further forward in understanding the significance of Mill's work, just as Hollander's systematic attempt to rewrite Mill's statement into modern notation only obscures the historical significance of the political economy of John Stuart Mill.

As anyone familiar with Hollander's earlier writings will know, and as the epigraph at the beginning of this review makes clear, Hollander reads classical economics as a modern economist. That is, the analytical armoury that is brought to bear on Mill's *Principles of Political Economy* is broadly the same as that which would be employed in reading the latest issue of the AER. What interests him are those aspects of the text that support a particular view of the nature and function of economic analysis; those parts that do not fit into this view are either overlooked or regarded as deviations or errors to be marked as such, but which are nonlethal to the overall validity of the text in question. The version of classical economics supplied by Hollander is then but a variant upon modern economics: its scope and limits, its analytical core, its theoretical preoccupations, and the manner in which proofs are constructed. The difficulty is that, weighed on these scales, texts of the early nineteenth century can never be anything but primitive versions of what comes later. Put another way, such an investigative technique is constantly registering a difference which has negative connotations. All the more puzzling that Hollander should subject the work of John Stuart Mill to his method, since the general result could have been anticipated at the very beginning: that John Stuart Mill comes between Ricardo and Jevons (sticking to the English tradition). Paradoxically, the thesis of this bulky book appears to be that the economics of John Stuart Mill are routine and unexceptional—read in terms of modern economics, he isn't really worth reading.

Maybe not as an economist; but this is an unsurprising conclusion, and an investigative apparatus which labors to produce such a conclusion must be faulty. There is a different approach that can be adopted, one which takes into account both Mill's motivation in writing what he did, and also the manner in which he was received by his contemporaries. It is the latter that should weigh heaviest in our preliminary evaluation: Mill is important to an understanding of the development of economic discourse because his writing, whatever its merits might be from a modern perspective, was so widely accepted and proved so durable. Some figures can be put on this: *Principles* went through seven Library editions in Mill's lifetime and in May 1865 was published in a cheap People's edition, which was reprinted in October of the same year and within five years had sold over 10,000 copies. This popular and cheap edition was reprinted six times during the 1870s, and six times during the 1880s. The Library edition was republished four times in the 1890s, and five times from the turn of the century to 1910. W.J. Ashley edited a new edition in 1909, and in his introduction described the book as:

> ...still one of the most stimulating books that can be put into the hands of students, if they are cautioned at the outset against regarding it as necessarily final in all its parts. On some topics there is still, in my opinion, nothing better in the English language; on others Mill's treatment is still the best point of departure for further enquiry (Ashley, 1909, p. xxiv).

Whatever one might think of Ashley's authoritativeness, or of Mill's *Principles* for that matter, the sheer durability of the text lends it an importance transcending our modern estimation of its substance. And it is precisely because this success was as a textbook that the application of modern evaluative criteria becomes so inappropriate. By and large textbooks summarise received opinion; the process of innovation here takes place as incremental improvement in exposition and pedagogic technique, not as major theoretical novelty. But what if we are interested in what this "received opinion" was, rather than tracing the "leading edge" of scientific progress? The very success of Mill's textbook is indicative both of the character of economic argument in the later nineteenth century, and of the theoretical and rhetorical resources available to Mill in the later 1840s. *Principles* is thus central to an understanding of the constitution of the domain of modern economic argument as a public domain, rather than one exclusively the property of scholars and specialists.

Having established this point in a very preliminary fashion, some consideration can be given to Mill's motivation in writing a book of the size and substance of *Principles*. In his original Preface he stated that he wished to incorporate into a systematic survey "the latest improvements which have been made in the theory of the

subject" (*CW*, 2, p. xci). As such, he expressed the belief that his book
was distinct from any treatise produced since that of Adam Smith,
where principles had been associated with applications; and where
therefore political economy was made accessible to general readers.
While the *Wealth of Nations* was seen as in many respects outmoded:

> No attempt, however, has yet been made to combine his practical mode of
> treating his subject with the increased knowledge since acquired of its theory,
> or to exhibit the economical phenomena of society in the relation in which
> they stand to the best social ideas of the present time, as he did, with such
> admirable success, in reference to the philosophy of his century (*CW*, 2, p.
> xcii).

It is important to note here that what Mill admires in Smith is a
particular form of exposition, distinct from the "abstract speculation"
that the science of political economy had more recently become.
Commentators have here sought to choose between Smith and
Ricardo as predominant influences on *Principles*, the former
representing a "broader," the latter a "narrower," concept of the
science associated with the term "Ricardianism." Hollander himself
is clearly concerned to deny the "Smithian" reading of Mill and
support the "Ricardian" option, but the utility of making such a
distinction is dubious.

While it is clear that Mill had by the later 1820s grown away from
the balder forms of argument by principle, this should not be
overemphasised. One of the more memorable passages of *Principles*
states that "there is nothing in the laws of Value which remains for
the present or any future writer to clear up" (*CW*, 2, p. 456)—a
passage often cited in evidence of Mill's woeful misreading of the
economic agenda. Likewise this could be seen as evidence of his shift
away from abstract speculation towards the more material problems
of economic development.

But there is another interpretation that can be placed on Mill's
statement: that he never regarded the disputes on value (which have
since Marx come to occupy a central place in approaches to classical
economics) as of any great import. For example, when lambasting
Malthus' characterisation of the "new school" of political economy
he was critical of the importance Malthus attached to a measure of
value, and argued:

[I]t is too much to attempt to persuade the public that Mr. Malthus is so wrapt up in the importance of his supposed discovery, as actually to believe that these insignificant disputes about value are the most important questions in political economy, questions upon which every thing depends—questions of more consequence than the theories of rent, profits, and foreign trade! (*CW*, 4, p. 30).

And if we ask: what then did Mill think was the most important principle of political economy? the answer is:

every increase of produce is obtained by a more than proportional increase in the application of labour to land.... This general law of agricultural industry is the most important proposition in political economy (*CW*, 2, p. 174).

The significance of this stance lies not only in the implicit assumption that "marginalism," as an abstract principle, is seen by Mill as the central concern of political economy; the actual effects of this principle in agriculture link rent, the rate of profit, wages and trade in a quite particular way—those very phenomena that Mill had in 1825 stated to be of greater importance than the measure of value. Even as a teenager, then, Mill had argued against a preoccupation with "abstract" principles to the neglect of their implications for strategically important economic phenomena.

Quite how misleading a search for a definite "break," an option for or against "Ricardianism," can be when considering the work of John Stuart Mill is lent further emphasis by some comments dating from 1834. Reviewing the last volume of Harriet Martineau's *Illustrations of Political Economy*, he suggests that many treatises in the subject practise a spurious abstraction and pretended generality, while in fact applying only to particular sets of relationship in one country. This statement is employed by Hollander to support his contention that Mill is, subsequent to his mental crisis and discovery of the romantic poets, critical of the "old school" of political economy on grounds of their abstractness and narrowness (Hollander, pp. 85-6). But in a passage immediately following the one cited by Hollander, Mill qualifies his criticism. First, he shows that the "three classes" of society have varying functions and are expressive of differing property forms in the West Indies, India and France; but he at once continues:

It must not, however, be supposed that the science is so incomplete and
unsatisfactory as this might seem to prove. Though many of its conclusions
are only locally true, its method of investigation is applicable universally; and
as he who has solved a certain number of algebraic equations, can without
difficulty solve all others, so he who knows the political economy of England,
or even of Yorkshire, knows that of all nations actual or possible: provided
he have sense enough not to expect the same conclusion to issue from varying
premises (*CW*, 4, p. 226).

It is only to be expected that Mill's views on the tasks and methods
of political economy altered over three decades, but it is misleading
to seek definite periods within these decades within which Mill can
be assigned to one or another "school of thought." Paradoxically,
this leads to an overemphasis on the degree to which Mill's ideas did
alter; a natural enough assumption given the thirty years separating
the publication of Ricardo's *Principles* and those of Mill. It can
nevertheless be argued that the basic propositions that Mill
expounded in 1848, and which proved so durable, are in fact entirely
compatible with those generally accepted in the 1820s. While such
a thesis certainly requires qualification, the implication is clear
enough: given the general assent to the agenda established by Mill
up to at least the 1870s and his persisting influence beyond that time,
this strongly indicates that a general understanding of the nature and
substance of political economy remained relatively stable throughout
the best part of the nineteenth century. This is not the same continuist
thesis as that embraced by Hollander; on the contrary, if correct, such
a contention illuminates the variant levels and different speeds upon
which economic discourse proceeds—that a "traditional" core of
teaching can co-exist with advances in theory that modify or even
overturn generally accepted principles, without however having a
direct or immediate impact on economic argument as public
property.

Further confirmation of this line of argument can be found if we
consider the relationship between John Stuart Mill and his father.
In his introduction to the 1909 edition of *Principles*, Ashley
emphasised the broad similarity between John Stuart's *Principles* and
James's *Elements* of 1821 (1909, p. viii). Comparison of the two texts
does reveal striking similarities, as well as interesting differences.
Books I-III of *Principles* are arranged in a similar manner to the first
three chapters of *Elements*, while substantial discussion begins in
both books on exactly the same point—the part played by labor and

nature in production. However, while James Mill began his "Introduction" with the following words:

> Political economy is to the state, what domestic economy is to the family (1966, p. 210).

John Stuart Mill rejected this idea, arguing in the essay on Definition that it overlooked the fact that while political economy was a science, domestic economy was an art, an assembly of precepts (*CW*, 4, p. 313). It is not an exaggeration to claim that the first three books of John Stuart Mill's *Principles* represent elaborations upon, modifications of, and disputes with, his father's *Elements of Political Economy*.

But this is not altogether such a novel finding, since *Elements* was itself based upon notes made by the son on lectures by the father. This was described later by John Stuart as follows:

> My father, therefore, commenced instructing me in the science by a sort of lectures, which he delivered to me in our walks. He expounded each day a portion of the subject, and I gave him next day a written account of it, which he made me rewrite over and over again until it was clear, precise and tolerably complete. In this manner I went through the whole extent of the science; and the written outline of it which resulted from my daily compte rendu, served him afterwards as notes from which to write his *Elements of Political Economy* (*CW*, 1, p. 31).

This took place in 1819, that is, when John Stuart Mill was 13. Although John Stuart did, in his assessment of his father's intellectual legacy, play down the importance of this book—*Elements* was described as "a very useful book when first written, but which has now [1853-4] for some time finished its work" (*CW*, 1, p. 213, cf. p. 212)— it could reasonably be argued that this was because John Stuart's *Principles* was a far more fitting work, not only in the manner in which principles were combined with applications (in the manner of Smith), but substantively as well. The link to *Elements* is important not because it thereby becomes an "early source" for the *Principles* of 1848, but because it is indicative of the longevity of a basic consensus on the principles of economic argument in the nineteenth century.

Why, then, if such a basic stability exists, could Mill claim in 1848 to have composed a text without equivalent since the appearance of *Wealth of Nations*; if there was such stability and consensus, why

did an authoritative and comprehensive modern treatise on the
subject already exist? Conversely, why did the political economy of
John Stuart Mill enjoy such longevity? His own comment from the
1860s was:

> It was, from the first, continually cited and referred to as an authority, because
> it was not a book merely of abstract science, but also of application, and
> treated political economy not as a thing by itself, but as a fragment of a greater
> whole: a branch of Social Philosophy, so interlinked with all the other
> branches, that its conclusions, even in its own particular province, are only
> true conditionally, subject to interference and counteraction from causes not
> directly within its scope: while to the character of a practical guide it has no
> pretension, apart from other classes of considerations (*CW*, 1, p. 243).

In his *System of Logic*, as well as in the essay on definition, John
Stuart Mill laid great emphasis on the place of political economy in
the moral sciences, considered as human sciences. General acceptance
of the configuration of these discourses did more or less coincide with
the appearance of *Principles*; in that respect it was published at an
opportune moment. Moreover, the 1850s and 1860s in Britain were
marked by growth, social and political stability, and reform; in this
respect also the period subsequent to publication was optimal for the
propagation of such a synoptic account of the scope and substance
of political economy. Broadly speaking, it was only with the
appearance of Marshall's *Principles of Economics* in 1890 that Mill's
*Principles* was presented with a competing text which was, over the
next two decades, to decisively displace it.

Here the change of name is also of significance, for a large question
mark should be placed over Hollander's attempt to write an account
of "Mill's economics." In some respects, this entity is a product of
Hollander's own investigative method, it is not interchangeable with
Mill's political economy. Mill devoted much effort to elaborating the
art and science of political economy as a broad enterprise; and if
historians have detected a "narrowing down" of the subject of
economics since the late eighteenth century, this is as much a product
of their own predilictions and modes of investigation as anything else.
The comments made above sketch out a way of approaching Mill's
political economy that does not rely on a framework drawn from
modern economics to organise investigation and evaluation. Rather
than simply dismiss such an approach as exemplified by Hollander,
I have suggested that in the case of Mill the application of this method

results in a curious paradox: rendered into the preoccupations and terminology of a modern economist, the stature of John Stuart Mill shrinks to that of the writer of a bulky and superseded textbook. Practised in this fashion, the history of economics is an exercise in negation: there seems to be no reason for pursuing it as a serious scholarly occupation.

But if we begin from the premise that Mill's political economy was important in its own time, and seek instead to understand why it was that it could gain and retain such a public stature—then we are led into a different form of investigation, one which promises to reveal to us aspects of the formation of modern economic argument that have hitherto been neglected. And this in turn leads to a more productive paradox than the one exemplified by Hollander: the prospect of gaining new insights through historical investigation: of employing historical studies to say new things.

## REFERENCES

CW = Collected Works of John Stuart Mill. 1963-1986. London: Routledge and Kegan Paul.

Ashley, W.J. 1909. "Introduction." In *Principles of Political Economy*, by John Stuart Mill, pp. v-xxvi. London: Longmans, Green and Co.

Cairnes, J.E. 1875. *The Character and Logical Method of Political Economy*, 2nd ed. London: Macmillan.

Collini, S., D. Winch, and J. Burrow. 1983. *That Noble Science of Politics*. Cambridge: Cambridge University Press.

Hollander, S. 1973. *The Economics of Adam Smith*. London: Heinemann.

———. 1979. *The Economics of David Ricardo*. London: Heinemann.

Keynes, J.N. 1891. *The Scope and Method of Political Economy*. London: Macmillan.

Malthus, T.R. 1824. "Political Economy." *Quarterly Review* 30:297-334.

Mill, J. 1966. *Elements of Political Economy*. Edinburgh: Oliver and Boyd.

Mill, J.S. 1836. "On the Definition of Political Economy: And On the Method of Philosophical Investigation in That Science." *London and Westminster Review* 4 and 26: 1-29.

Mill, J.S. 1843. *A System of Logic*. London: Longmans, Green and Co.

Mill, J. S. 1970. *Principles of Political Economy*. London: Penguin Books.

Smith, A. 1970. *The Wealth of Nations*. London: Penguin Books.

Sraffa, P., and M.H. Dobb, eds. 1970. *On the Principles of Political Economy and Taxation*, Vol. 1: *Works and Correspondence of David Ricardo*. London: Cambridge University Press.

Whewell, W. 1837. *History of the Inductive Sciences, From the Earliest to the Present Times*, 3 vols. London: William Parker.

Winch, D., ed. 1966. *James Mill. Selected Economic Writings*. Edinburgh: Oliver and Boyd.

# SAMUEL HOLLANDER'S VIEW
# OF *CLASSICAL ECONOMICS*
## A REVIEW ESSAY

Salim Rashid

*Classical Economics*
**By Samuel Hollander**
**Oxford: Basil Blackwell, 1987. Pp. xiv, 485.**

This volume is Professor Hollander's attempt to summarize, for advanced undergraduates and graduates, the substance of his earlier studies on Adam Smith, David Ricardo and John Stuart Mill. After two brief chapters dealing with the Precursors of Adam Smith and with the Physiocrats, the main body of the text is organized by topic. First, we have value and distribution, then capital, employment and growth, followed by money and, finally, method. Two general chapters, one on Classical Features in Marxian Economics and the other on Intellectual Linkages, come before the conclusion. The book

Research in the History of Economic Thought and Methodology, Volume 9, pages 247-253.
Copyright © 1992 by JAI Press Inc.
All rights of reproduction in any form reserved.
ISBN: 1-55938-428-X

is well produced and printed and Hollander is commendably clear in his account. One of his main interests is to combat the Italo-Cambridge School's claim that Distribution and Exchange were differently treated by the classicals—especially the Ricardians—and by the neoclassicals. This is a dichotomy that has long been accepted and readers familiar with any of Hollander's recent works are no doubt aware of his strenuous objections to the purported dichotomy:

> The present text envisages matters very differently. It will be my major theme that the notion of alternative 'paradigms' does not adequately describe the development of nineteenth-century economics (p. 6).

This is a thesis that has been vigorously criticized in the past and reading the critiques and counter-critiques of Hollander's volume on Ricardo, in particular, forms a minor task in itself. Hollander's determination to present his thesis in textbook form necessitates focus upon this issue.

It is convenient to begin with Microeconomics. Hollander notes, "A tradition exists that demand theory played a small part, if any at all, in Ricardian analysis. Nothing could be further from the truth" (p. 89). Hollander proceeds to provide examples where Ricardo can be said to have recognized the role of demand. Let us grant that the half-dozen quotes he provides are entirely to the point. How can these quotes be brought to bear against the explicit theorizing on labor-values in chapter 1 of the *Principles* and subsequently? Anyone can make observations about the market. Theorists are supposed to theorize. When Ricardo *did* theorize, he did neglect demand. In the penultimate paragraph of this section, Hollander substantially concedes this:

> Ricardo is frequently said to have rejected demand-supply analysis. From the above evidence, this is obviously a misconception. What he actually complained of was "the opinion that the price of commodities depends solely on the proportion of supply to demand, or demand to supply" (I, 382), a complaint alluding to those formulations which appeared to exclude a role for cost conditions in the mechanism. Thus his observation to Say: "You say demand and supply regulates the price of bread; that is true, but what regulates supply? the cost of production ..." (IX, 172). The essence of the matter is also captured in a letter to Malthus: "You say demand and supply regulates value—this I think is saying nothing... —it is supply which regulates value—and supply is itself controlled by comparative cost of production" (VII, 279).

Since Malthus had carefully and clearly emphasized that cost conditions have a role to play only insofar as they influence supply, Ricardo's complaints are groundless.

A second point on which Hollander lays great stress is the inverse relationship between wages and profits. In a section headed, "The Inverse Relation a Truism?" Hollander begins:

> The inverse relation between profits and wages—"profits depend upon wages"—may seem to be a mere truism, since by a change in wages is meant a change in proportionate wages. But this is not so. It is obviously true that an increase in a proportionate share must imply a decrease in the residual proportionate share. But Ricardo's efforts were not devoted to proving this proposition; his concern was with the preceding stages of the argument (p. 113).

Let it be granted for the sake of argument that Ricardo's efforts were directed to the "preceding stages of the argument." To what end were the preceding stages being developed? To present us with a truism! If the preceding stages are worth knowing, they have to stand on their own feet, not as a preliminary to a truism. The subsequent attempt to show support for such an inverse relationship is forced. It is quite misleading to emphasize John Stuart Mill's "allocation economics" in support of the inverse relationship on page 145 when Mill has been carefully quoted on page 144 as referring to the inverse relationship as "resting on a law of arithmetic, from which there is no escape."

The Ricardian emphasis upon the importance of agricultural profits is not duly emphasized. By referring to Ricardo's *Principles* as a theoretical work, the point is dealt with only in passing. When Malthus challenged Ricardo on this issue, it would have been easy for Ricardo to argue that Malthus had mistaken his emphasis. Instead, Ricardo reiterates the importance of agricultural profits. The significance of the following passage has been noticed earlier by Jacob Hollander and is worth repeating:

> Malthus: "I should feel no doubt of an increase in the rate of profits in this country for 20 years together, at the beginning of the 20th century, compared with the 20 years which are now [circa 1820] coming on; provided this near period were a period of profound tranquility and peace and abundant capital, and the future period were a period in which capital was scanty in proportion to the demand for it owing to a war, attended by the circumstances of an

increasing trade, and an increasing demand for agricultural produce similar
to those which were experienced from 1793 to 1813."

Ricardo: What a number of conditions! The only one of importance is the
abundance or scarcity of capital compared with the demand for it, which is
saying in other words that if in the [beginning of the] 20th century the
comparative quantity of capital and labor should be such that the laborers
should [not be able to command so large a] proportion of the produce
obtained on the last land profits will [then] be higher. On these conditions
there is no denying the conclusion. Whether they will be so [or] not must
depend on improvements in agriculture—or on the permission by law to
import corn [freely and] without restrictions from other countries (p. 150).

When Hollander turns to Ricardo's use of abstract models to deal
with real-life policy, we find the same puzzling approach. The
discussion of Say's Law is conducted so as to suggest that Ricardo
did not really believe that supply and demand were constantly equal:

Ricardo may then be understood (like Say) as insisting not upon an identify
of aggregate supply and demand but rather upon their long-run or secular
equality (p. 248).

This theme is then developed by providing us with two supporting
quotes. Immediately following, however, we have the following
paragraph:

We are not, however, yet out of the woods. For Ricardo approached the post-
war depression in terms of a model which incorporated the full-employment
assumption and he insisted that an increase in government expenditure implies
an equivalent reduction in private expenditure—in our century labelled the
"Treasury View"—despite awareness of severe unemployment and underutilization of capacity over the years 1815-21 (p. 249).

Not only are we not out of the woods, to the untutored mind it seems
as though we are very closely entangled in the underbrush. Why
would Ricardo wish to deny the depression? Hollander explains:

In the *Principles*, he referred to an alternative account of the post-war
difficulties that emphasized an actual reduction in aggregate capital; he
admitted that the characteristics of crisis due to such a cause would be no
different from those due simply to the frictions he had in mind, but *since there
was at hand a simple hypothesis, he felt it unnecessary to look further for
an explanation* (p. 250, emphasis added).

The last (emphasized) sentence grants everything that the "Ricardian Vice" would require.

Hollander appears to be convinced that classical economics is the beginning of worthwhile economic analysis—this is the only way I can account for the poor chapter on "The Precursors of Adam Smith"—and that there was continuity in economic doctrine and method from Adam Smith to Alfred Marshall (and beyond?). The focus upon continuity leads him to highlight the fact that, on several issues, Ricardo and Smith held similar views. This is a valuable point to emphasize and Hollander does well to note how wedded Smith was to his own *system* (pp. 322-23). The proper conclusion would appear to be that classical economics contained inconsistencies and that the classical economists could be quite enamoured of certain policy prescriptions without having a "sound" economic basis for them. These policies could be chosen because of their political attractiveness—but this is an aspect that Hollander consistently minimizes. On page 415, we are told that Smith was the real inspiration for the labor writers of the 1820s and 1830s who believed rent and profits to be *deductions* from the efforts of labor. This important point is not dealt with any further and it is even trivialized in an earlier statement:

> What Smith has to say regarding capital productivity makes it certain that his statements defining profits as "deductions from the produce of labor" were intended as a criticism of contemporary capitalism—the ownership of capital by a separate class of capitalists (p. 75).

If Smith really did believe that the ownership of capital by a separate class was tantamount to theft, this is scarcely the sort of issue to be treated in such brief and disjointed fashion.

It is a pity that Hollander is so wedded to his main thesis. He has read Smith, Ricardo and Mill with perhaps greater care than any other scholar in recent times. On some occasions, such as John Stuart Mill's emphasis on habit in determining the expenditures of the retail consumer, Hollander casts considerable light on particular aspects of an economist's thoughts. Hollander's ability to see, and to dig out, every theoretical nuance in an earlier work is almost daunting. The Introduction also contains some valuable comments on exercising due caution in interpreting the analytics of a pre-analytic age. And yet these most worthwhile qualities run aground because of a want of attention to some basic methodological issues. Hollander justifies his use of modern terminology as follows:

> Now it is self-evident that we must strenuously avoid superimposing on an early writer reference frameworks that were developed only after his death or even after a particular moment in his career. But this does not require that we avoid modern vocabulary and categories in tracing the filiation of ideas (p. 12).

This argument relies, to an indefensible extent, on a disassociation between concepts and words. It is misleading to speak of Adam Smith's use of "marginal demand price" not only because Smith did not have such a phrase available but, more importantly, because the phrase is much more well-defined and unambiguous than any of Smith's views on demand appear to be. Since modern economists carry this theoretical penumbra within themselves, it is wrong to expect them to use the modern phrase but divest it of all modern connotations.

When Hollander refers to Ricardo's analysis of the effects of a general increase in wages as a "general-equilibrium" analysis, he is right insofar as Ricardo's analysis is not partial equilibrium analysis. But "general-equilibrium" has a well-defined meaning today and this includes the impact upon demand, a feature missing in Ricardo. Industry-wide analysis of the sort conducted by Ricardo is visible as early as John Locke and later in the Physiocrats. In describing this lack of demand repercussion in Ricardo's analysis, Hollander states:

> Ricardo failed to spell out the playback on distribution; but there is nothing in the logic of his system to preclude it (p. 97, also see p. 439).

"Nothing to preclude it!" What a powerful methodological tool is being introduced with virtually no discussion of its attendant dangers. When Hollander says that Adam Smith "did not fear the exhaustion of sources of new technology" (p. 167) does he mean that Smith explicitly stated such a view or is he using the absence of any reference to this issue to *infer* such a view in Smith? Similarly, when Hollander describes Smith's "model of value and distribution" (pp. 82-84) without adverse comment, does he mean to imply that this strange construct is correct?

This volume cannot be recommended as a basic *text* for either undergraduates or graduates. If one can avoid being ensnared in the main thesis, since the book contains many worthwhile, and frequently neglected, points it will be a fruitful second text or a source of provocative seminar discussions.

## REFERENCES

Hollander, Jacob (Editor). 1928. *Notes on Malthus*. Baltimore, MD: Johns Hopkins University Press.

# THE COWLES COMMISSION IN
# THE HISTORY OF ECONOMETRICS:
## A REVIEW ESSAY

Christopher L. Gilbert

*A History of Econometrics*
**By Roy J. Epstein**
**Amsterdam: North-Holland, 1987, 254 pages.**

The history of econometrics has only recently begun to be written. In the 1950s and 1960s, econometrics was continually pushing back computational constraints, and the rapidity of "progress" left little time for either historical or methodological reflection. In the 1990s, econometricians can do more in a couple of minutes on their desktops than was possible fifteen years earlier overnight on the university mainframe and the computational constraint has effectively dissolved. Instead, the profession finds itself possessing a number of competing methodologies urging radically different

Research in the History of Economic Thought and Methodology, Volume 9, pages 255-264.

research strategies. This has induced a mood of methodological reflection which has reawakened interest in the history of the subject. Roy Epstein's study is therefore very timely.

The initial contributions to the rapidly growing literature on the history of econometrics combine historical analysis and personal reminiscences in roughly equal proportions. One major conclusion stands out: the crucial importance of the work undertaken at the Cowles Commission in Chicago during the 1940s, and in particular of Haavelmo's methodological manifesto *The Probability Approach in Econometrics* (1944, mimeo version circulated in 1941).

Epstein's discussion ranges widely. An initial chapter is devoted to the pre-Cowles period with particular attention devoted to H.L. Moore, Elmer and Holbrook Working, and Sewall Wright. Later chapters discuss postwar European contributions to econometrics (the Department of Applied Economics at Cambridge under Richard Stone, time-series work at the London School of Economics associated in particular with Bill Phillips and Denis Sargan, the Netherlands Centraal Planbureau under Jan Tinbergen and Henri Theil, and Hermann Wold's work at Uppsala); and contemporary methodology (exogeneity, rational expectations, and vector autoregressions). But the three central chapters on structural estimation and the Cowles methodology form the core of Epstein's contribution. It is on this that I shall concentrate.

It is natural to start with Haavelmo's manifesto. It would be quite incorrect to see Haavelmo as initiating modern econometrics; and Epstein devotes his initial chapter to the pre-Cowles period (more fully covered in Morgan (1987, 1989). Karl Fox has emphasized the long tradition of regression-based applied research undertaken by American agricultural economists (Fox, 1986, 1988, 1989). Nevertheless, as Morgan (1987) persuasively argues, much of this activity should be seen as using statistics to *measure* unknown constants (e.g. price elasticities) in a structure which may be regarded as known, rather than to *model* the economic processes, (and even less to model the data). Furthermore, this measurement process was undertaken without the benefit of any agreed theory of the relation of the empirical data to the underlying structure.

Many, perhaps most, nonagricultural economists remained deeply sceptical. In 1901, Marshall wrote "I regard the method of Least Squares as involving an assumption with regard to symmetry that vitiates all its applications to economic problems with which I am acquainted."[1] Better known is Robbins (1932) caricature of Dr. Blank's demand function for herrings with the implication, in current parlance, that such estimated functions would be pathologically structurally unstable. And Keynes' (1939) famous and in places perspicacious criticism of Tinbergen's League of Nations business cycle models (quoted by Epstein, 1989) reveals a hostility to the application of formal statistical methods in economics on a par with Marshall's.

Robbins and Keynes were on opposite sides of the economic debate in Britain in the 1930s but they shared a methodological position which may be traced back to Mill[2] and which regarded economic theory as exact and true, but incomplete (i.e., true so far as it goes). The implied nonconstancy or nonhomogeneity through time of economic data were held to preclude the use of formal statistical methods. These two traditions had combined to limit the role of statistics in economics to verifying theory or to establishing just how large the gaps are between the predictions of (true) theory and the facts. The true theory, of course, embodied the main causes thought to be present and operating in a wide variety of cases; the supposedly minor, and irregular or "disturbing causes" were put into the *ceteris paribus* pound.

Haavelmo's manifesto is an outright rejection of this position. He insisted that economic theory is best modelled as "stochastical" not exact (1944, in particular, sections 11-13). He also confronted typical objections to applying probabilistic methods to economic time-series, arguing that the difficulties of fulfilling the *ceteris paribus* condition, and of obtaining enough variation to extract from the whole underlying set of causes the separate relations responsible for the movements in the series, are neither peculiar to time series data nor insurmountable in practice (1944, section 6). Finally, he urged that the fact that economic observations are not experimentally generated does not preclude treating them for practical purposes as if they were (1944, pp. 43, 48). The crucial move was to see that although individual time-series observations may not in general be taken as a random drawing from a stable population (contrast tosses of a coin or individual mortalities), we may legitimately regard an entire historical time-series as a drawing from a hypothetical population of possible series (but all populations are hypothetical) (1944, p. 51). History was uniquely what it was, but it could nevertheless have been otherwise.

Epstein stresses the importance of structural modeling of complete systems, starting with supply and demand analysis in a single market but moving on to Tinbergen's work on the structural modeling of entire economies. Consideration of complete systems naturally gives rise to issues of statistical simultaneity. In his important 1943 *Econometrica* article, Haavelmo showed the behavior of variables in a complete system depends on the stochastic specification of the entire model and that, in particular, Ordinary Least Squares (OLS) applied to an individual equation would result in biased and in general inconsistent estimates (Haavelmo, 1943); the argument recurs in Haavelmo (1944, section 21). This stresses the importance of the stochastic specification of economic models. Haavelmo described simultaneity bias as "the statistical side of the problem of autonomous relations" (1944, p. 84).

That OLS might give biased results was not a new insight. Frisch (1934) had used a model in which exact relationships held between unobserved latent variables, all of which in principle are measured with error. It was known that in this model, OLS estimates in each regression direction put bounds on the parameters in the latent relationships, but in general would not coincide with any one of these relationships. In his work, Haavelmo had rejected this model in favor of the more tractable errors in equations model in which stochastic relationships hold between accurately measured variables. That OLS might still be biased in the errors in equations model was new, and had been overlooked by Tinbergen (1930) who had derived the reduced form of a supply-demand model and had supposed that the differences in the direct and indirect least squares estimates of the parameters were due to rounding, and so on. The next step in the Cowles research program was to find an appropriate consistent estimator.

The mathematical statisticians at Cowles were aware of Fisher's new maximum likelihood (ML) methods (Fisher, 1925), which gave consistency under very weak conditions, and so it is natural that they should look in this direction. Full information ML methods (as we would now call them) imposed an impossible computational burden even for small pedagogic models in an era of "computors" who sat at hand-calculating machines. However, in 1945 Ted Anderson, drawing upon an obscure ("black magic") suggestion made in a letter from Girshik to Marschak recently rediscovered by Mary Morgan (see Epstein, 1989), developed a limited information or single equation ML estimator (LIML) which made the program feasible. LIML was central to the Cowles program: the technique was their own, and LIML was significant because it was an application of statistical theory specifically developed for economics, an innovation almost made to order to silence those who had insisted for so long that economic data precluded any meaningful application of statistics in that discipline.

The next few years were devoted to coloring in the theoretical map and to empirical implementation. But as Epstein notes, there was little new work on econometric theory at Cowles after 1947, and the famous Cowles monographs 10 and 14 (Koopmans, 1950; Hood and Koopmans, 1953) reported work substantially undertaken considerably earlier than their publication dates. From that time, Cowles' research activity was predominantly devoted to economic theory, and in particular to the important new discovery of activity analysis.

Epstein provides the detail of this story but fails to communicate the excitement or controversy it engendered. Haavelmo in 1944 was a revolutionary, set to change both the way we do applied economics and the way we talk about what we do, but that fervor is absent from Epstein's account. More specifically, why did Keynes object so strenuously to Tinbergen's almost "Keynesian" business-cycle models? Why so little detail on the fascinating detective story on the discovery of LIML (filled out in Epstein, 1989)? Does not the enormous gulf in perception between Koopmans and Vining in the "measurement without theory" debate (Koopmans, 1947, 1949; Vining, 1949; but only two paragraphs in Epstein), in which Vining refers (jocularly?) to Koopmans as a Commissar of Research, indicate the enormity of the Cowles claims for their new methodology? Most tantalizing, however, is the longer discussion of Friedman's criticisms of Cowles, which in fact led Friedman to comment unfavorably on continued Rockerfeller funding. Were Friedman's worries purely intellectual (economists simply did not know enough to build models as ambitious as those attempted by Cowles, but what they did know suggested that those models were far too simple), or was there also the suspicion that the Cowles models were Keynesian[3] and that the intentions of the modellers were anti-free enterprise? And why the retreat from econometrics? Had it failed to deliver, or was it simply that there were new crusades to be waged?

A related deficiency in Epstein's account is the lack of any attempt to provide an assessment of the Cowles achievement. Are monographs 10 and 14 the pinnacle of econometric achievement or were they a distraction from more important endeavors? Epstein stresses the 'problem of multiple hypotheses', which worried the Cowles econometricians and, in an argument which echoes Leamer's recent discussions (Leamer, 1978, 1983), he suggests that this invalidates conventional Neyman-Pearson inference. I would stress other concerns. In particular, although the Cowles workers intended to make their inquiries dynamic, this never was accomplished, and in part this must be attributed to their prior commitment to simultaneity (see Morgan, 1991). The commitment was reinforced by computational problems (forcing them to estimate at a high level of aggregation) and data limitations (most series were of annual observations), both of which tended to suppress the dynamic properties of the data. This was in contrast to the emphasis on dynamics in Tinbergen's business cycle models. Errors in measurement were also more or less left off the Cowles agenda.

The implication is that if the Cowles work is to stand as the major achievement of the first generation of econometricians this must be through the analysis of simultaneity, and in particular through the discovery of the LIML estimator. I do not wish to deny that simultaneity is an important chapter in the econometrics textbook. Furthermore, simultaneity bias can in principle be enormous. In practice, however, particularly in macroeconometric applications, the OLS biases often turn out to be quite small—most notably so in the estimation of consumption functions, where, in any case, one may prefer to use a conditional model. It is notable that Klein very rapidly reverted to OLS after leaving Cowles.

One could accept this argument, but still note that one requires an estimator known to be consistent to check on the extent of OLS bias, as in the Hausman (1978) test. LIML provides this. However, one can further question the whole ML direction which econometric theory was to take in the post-Cowles decades. ML methods require specification of the error distribution, and indeed it is implicit in Haavelmo (1944) that the properties of that distribution will determine the stochastic properties of the observed variables. It is almost universal to assume joint normality. In linear models, the assumption is of little consequence, at least with regard to the consistency of parameter estimates. But in the increasingly complicated nonlinear models which we are now able to entertain, this gratuitous assumption may do much of the work (Amemiya, 1977). This suggests an alternative nonparametric approach, consistent in a considerably wider class of circumstances but less efficient if normality is correct. These concerns underlie the recent interest in Generalized Methods of Moments (GMM) estimators.[5] Instrumental variables (IV) estimators are members of the GMM class, and Two Stage Least Squares (TSLS) is simply a particular IV estimator. If disturbances are normal, the small sample distribution of the LIML estimator is to be preferred to that of the TSLS estimator (Anderson, Kunitomo, and Sawa, 1982), but this result may not be robust. Did the existence of LIML delay the discovery of OLS analogue, Two Stage Least Squares?

A weaker position would be to argue that the details of the Cowles econometric program were relatively unimportant. Haavelmo's major contribution was to make economics stochastic. This prompts the question: have the probabilists won the day? One answer is that, in fact, the Haavelmo agenda has been only partly implemented. It is true that econometrics is now a compulsory component of almost every graduate program in economics; and that it would be as reasonable to expect any professional economist to be familiar with basic econometric methods as with intermediate micro- and macroeconomic theory. It is also true that the journals carry a huge volume of regression-based empirical work; although this remains small relative to the volume of pure theory. At the same time, most economic theory is developed as deterministic (game theory notwithstanding). Dr. Blank's contemporary counterpart derives his "theoretical" relationship within the prescribed optimizing framework and then adds on disturbance terms which take into account errors in optimization, factors not taken into account in the model, and so on. So at the theoretical level economics remains deterministic and deductive (and indeed, one can read Haavelmo (1944) as himself holding this instrumentalist position).

Much of what modern econometricians do bears little relation to the Cowles methods or concerns, and much applied economics owes more to the interwar agricultural economists than to Haavelmo. This is not to deny the historical importance of the Cowles Chicago period but more to note how much the subject has grown and advanced over the intervening decades. But in view of the claims that the Cowles workers made for their new and revolutionary approach it would be useful to have a balanced and historical assessment. Sadly, neither Hildreth (1986) nor Epstein can be said to have provided this. Hildreth contents himself with a static ahistorical snapshot of the Cowles results; its main value to the historian is a useful list of all the Cowles Commission members and visitors over the Chicago period. Epstein's book is a considerable advance but it avoids some of the most interesting questions, and manages to eliminate much of the excitement from those it does discuss (as if the history of econometrics requires a PG rating). Nevertheless, this book will provide a useful point of reference until the time that its section headings are replaced by chapters of succeeding volumes. At the very least, Epstein has suggested half a dozen topics for useful doctoral dissertations.

## NOTES

1.   Letter to Bowley dated 21.ii.1901 (Pigou, 1956, p. 419). The discussion in this and the following paragraph draws on de Marchi and Gilbert (1989). I am grateful to Neil de Marchi for permission to use this material.
2.   Mill (1967), (first published 1844), pp. 326, 329.
3.   See page 108, footnote 38 in Epstein. This reviewer found the absence from the reference of "Friedman (1951)," discussed throughout page 109, extremely irritating.
4.   Fox (1989) makes the same claim for agricultural supply-demand models.
5.   The seminal paper is Hansen (1982).

## REFERENCES

Amemiya, T. 1977. "The Maximum Likelihood and the Nonlinear Three-Stage Least Squares Estimator in the General Nonlinear Simultaneous Equation Model." *Econometrica* 45: 955-968.
Anderson, T.W., N. Kunitomo and T. Sawa. 1982. "Evaluation of the Distribution Function of the Limited Information Maximum Likelihood Estimator." *Econometrica* 50: 1009-1027.
de Marchi, N., and C.L. Gilbert. 1989. "Introduction." In *Oxford Economic Papers* 41: 1-11.
Epstein, R.J. 1989. "The fall of OLS in structural estimation." In *Oxford Economic Papers* 41: 94-107.
Fisher, R.A. 1925. *Statistical Methods for Research Workers*. Edinburgh: Oliver and Boyd.
Fox, K.A. 1986. "Agricultural Economists as World Leaders in Applied Econometrics, 1917-33." *American Journal of Agricultural Economics* 68: 381-386.

Fox, K.A. 1988. "Econometrics Needs a History: Two Cases of Conspicuous Neglect." In *Econometrics of Planning and Efficiency*, edited by J.K. Sengupta and G.K. Kadekodi. Boston: Kluwer.

Fox, K.A. 1989. "Agricultural Economists in the Econometric Revolution: Institutional Background and Leading Figures." *Oxford Economic Papers* 41: 53-70.

Frisch, R. 1934. *Statistical Confluence Analysis by Means of Complete Regression Systems*. Oslo: Universitets/Økonomiske Institutt.

Haavelmo, T. 1943. "The Statistical Implications of a System of Simultaneous Equations." *Econometrica* 11: 1-12.

Haavelmo, T. 1944. "The Probability Approach to Econometrics." *Econometrica* 12(Supplement).

Hansen, L.P. 1982. "Large Sample Properties of Generalized Method of Moments Estimators." *Econometrica* 50: 1029-1054.

Hausman, J.A. 1978. "Specification Tests in Econometrics." *Econometrica* 46: 1251-1271.

Hildreth, C. 1986. *The Cowles Commission in Chicago, 1939-55*. Lecture Notes in Economics and Mathematical Systems, 271, Berlin: Springer-Verlag.

Hood, W.C., and T.C. Koopmans, eds. 1953. *Studies in Econometric Methods*. Cowles Commission Monograph 14. New York: Wiley.

Keynes, J.M. 1939. "The Statistical Testing of Business Cycle Theories." *Economic Journal* 49: 556-568.

Koopmans, T.C. 1947. "Measurement Without Theory." *Review of Economics and Statistics* 29: 161-172.

Koopmans, T.C. 1949. "Reply to Rutledge Vining." *Review of Economics and Statistics* 31: 86-91.

Koopmans, T.C., ed. 1950. *Statistical Inference in Dynamic Economic Models*. Cowles Commission Monograph 10. New York: Wiley.

Leamer, E.E. 1978. *Specification Searches: Ad Hoc Inference with Non-experimental Data*. New York: Wiley.

Leamer, E.E. 1983. "Let's Take the Con Out of Econometrics." *American Economic Review* 73: 31-43.

Mill, J.S. 1967. "On the Definition of Political Economy; And On the Method of Investigation Proper To It." In *J.S. Mill, Collected Works*, Vol. IV, edited by J.M. Robson. Toronto: University of Toronto Press. (Originally published 1844 in *Essays on Some Unsettled Questions of Political Economy*).

Morgan, M.S. 1987a. "Statistics Without Probability and Haavelmo's Revolution in Econometrics." In *The Probabilistic Revolution*, Vol. 2, edited by L. Kruger, G. Gigerenzer and M.S. Morgan. Cambridge MA: MIT Press.

Morgan, M.S. 1991. "The Stamping Out of Process Analysis from Econometrics." In *Appraising Economic Theories*, edited by N. de Marchi and M. Blaug. Aldershot: Edward Elgan.

Morgan, M.S. 1989. *The History of Econometric Ideas*. Cambridge: Cambridge University Press.

Pigou, A.C., ed. 1956. *Memorials of Alfred Marshall*. New York: Kelley and Millman.

Robbins, L. 1932. *An Essay on the Nature and Significance of Economic Science*. London: Macmillan.

Tinbergen, J. 1930. "Bestimmung und deutung von angebotskurven: ein beispiel." *Zeitschrift für Nationalökonomie* 1: 669-679.

Vining, R. 1949. "Koopmans On the Choice of Variables to Be Studied and On Methods of Measurement." *Review of Economics and Statistics* 71: 77-86.

# UNDERSTANDING THE POPPERIAN LEGACY IN ECONOMICS:

## A REVIEW ESSAY

Lawrence A. Boland

---

**The Popperian Legacy in Economics: Papers presented at a Symposium in Amsterdam, December 1985**
**By Neil de Marchi**
**Cambridge: Cambridge University Press, 1988**

> *I shall start with two general theses. My first thesis is this.*
>
> *(1) If anyone should think of scientific method as a way which leads to success in science, he will be disappointed. There is no royal road to success.*
>
> *My second thesis is this.*
>
> *(2) Should anybody think of scientific method...as a way of justifying scientific results, he will also be disappointed. A scientific result cannot be justified. It can only be criticized, and tested.*
>
> —Karl Popper
> (1961/72, p. 265)

Research in the History of Economic Thought and Methodology, Volume 9, pages 265-276.
Copyright © 1992 by JAI Press Inc.
All rights of reproduction in any form reserved.
ISBN: 1-55938-428-X

*Similarly, it is helpful to formulate the task of scientific method as the elimination of false theories (from the various theories tentatively proffered) rather than the attainment of established truths.*

—Karl Popper
(1963, Vol. 1, p. 285)

*From the point of scientific method,... we can never rationally establish the truth of scientific laws; all we can do is to test them severely, and to eliminate the false ones (this is perhaps the crux of my* The Logic of Scientific Discovery).

—Karl Popper
(1963, Vol 2, p. 363)

In the minds of many, Karl Popper is the most important philosopher of science of the twentieth century. For some, this is because they love his vision of science as a progressive and critical enterprise, while for others it is because they hate his rude dismissal of any traditional philosophy that would see science as a means of justifying beliefs. Those who love Popper's vision, and think economics should be considered scientific, often think there ought to be a Popperian legacy in economics. Unfortunately, in his many writings Popper is of little help to his economist fans. In his infrequent references to economics he treats economics, so gingerly as to leave considerable doubt about his views of economics or his view of the applicability of his philosophical concerns to the study of economics.

Some of the economists interested in the possibility of a Popperian legacy in economics were brought together in a 1985 symposium to consider the issue. The purpose of this paper is to examine the main results of this symposium as presented in *The Popperian Legacy in Economics*.[1] In his summary of the symposium, de Marchi concludes that there is no Popperian legacy (1988, p. 12). While it is easy to agree with his conclusion, I find the reasons provided in the symposium to be unsatisfactory. Is the absence of a Popperian legacy in economics due to (1) a fault of Popper, (2) the essential nature of economics, or (3) a failure of proponents to understand or correctly apply Popper's views? Only one participant seemed to think the absence of a Popperian legacy is entirely due to Popper. The rest seemed to think it is due to one or another peculiarity of economics that distinguishes economics from scientific disciplines such as physics or chemistry. None of these participants were willing to admit that there may have been a failure on the part of economists to understand or correctly apply Popper's views to economics.

Three of the prominent participants of this symposium have major Popperian credentials. There is Terence Hutchison who is credited by almost everyone with being the first to introduce economists to Popper's views in 1938. Although he claims to have tempered his views since then, he still is the strongest advocate of an essential role in economics for Popper's falsifiability.[2] There is the self-professed "neo-Popperian" (p. 38) Mark Blaug, who is famous for promoting what the participants call "falsificationism" and for complaining that economists give only lip-service to falsifiability.[3] And there is Joop Klant who is considered the leading proponent of Popper's views in economic methodology in the community of European economists. Regrettably, most of the other participants fail to understand Popper's views and thus too often seem willing to throw the baby out with the philosophically dirty bath water.

## I. CRITICISM OF POPPER'S VIEW OF SCIENCE

In one sense, the critics of Popper's view of science are correct: Popper's view of science does not do a good job of solving the problems that these critics think must be solved. Most of his critics insist that any good philosopher of science must be able to provide criteria by which good theories can be distinguished from bad theories—that is, it must solve the problem of theory choice.[4] Of course, I think it is silly to criticize Popper for failing to solve problems that he obviously rejects. The root of the issue is the common view that anyone who discusses the philosophy of science must be promoting their form of a "scientific method" and claiming that, if properly followed their method will always produce scientifically acceptable results. For some people, the scientific method is needed in order to specify conventional criteria by which one would rationally choose the best theory from a list of competitors. For others it is a means of justifying or verifying the truth of one's prior beliefs.[5]

As the above quotations from Popper's well-known work clearly show, he is not promoting or recommending a particular scientific method. Anyone reading Popper's work to find a recommended scientific method is doomed to disappointment. Typically, critics (and even some proponents) identify Popper with a normative view which says that true scientists should go out of their way to make their theoretical statements falsifiable. A superficial reading of Popper would seem to support this identification. Critics will then argue that many scientifically useful statements are not obviously falsifiable and very few scientific propositions are independently falsifiable (i.e., without depending on an assumption of other propositions being true and thereby begging more questions). They thus say it should be concluded that Popper's normative view of science is wrong.[6] If readers of Popper's early work are more careful to observe the intended audience of his argument, they will find a much more cautious position. Specifically, the context must always be recognized in his arguments in favor of falsifiability. With regard to the importance of falsifiability he sees himself arguing against the common view of the 1920s and 1930s that theories are scientific because they are verifiable. And Popper counters that falsifiability rather than verifiability would be a more appropriate means of demarcating science from nonscience (e.g., 1965, p. 40). But Popper is not claiming that falsifiability, as a static attribute of scientific theories, is a sufficient condition for anything. Obviously, many false propositions are falsifiable.

Since almost all of Popper's early discussion of science is concerned with disciplines such as chemistry and physics, there is no question of scientific status, but rather a question of just what makes chemistry or physics scientific. In his early work, he was merely claiming that verifiability, as a means of demarcation, is logically inadequate since every explanation requires universal propositions[7] which can never be verified (even when true). Such explanatorily essential propositions are, however, at least falsifiable—so, if one wants a means of demarcation then logically one should require falsifiability rather than verifiability. In this context falsifiability is not obviously being promoted as a foundation for a normative scientific method. Besides, to the extent that every explanation involves universal propositions, falsifiability is assured. Unless one is defending verifiability as a means of demarcating scientific explanations, it is hard to imagine how one can fault Popper's view that falsifiability is an essential attribute of any scientific explanation.

## II. FALSIFIABILITY IN ECONOMICS

To the extent that every economic theory, model, or explanation involves assumptions in the form of universal propositions, Popper's views are obviously applicable in economics. So what are the alleged problems that arise when one claims that economic explanations should be falsifiable? During the 1985 symposium, the central problem often referred to was what Klant called the "parametric paradox."[8] The paradox seems to be an alleged conflict between the explanatory method of comparative statics and the common presumption that all testing requires constant parameters. While comparative static analysis requires that we change one of the exogenous variables and determine the effect on the endogenous variables (a common example is the calculation of multipliers in macroeconomics), Klant claims that, "If you assume parameters to be variables, you imply that your theory is not falsifiable" (p. 30). If Klant's parametric paradox is a problem, then it would be a central obstacle to any fulfillment of the requirement of falsifiability in economics.[9]

Personally, I find the acceptance of Klant's claim—that the parametric paradox is a proof that modern economics is essentially unfalsifiable—to be astounding. The reason is that in my 1960s PhD thesis I *required* the assumption of the variability of both parameters and exogenous variables so that I could show what it takes to unambiguously refute some typical macro-economic models (see Boland, 1989, chapters 2 and 3).

One of the reasons why many people think falsifiability is difficult to apply in economics is the claim (and possible observation) that few if any fundamental theories have ever been empirically refuted. And, presumably, these same people think refutation of fundamental theories in physics is an everyday occurrence. The main difficulty is that methodologists and historians of economics too often are concerned with grand theories rather than the everyday business of economics. The everyday business of economics is more involved with model building and, as is well known, a refutation of a model would seldom constitute a refutation of the theory represented (or presumed) by the refuted model (Boland, 1977, 1989, chapter 7; Cross, 1982).[10] But particular modeling assumptions are refuted or rejected everyday. Whenever a model builder finds that a linear model cannot fit the available data, that linear model is being rejected as refuted—that is, the linear *model* is considered in some sense false. Similarly, econometricians who reject ordinary least-squares in favor of generalized least-squares as a means of estimating a model's parameters do so because they have found models based on the former to be false in some important respect. Such considerations would lead me to conclude that a very modest form of falsification is quite commonplace in economics and certainly not inapplicable.

Even if it is accepted that there is a modest form of falsification employed on a regular basis in economics, this does not constitute evidence in favor of a Popperian legacy in economics. The practice of this modest form of falsification is more a consequence of economists accepting Paul Samuelson's methodological prescriptions. And, most important, the primary reason for requiring falsifiability is to assure that any verified theories will not be confused with tautologies (see Boland, 1977). Recall that the avoidance of tautologies was one of the main objectives of Hutchison's promotion of falsifiability in his 1938 book.[11]

## III.  ATTEMPTS TO CREATE A POPPERIAN LEGACY

In a very interesting paper, de Marchi recounts the history of a group of well-known economists who in the late 1950s and early 1960s explicitly attempted to use Popper's view of science in economics. Their hidden agenda was to push economics beyond the dominating methodological views of the alleged arch-apriorist, Lionel Robbins, who opposed quantification. It did not take them long to declare failure in their Popperian research programme. According to de Marchi, Chris Archibald tried to apply Popper's views to some fundamental theoretical questions but eventually decided that the variability and/or ambiguity of "parameters" in comparative static explanations implies that refutations are logically impossible. Dick Lipsey was more concerned with emphasizing the role of quantitative testing of economic theories but eventually decided that all testing must be based on statistical models and, according to de Marchi, this led to the conclusion that economic theories are irrefutable.[12] In both cases, I think a more accurate conclusion might be that neither Archibald nor Lipsey understood Popper's views very well.[13]

Almost everything presented at this symposium misses the point of Popper's approach to the philosophy of science. In his introduction de Marchi acknowledges that many of us think that the importance of Popper's work is not that it sees science as an enterprise devoted to the growth of knowledge but that it sees science primarily as an instance of learning by criticism (p. 7). For many of us, Popper is seen to be interested in science as an ongoing human activity, a process, which is based primarily on a critical attitude. He is not interested in science as a static method of justification or as a formula for success. Unfortunately, hardly anyone pursued this learning aspect of Popper's work.

In my opinion, the role of falsification in the growth of knowledge is promoted by Popper more to emphasize that *science is a process* than to argue that it embodies a method that assures progress. By his noting that anyone's claimed advance represents more a refutation than anything else, Popper's argument is always against those who think science progresses in a positive, verificationist manner. His idea of progress is more like Socratic learning—namely, one where we always learn by exposing our ignorance (i.e., false theories and beliefs). But most important, he continually notes that the absence of a scientific method (one which would guarantee success) is not a problem since science is an ongoing process which is always going in the right direction.

The idea of emphasizing process and direction sounds to me like Austrian economics. It is easy to see a similar sentiment in Hayek's early emphasis on the market-based price system as an ongoing process where (in the absence of external influence) there is always movement in the right direction (namely, toward an equilibrium where resources are optimally used and everyone is maximizing). Moreover, the competitive price system is best understood as a commendable process even though it may not always reach an equilibrium. Popper similarly wishes us to recognize that it is not a guarantee of the successful attainment of true theories which motivates scientists but that refuting ignorance is always a movement in the right direction.

Market-oriented economists will often observe that by bidding up the price when there is excess demand, demanders always give the right signal and incentive to producers. As a process, the market forms a basis for social coordination that is always moving in the right direction (toward universal maximization). Popper similarly notes that by putting forth falsifiable explanations, scientists are in a position to improve our knowledge by refuting our ignorance. As a mere practical matter it is easy to see that the more falsifiable our explanations, the better will be our opportunity to learn. For Popper, science as an ongoing social enterprise must be based on falsifiable theories since it is devoted to eliminating ignorance even though complete elimination may never be achieved.

## IV.   THE RHETORIC OF POPPER'S VIEW OF SCIENCE

As argued above, practicing economists and econometricians refute particular modeling assumptions every day even though they may only wish to be modest and say the assumptions are rejected as not being "satisfactory" (e.g., pp. 204-208). Of course, such modesty is merely rhetorical. Moreover, when practicing economists do talk of falsifiability, they are almost always following Paul Samuelson's lead. Rather than a symposium on a Popperian legacy in economics, I think there should be more discussion of the methodological legacy of Samuelson.

It is surprising that with all their talk of the rhetoric of economics, Don McCloskey and Arjo Klamer fail to examine the rhetoric involved in the typical discussion of Popper's view of science in economics or even of philosophy itself. Neither seems to practice what they preach! Although McCloskey does offer his criticisms of Popper's view of science, nowhere does he seem to appreciate the rhetorical aspect of Popper's writings. Specifically, Popper is always willing to put his discussion in the terms of his intended audience (as noted above) and thus one must be very careful to separate Popper's views from those he is debating. McCloskey does engage in a little rhetorical inquiry by accusing the philosophy of science of being "too thin." One lesson that I think can be learned from McCloskey's general discussion on the rhetoric of the history of economics and of methodology is that we should not take philosophers of science as seriously as they take themselves. Unfortunately, in response to McCloskey's and Klamer's continued promotion of the rhetoric of inquiry, some of the participants eventually complained that the discussion of the rhetoric of economics was itself wearing thin.

Perhaps McCloskey and Klamer could have devoted some of their time to an inquiry into the rhetoric of the symposium. For example, it might have been possible for the participants to spend some of the symposium's time discussing Popper's "critical rationalism" (1963, chapter 24), or his logical "negativism" (1965, p. 228), with respect to science as a critical process. Instead, the participating economists and methodologists seemed to be victims of the rhetoric of Latakos who emphasized the *growth* of knowledge, thus, they spent too much time on questions of whether neoclassical economics is an "empirically *progressive*" research programme (p. 247). Unfortunately this seemed to be a matter of design since the symposium was almost exclusively limited to the discussion of falsifiability and its relationship to the question of the growth of knowledge (pp. x, 2, 6-7). Such a limitation allowed only a thin slice of Popper's view of science to be discussed. The thinness of the slice served up by this symposium is distressing to many of us interested in Popper's more general views of science and learning. And silly criticisms of the chosen thin slice of Popper's work seemed to be distressing for some proponents of falsifiability in economics such as Hutchison:

> What alarms me is that we are not building on the advances of the 1930s. In some respects, we are going back to the 1930s. The barbarians really *were* at the gates then, and in some ways they still are. (p. 25)

Judging by the thinness of the discussion of Popper's work in this symposium and the exclusive concern for thin questions such as whether falsifiability should be a guiding rule in economics, I think Hutchison should look around him. The barbarians are no longer at the gates—now they are within the gates.

## NOTES

1. Since I will be focusing primarily on this book (de Marchi, 1988), unless specifically noted, all page references will be to this book.
2. Hutchison urges us not to abandon falsifiability as a primary operating rule in economics because economics is ultimately used to support politics and ethics. He argues that falsifiability is an essential tool against dishonesty.
3. Blaug's paper critically examines the methodological views of John Hicks and finds them incoherent.
4. See Tarascio and Caldwell (1979). Very many methodologists in economics consider the primary concern of methodology to be that of determining conventional criteria to enable us to choose among competing theories much like consumers choose between apples and oranges. I have often criticized this view of methodology as well as the related view that is concerned with determining the attributes of

scientific theories which allows them to be considered contributions to the growth
of knowledge (see Boland 1982, chapter 10, 1989, chapters 4 and 5).

5. For a critical discussion of conventionalist criteria, see (Boland 1982, chapter
1, 1989, chapters 4 and 5).

6. Dan Hausman's contribution to the symposium is just such a critique. From
my perspective, such criticism seems to be an attempt to sculpture a representation
of Popper from a piece of rotten wood. What Hausman's paper does, however, is
to whittle the wood down to a square peg which he tries to cram into an analytical
philosopher's round hole. Of course, square pegs do not fit into round holes—and
Hausman wants us to think it is due to a flaw in the peg. I think it is the fault of
the hole.

7. Such as "all consumers are maximizers."

8. The alleged parametric paradox is not explicitly defined in de Marchi's
book and Klant points out that it was introduced elsewhere to criticize Samuelson's
methodology. Together these considerations make it difficult to understand the
reported discussion. In what follows I am conjecturing what the participants
understood as Klant's concept of a parametric paradox (Blaug is explicit in his
puzzlement and wonders why Klant would promote Popper given the paradox
[p. 30]).

9. The reason why variability of parameters is an issue is probably the
recognition that on the one hand in the natural sciences, for all practical purposes,
there are many constants (gravitational acceleration at a given height, absolute zero
temperature, the speed of light) but on the other hand, as noted by John Hicks,
"there are no such constants in economics" (1979, p. 39). Judging by the reported
discussion, it seems that many feel that Popper's view of falsifiability and testability
is thus appropriate only when there are such natural constants.

10. In Mary Morgan's review of the history of econometrics with respect to
whether econometricians have been concerned with refuting or even verifying
fundamental economic theories, she notes:

> econometricians have been primarily concerned with finding satisfactory
> empirical models, not with trying to prove fundamental theories true or untrue
> (p. 199).

11. This idea of promoting falsifiability in opposition to tautologies was
essentially the focus of the critical argument developed by Klappholz and Agassi
in their well-known debate with Hutchison (Klappholz and Agassi, 1959; Hutchison,
1960; Agassi, 1971).

12. This reaction to the problem of testing grand theories with specific models
is, of course, an instance of the well-known Duhem-Quine thesis (see Cross, 1982).
Virtually everyone thinks it means that testing of grand theories is impossible (e.g.,
p. 20). I think this is a mistaken conclusion about testing in economics. Specific
general statements can be tested in economics. As Klant points out, even without
absolute refutations testing can necessitate adjustments in our general theories (p.
104). If one carefully defines the test criteria, it is sometimes possible to test grand

theories with specific models subject only to an agreement concerning ordinary test criteria (see, further, Boland, 1989, chapter 8).

13.   De Marchi's paper solved an old puzzle for me. Both Lipsey and Archibald have a reputation for being what some people might call methodologists. Yet:

(a)   I met Lipsey many years ago and he told me that he learned everything he knew from my teacher Joseph Agassi. I ran to the library to look up Lipsey's famous book to see what he had to say about methodology. I was very disappointed.

(b)   In 1967, or there about, I had a long conversation with Archibald. He tried in vain to convince me to switch my interests from methodology to something— anything—else.

Given their reputations, how was it possible for them to be so far divorced from my understanding? Nevertheless, I credit Archibald with providing me with a very important viewpoint. In our three-hour conversation he stressed that if I was going to study or promote the study of methodology, it was my obligation to always show that the methodology I wished to discuss matters to economists. I always try to apply this both as a consumer of methodology and as a methodologist. As a consumer I always ask: What have I learned that matters? As a methodologist, I always assume my audience is poised to ask whether methodology can matter.

# REFERENCES

Agassi, Joseph. 1971. "Tautology and Testability in Economics." *Philosophy of Social Science* 1: 49-63.

Boland, Lawrence. 1977. "Testability in Economic Science." *South African Journal of Economics* 45: 93-105.

Boland, Lawrence. 1982. *The Foundations of Economic Method.* London: George Allen & Unwin.

Boland, Lawrence. 1986. *Methodology for a New Microeconomics.* Boston: Allen & Unwin.

Boland, Lawrence. 1989. *The Methodology of Economic Model Building.* London: Routledge.

Cross, Rodney. 1982. "The Duhem-Quine Thesis, Lakatos and the Appraisal of Theories in Macroeconomics." *Economic Journal* 92: 320-40.

de Marchi, Neil, ed. 1988. *The Popperian Legacy in Economics: Papers presented at a Symposium in Amsterdam, December 1985.* Cambridge: Cambridge University Press.

Hicks, John. 1979. *Causality in Economics.* Oxford: Basil Blackwell.

Hutchison, Terence. 1960. "Methodological Prescriptions in Economics: a Reply." *Economica* 27(NS): 158-61.

Klappholz, Kurt, and Joseph Agassi. 1959. "Methodological Prescriptions in Economics." *Economica* 26(NS): 60-74.

Popper, Karl. 1945. *The Open Society and its Enemies.* New York: Harper & Row. (Reprinted 1963).

Popper, Karl. 1965. "Science: Conjectures and Refutations." In *Conjectures and Refutations: The Growth of Scientific Knowledge*, pp. 33-65. New York: Harper & Row. (First published 1957).

Popper, Karl. 1972. "Evolution and the Tree of Knowledge." In *Objective Knowledge: An Evolutionary Approach*, pp. 256-284. Oxford: Oxford University Press. 1972. (First published 1961).

Tarascio, Vincent, and Bruce Caldwell. 1979. "Theory Choice in Economics: Philosophy and Practice." *Journal of Economics Issues* 13: 983-1006.

# SMITHIAN EXCAVATIONS:

## A REVIEW OF MAURICE BROWN'S

## *ADAM SMITH'S ECONOMICS*

Rajani Kanth

---

***Adam Smith's Economics***
**By Maurice Brown**
**London: Croom Helm, 1988. Pp. vii, 189.**

Any attempt at a grand re-evaluation of well-consecrated myths in the evolution of a discipline must of necessity arouse two rather diverse emotions in the potential reviewer: on the one hand, there is tremendous curiosity and enthusiasm—perhaps something dramatically new and different might actually be in the offing, maybe even a major revolution in interpretation. Yet, on the other hand there is the perennial dread: perhaps nothing new is being said at all, just a rehash of hoary old arguments with novel faces and titles to them. We might wish to term these separate responses, the optimism of the will reflex versus the pessimism of the intellect response. Both,

Research in the History of Economic Thought and Methodology, Volume 9, pages 277-284.
Copyright © 1992 by JAI Press Inc.
All rights of reproduction in any form reserved.
ISBN: 1-55938-428-X

however, are preliminary responses and should probably be discounted appropriately. Yet, there is another, more noetic, disquiet, that stems from the very nature of the effort to reinterpret a classical work performed in a past, historical setting which may not, easily, be recreated even in the mind. The fear here is that a previous tradition might now be interpreted through the refractive medium of current discourses quite alien to the period in question of the study under consideration.

In such an instance, the danger is that a very real history is then being artificially rewritten to make it "fit" within modern-day prejudices (even if such prejudices were to be dignified by a "scientific" veneer). An instance that comes to mind is that of Schumpeter magisterially dismissing all economic traditions prior to neoclassical innovations as being just so much offal. Connected sometimes with this temporal centrism is the tendency to imply a teleology to history such that all past efforts in a social science are seen as lumbering efforts that finally bear fruit only in the present. Here one is reminded of various Marxist statements to the effect that the search for the holy grail of surplus value commenced with Petty and culminated in Marx with all the intermediate scholars being just so many stepping stones to—or detours from—current wisdom; or Schumpeter, again, seeing the marginal utility theory of value as the summation of generations of partial efforts and failed insights. Such transcendent schemes of history fail to notice that different periods, quite simply, have different agendas of their own quite unrelated to any grand designs that might be identified post factum.

It is a relief, therefore, to note that Maurice Brown's revival of Adam Smith's economics steers clear, in a purely emotive sense, of the Scylla of enthusiasm for revolutionary departure and the Charybdis of despair at seeing old wine in new bottles. For the book generates neither enthusiasm nor despair. Rather like the vaunted "theories of the middle-range" of Merton's fancy, it is a comfortable and self-assured piece of work that distills moderate insights from Smith's rather copious writings. Of course, the title is a spectacular misnomer in the current context (although it would have been quite appropriate in Smith's time!) because the book is not really about Smith's "economics" but rather the *weltanschauung* contained within it and the underlying epistemology that sustains the Smithian view of the social world. Overall, the treatment is scholarly, studious, and studied, although notably lacking in any feats of inspiration; the results are, equally, sound but unspectacular. We do learn a little more about Smith, ultimately, but not enough to fundamentally rethink the whole matter. Notably, the book is free of any unsustainable grid reading; there is no holy grail at stake, apparently, either neo-classical or Marxist. And that's a relief all in itself. Now to turn to the specific evaluations offered by Brown, in sequence.

## II

On matters of epistemology we glean that, ultimately, Smith was a cautious materialist (for there can be "no question of a realist view of perception") in the Scottish historical tradition placing a great deal of emphasis on the determining influence of the material sphere on other social institutions. Further, Smith was, ontologically speaking, a monist who saw no fundamental distinction between the physical and moral sciences; indeed, Smith actually considered the *latter* to be the harder of the two. Finally, Smith conceived of social knowledge in a dynamic, interactive sense of evolution and development. For the scholar who is aware of eighteenth century traditions in this regard—especially the work of the Hutchinson school—none of this can come as a great surprise. On the other hand, the interpretations themselves are quite unobjectionable, if sometimes a trifle trivial.

On the relationship between the atom and the whole (ch. 4)—or the individual and society—we are told that Smith's work sustains a tension between the associationist view of knowledge and a progressive view of humankind, but that the tension is ultimately displaced—resolved ?—because the Smithian apparatus allowed for the possibility of an "interactive" dimension between individual and society such that the individual grows "dialectically" in and through changing social modes. The argument—by no means novel—is that the individual shapes society and is—as much—shaped by it.

The following chapter on specialisation and social change is equally bland. We are informed—no surprises at all—that the way in which human labor is organized affects social development as a whole; to quote, "the division of labour is both the cause of the economic and institutional development of society and its effect..." (p. 78). Again, we are reminded that this is a "dialectical" proposition.

The ensuing chapter, somewhat amorphous and sometimes rather belabored for my taste, points to the often contradictory nature of the interaction between individual and society as a process of "creative destruction"; the division of labor produces both good and bad, material wealth and alienation. However, it was clear to Smith that material wealth, nonetheless, was the basis for the possibility of a subsequent evolution of nonmaterial wealth and values. However homeostatic the economic life of society, there is yet a positive role for the science of legislation and policy formation.

The penultimate chapter, titled "Purposive Action and Unintended Consequences," is possibly the best section of the book. Here, clearly and eloquently, the important point is made that Smith saw the interaction between greed and sympathy, rationality and passion (if left alone), with the development of the division of labor, as producing a society wherein all human possibilities are made realizable. Short-run avarice may engender a long run escalation of social wealth and an extension in the range of human freedom within society. Clear and eloquent as the chapter is, it goes but little beyond a sophisticated appreciation of Smith's oeuvre already available in sources—albeit few—other than Brown.

The final chapter makes a point that cannot be repeated often enough for my satisfaction, that any reading of Smith must take Smith's meanings from the contextual boundaries of the texts, instead of ascribing metahistorical meanings to them. To state it differently, Smith's ideas, always located in a dynamic context, need to be allocated an integrity all their own rather than simply being accorded the common ascription of inspired anticipations of the ideas of others, a left-handed compliment paid to Smith both by Marxists and by the neoclassicals. Our class struggles were not his; as such, so to transplace them is a grave historical sin.

## III

That, in desperate and unjust brevity, is the book and its salient ideas: what then is one to make of its achievement? Regrettably, for it is both a well-conceived and well-executed study, our sights on Smith are not lifted appreciably. Perhaps this austere judgement is influenced by the presumption that epistemology is really a bastard science that one discovers *post factum* rather than something that might be said to have moved Smith *consciously* in his writings. On the other hand this derision cannot apply to the issue of *methodology* in a social science, of which Smith was well aware, being a late member of the Scottish Historical School. In fact, the best part of Brown's work resides in its laying bare this methodology and making it explicit. The materialism, the historical perspective, and the idea of progress, which fundamentally inform the Smithian view, are stressed as never before since the work of the late Ronald Meek.

Secondly, an overemphasis on the Lakatosian framework of "paradigm-shift"—a gravely deficient and idealist framework— seriously flaws the Brownian treatment. Stated simply, the Lakatosian view makes the idea of scientific change an *internal* matter contained within the logical properties of the science. The fact that such a categorisation better fits the natural than the social sciences seems to have escaped Brown altogether, although he does seem to recognise the countertrend evident in the Kuhnian vision which scales in a correct, but improperly specified, social-selection process on the issue of paradigm change. As my own work on Ricardo makes explicit, Lakatosian criteria are far less important than social-selection processes in the realm of social science. This lapse of judgment is rather curious given Brown's favourable reviews of the Scottish Historical School, of Smith and materialism itself; the naivete of an idealist view of science becomes rather surprising in contrast. Perhaps he might have heeded Smith's own suggestion that science is ultimately undertaken—by the scientist—for its shock value, for its power to impress the lay ignorati, which errs, at least, in the right direction!

Furthermore, no discussion of the question of epistemology is complete without a prior statement of ontology; in fact, I go one step further and argue that epistemological possibilities are limited, ultimately, by real ontological properties themselves. Brown provides no view of a coherent connection between the two. Further, errors abound on matters philosophical such as the confusion of a "realist" epistemology with an "empirical" one, surely a positivist travesty bearing little kindred with a scientific realism where "reality" is much more complex and stratified than the one-dimensionality of the "empirical" would suggest. Nor does the idea that external reality is somehow unknowable fit in easily with the materialism of the Scottish Historical School, despite the Brownian attribution. Unless I have misunderstood, it might be that Brown is really referring to the more abstract argument that nothing really conclusive can be proved from some independent standpoint other than the direct evidence of the senses. But the "nonprovability" of reality is no disproof of the existence of reality in itself.

Additionally, there is some straining in Brown's account of the importance of the "dialectical interaction" between man and nature. It is unclear which version of the dialectic is being referred to (there being a whole family of species in this regard stretching from Heraclitus through Hegel to Marx, and even Engels). Nor can too much credence be attached to the strong assertion that Smith's overall system is a product of his general epistemological position, for either this is a statement of tautology or it is altogether too strong. Indeed, how would one go about trying to "verify" such a statement? Showing merely a "correspondence" between theory and epistemology will not do, for that reduces to a truism. It is almost as if it is a short space, indeed, that separates the profound from the trivial in Brown's work. We are told that, for Smith, "scientific systems are constructs of the imagination which seek to render reality coherent. Their task is to generate explanations of observed events" (p. 182). Give or take a word or two, I submit, this would fit almost anybody's version of science (outside of Milton Friedman's).

One final danger remains in the entire presentation. There is a distinct effort made in this work to make Smith compatible with Marx (if not exactly as a forerunner) even if it is only latent; in fact, even in the introduction, we are informed that the term "dialectical materialism" can be applied to Smith's work. While clearly an overstatement in the instance of Smith, I wonder if even Marx's work could bear the weight of that characterisation (this point is made clearer in the concluding passage of this review). Nor does it follow, as Brown seems to think, that the dialectical materialism of Smith rules out his being a champion of capitalism; for he was that, if anything at all, although he was emphatically not a champion of the merchants and manufacturers. For one may find the behaviour of a class pernicious and still regard the material achievements of the mode of production (succoring the class) favourably. Smith was *not* an apologist for merchants and manufacturers; but he did champion the principles of "commercial" society, that is, capitalism as *he* knew it. Given the context of mercantilist protectionism, laissez-faire and free trade could only, objectively, augment the fortunes of the emergent industrial bourgeoisie; so Smith, by virtue of his policy thrust, *indirectly* assisted the fortunes of the industrial capitalist. Distrusting the perfidy of the commercial spirit, Smith, aristocratic disdain notwithstanding, had admiration for the possibilities of the accumulation of social wealth inherent in the economic order of commercial society.

## IV

However, there are other matters that take precedence over these internal quibbles about detail. Curiously, for someone with an abiding sympathy for dialectical materialism, there is no *materialist* accounting of the Smithian oeuvre; no discussion of the political economy of eighteenth-century England is made available, nor any accounting of Smith's role in it. Importantly, no sketch is attempted, let alone detailed, as a means of fleshing out the connections between perceived policy needs and the soundings of theory. Was Smith merely an innocent—albeit bright—country gentleman with innocuous interests in philosophy and political economy, or was he an active and important participant in the policy debates of the time? One can be quite categorical about this failing; there is simply no material delineation of the Smithian enterprise: both Brown's dialectics and his materialism apparently fail him in this respect.

Finally, these prejudices toward a full-blooded inquiry along materialist lines are easily implicit in Brown's embrace of Lakatosian positions in the philosophy of science which also views science, ultimately, as an *internal* matter settled within the scope of theoretical matters. Where, one might ask, is the intrusion of material life? Of the calculus of greed? Of the logic of class and power? But in this one need not fault Brown at length, for even the great Meek, Marxist sympathiser as he undoubtedly was, failed to carry out such an accounting of classical economics. And, in fact, we can even forgive Meek readily; for the astonishing truth is that even Marx, the fountainhead, lost his bearings in attempting an *internal* critique of the classicals (to show that necessary conclusions from classical premises pointed to opposite trends than those suggested by Smith and Ricardo) so that he too, in Capital, offers an "economic theory" instead of a *political economy* soundly resting on historical materialism. It is high time that Marx-inspired scholarship took its cues from the tenets of historical materialism, for the ideas of the classical economists do need to be understood anew. Regrettably, Brown does not take us (despite many useful insights) far enough toward such an undertaking.

## REFERENCES

Bhaskar, R. 1986. *Scientific Realism and Human Emancipation*. London: Verso.
Kanth, R. 1985. "The Decline of Ricardian Politics: Some Notes on Paradigm Shift in Economics." *European Journal of Political Economy* 1(2): 157-187.
_____. 1986. *Political Economy and Laissez-Faire*. Totowa, NJ: Rowman and Littlefield.
Meek, R. 1956. *Studies in the Labor Theory of Value*. 2nd edition. New York: Monthly Review Press.

# NEW BOOKS RECEIVED

Backhouse, Roger. *Economists and the Economy*. New York: Basil
Blackwell, 1988. Pp. x, 224. $49.95.

Balabkins, Nicholas W. *Not by Theory Alone: The Economics of
Gustav von Schmoller and Its Legacy to America*. Berlin:
Duncker & Humblot, 1988. Pp. 115. 44DM, paper.

Benn, Stanley I. *A Theory of Freedom*. New York: Cambridge
University Press, 1988. Pp. xiv, 338.

Black, Eric. *Our Constitution: The Myth that Binds Us*. Boulder:
Westview, 1988. Pp. xiii, 176. $27.95, cloth; $12.95, paper.

Blaug, Mark. *Great Economists Before Keynes*. New York:
Cambridge University Press, 1988. Pp. xi, 286.

Blaug, Mark. *Great Economists Since Keynes*. New York:
Cambridge University Press, 1988. Pp. xi, 267.

Buchanan, James M. *Essays on the Political Economy*. Honolulu:
University of Hawaii Press, 1989. Pp. xii, 85. $15.95.

Research in the History of Economic Thought and Methodology, Volume 9, pages 285-288.
Copyright © 1992 by JAI Press Inc.
All rights of reproduction in any form reserved.
ISBN: 1-55938-428-X

Cannon, John, et al., eds. *The Blackwell Dictionary of Historians.* New York: Basil Blackwell, 1988. Pp. xiv, 480. $75.00.

Clarke, Peter. *The Keynesian Revolution in the Making, 1924-1936.* New York: Oxford University Press, 1988. Pp. xii, 348. $64.00.

Clarke, Simon. *Keynesianism, Monetarism and the Crisis of the State.* Aldershott: Edward Elgar, 1988. Pp. viii, 368. $49.95.

deLeon, Peter. *Advice and Consent: The Development of the Policy Sciences.* New York: Russell Sage, 1988. Pp. xii, 131. $17.50.

Douglass, R. Bruce, ed. *The Deeper Meaning of Economic Life.* Washington, DC: Georgetown University Press, 1986. Pp. xxiv, 223. $19.95, cloth; $12.95, paper.

Dugger, William M., ed. *Radical Institutionalism: Contemporary Voices.* Westport: Greenwood Press, 1989. Pp. xii, 150. $39.95.

Dworkin, Gerald. *The Theory and Practice of Autonomy.* New York: Cambridge University Press, 1988. Pp. xiii, 173.

Crowley, Brian Lee. *The Self, the Individual, and the Community.* New York: Oxford University Press, 1987. Pp. ix, 310. $59.00.

Fuller, Steve. *Philosophy of Science and Its Discontents.* Boulder: Westview Press, 1989. Pp. x, 188. $32.95.

Gale, David. *The Theory of Linear Economic Models.* Chicago: University of Chicago Press, 1989. Pp. xxi, 330. $14.95, paper.

Giere, Ronald N. *Explaining Science: A Cognitive Approach.* Chicago: University of Chicago Press, 1988. Pp. 21, 321. $34.95.

Griliches, Zvi. *Technology, Education, and Productivity.* New York: Basil Blackwell, 1988. Pp. 378. $39.95.

Heilbroner, Robert, and Peter Bernstein. *The Debt and the Deficit.* New York: Norton, 1989. Pp. 144. $5.95, paper.

Hoover, Kevin D. *The New Classical Macroeconomics: A Sceptical Inquiry.* New York: Basil Blackwell, 1988. Pp. xiv, 310. $49.95.

Hull, David L. *Science as a Process: An Evolutionary Account of the Social and Conceptual Development of Science.* Chicago: University of Chicago Press, 1988. Pp. xiii, 586. $39.95.

Hyman, Sidney. *Marriner S. Eccles: Private Entrepreneur and Public Servant.* Stanford: Graduate School of Business, Stanford University, 1976. Pp. xviii, 456. $15.00.

Kahan, Arcadius. *Russian Economic History: The Nineteenth Century.* Roger Weiss, ed. Chicago: University of Chicago Press, 1989. Pp. xii, 244. $47.50, cloth; $18.95, paper.

Krausz, Michael, ed. *Relativism: Interpretations and Confrontation.* Notre Dame: University of Notre Dame Press, 1989. Pp. 503. $34.95.

Levinson, Sanford, and Steven Mailloux, eds. *Interpreting Law and Literature: A Hermeneutic Reader.* Evanston: Northwestern University Press, 1988. Pp. xvi, 502. $62.95, cloth; $29.95, paper.

Long, Edward LeRoy, Jr. *Academic Bonding and Social Concern: The Society of Christian Ethics 1959-1983.* Washington, DC: Georgetown University Press, 1984. Pp. xi, 178. $17.95, cloth; $5.95, paper.

Machan, Tibor R., ed. *Commerce and Morality.* Savage, MD: Rowman & Littlefield, 1988. Pp. xi, 252. $34.50, cloth; $15.95, paper.

Mitchell, Neil J. *The Generous Corporation: A Political Analysis of Economic Power.* New Haven: Yale University Press, 1989. Pp. x, 163.

Murphy, Antoin E. *Richard Cantillon: Entrepreneur and Economist.* Oxford: Oxford University Press, 1986. Pp. xv, 336. $49.95.

Parker, William N., ed. *Economic History and the Modern Economist.* New York: Basil Blackwell, 1986. Pp. xi, 105. $29.95, cloth; $12.95, paper.

Persson, Karl Gunnar. *Pre-Industrial Economic Growth.* New York: Basil Blackwell, 1988. Pp. viii, 159. $45.00.

Sargan, Denis. *Lectures on Advanced Econometric Theory.* Meghnad Desai, ed. New York: Basil Blackwell, 1988. Pp. xi, 176. $39.95.

Sen, Amartya. *On Ethics and Economics.* New York: Basil Blackwell, 1987. Pp. xv, 131. $39.95.

Shaffer, Ron. *Community Economics: Economic Structure and Change in Smaller Communities.* Ames: Iowa State University Press, 1989. Pp. xii, 322.

Tool, Marc R., and Warren J. Samuels. *The Methodology of Economic Thought.* 2nd edition. New Brunswick: Transaction Publishers, 1989. Pp. xvi, 590. $19.95, paper.

Turner, Marjorie S. *Joan Robinson and the Americans.* Armonk, NY: M. E. Sharpe, 1989. Pp. xv, 313. $29.95.

Walker, Donald A., ed. *Perspectives on the History of Economic Thought: Classical and Neoclassical Economic Thought.* Brookfield, VT: Edward Elgar, 1989. Pp. x, 216. $42.95.

Walker, Donald A., ed. *Perspectives on the History of Economic Thought: Twentieth-Century Economic Thought.* Brookfield, VT: Edward Elgar, 1989. Pp. ix, 256. $48.95.

Weiss, Linda. *Creating Capitalism: The State and Small Business Since 1945.* New York: Basil Blackwell, 1988. Pp. xii, 272. $49.95.

Winch, Donald. *Malthus.* Oxford: Oxford University Press, 1987. Pp. viii, 117. $18.95, cloth; $4.95, paper.

# Research in the
# History of Economic Thought
# and Methodology

Edited by **Warren J. Samuels,** *Department of Economics,
Michigan State University*

**Volume 5,** 1987, 248 pp. $63.50
ISBN 0-89232-832-0

**Volume 6,** 1989, 283 pp. $63.50
ISBN 0-89232-928-9

**Are the Real Dissenters?**, *William M. Dugger, DePaul University.* **Comment on the Comparing of the Austrian and Institutionalist Schools of Economic Thought**, *Richard A. Gonce, Grand Valley State College.* **Comparing Austrian and Institutional Economics**, *Wendell Gordon, University of Texas.* **Comment on Samuels and Boettke**, *William S. Kern, Western Michigan University.* **Comment on Boettke and Samuels: Austrian and Instituitional Economics**, *Edythe S. Miller, Littleton, Colorado.* **Some Issues in the Comparison of Austrian and Institutional Economics**, *Malcolm Rutherford, University of Victoria.* **Of Paradigms and Discipline**, *J. R. Stanfield, Colorado State University.* **Austrian Institutionalism: A Reply**, *Peter J. Boettke, George Mason University.* **Comparing Austrian and Institutional Economics: Response**, *Warren J. Samuels, Michigan State University.* **REVIEW ESSAYS. Brems's Pioneering Economic Theory, 1630-1980: A Mathematical Restatement: Review Essay**, *Larry Samuelson, Pennsylvania State University.* **Backhouse's A History of Modern Economic Analysis and Dasgupta's Epochs in Economic Theory: Review Essay**, *Salim Rashid, University of Illinois.* **Jones's Conflict and Control in the World Economy: Contemporary Economic Realism and Neo-Mercantilism: Review Essay**, *James P. Henderson, Valparaiso University.* **Rhoads's The Economist's View of the World and Whynes's What is Political Economy: Review Essay**, *William M. Dugger, DePaul University.* **Dow's Macroeconomic Thought: A Methodological Approach: Review Essays**, *John Lodewijks, University of New South Wales and Nina Shapiro, Rutgers University.* **New Books Received.**

**Archival Supplement 1 - Lectures By John Dewey: Moral and Political Philosophy**
1989, 248 pp.                                                    $63.50
ISBN 0-89232-868-1

Edited by **Warren J. Samuels,** *Department of Economics, Michigan State University* and **Donald F. Koch,** *Department of Philosophy, Michigan State University*

**CONTENTS: Introduction: Archival Supplements,** *Warren J. Samuels.* **Editor's Introduction: Notes From John Dewey's Lectures on Moral and Political Philosophy and Their Relevance to the Study of the History of Economic Thought,** *Warren J. Samuels, Michigan State University.* **Editor's Introduction: International Conflict and the Development of Dewey's Moral, Political, and Legal Philosophy,** *Donald F. Koch, Michigan State University.* **Notes From John Dewey's Lectures on Moral and Political Philosophy: October 1915-January 1916,** *Robert Lee Hale.* **Notes From John Dewey's Lectures on Moral and Political Philosophy:, October 1915-May 1916,** *Homer H. Dubs.* **References: Hale Notes and Dub Notes. Advances in Industture,** *Robin Roslender, Napier College of Commerce & Technology.* **The Relevance of Weberianism to Class Analysis of Accounting: A Reply to Roslender,** *Trevor Hopper, University of Manchester.*

**Volume 7,** 1990, 294 pp.                    $63.50
ISBN 0-89232-040-3

**Volume 8,** 1990, 288 pp.                    $63.50
ISBN 1-55938-233-3

_University._ **Fraternity, Free Association, and Socio-Economic Analysis,** _Mark Perlman, University of Pittsburgh._ **From Utopian Capitalism to the Dismal Science: The Effect of the French Revolution on Classical Economics,** _William M. Dugger, DePaul University._ **Reflections on the Age of Sophisters, Economists, and Calculators,** _Y.S. Brenner, University of Utrecht._ **Burke, The French Revolution and Public Choice Theory,** _E. Ray Canterbery and Edgar Fresen, Florida State University._ **Karl Marx and the French Revolution,** _John E. Elliott, University of Southern California._ **REVIEW ESSAYS. Campen's Benefit, Cost, and Beyond: Review Essay,** _A. Allan Schmid, Michigan State University._ **Has There Been Advances in our Understanding of "Scientific Advances" in Economics?: Deutsch Et Al's Advances in the Social Sciences 1900-1908: What, Who, Where, How?: Review Essay,** _William J. Barber, Wesleyan University._ **Raising** _Petitio_ to a _Principii:_ A Review Article, _Murray Wolfson, California State University-Fullerton._ **JKG's** _Economics in Perspective:_ Review Essay — Countervailing Perspective. New Books Received.

**Archival Supplement 2,** 1991, 255 pp.                                    $63.50
ISBN 1-55938-245-7

CONTENTS: Introduction. Frank A. Fetter's PRESENT STATE OF ECONOMIC THEORY IN THE UNITED STATES OF AMERICA, 1927. Introduction, _Warren J. Samuels, Michigan State University._ **Present State of Economic Theory in the United States of America, 1927,** _Frank A. Fetter, (deceased)._ **Frank H. Night's THE CASE FOR COMMUNISM, 1932.** Introduction, _Warren J. Samuels, Michigan State University._ **The Case for Communism, From the Standpoint of an Ex-Liberal, 1932,** _Frank H. Knight, (deceased)._ **Jacob Viner's THE SEARCH FOR AN IDEAL COMMONWEALTH, 1914.** Introduction, _Douglas A. Irwin, Columbia University._ **The Search for an Ideal Commonwealth, 1914,** _Jacob Viner, (deceased)._ **John Maynard Keynes on the 1914 Financial Criss: A Note with Documents,** _D.E. Moggridge, University of Toronto._ **Professor A.P. Lerner on "ISRAEL AND THE ECONOMIC DEVELOPMENT OF PALESTIONE": TWENTY YEARS LATER,** _Arie Arnon, Ben-Gurion University._ **Lewis K. Zerby's YOU, YOURSELF, AND YOUR SOCIETY.** Introduction, _Warren J. Samuels, Michigan State University._ **YOU, YOURSELF AND YOUR SOCIETY,** _Lewis K. Zerby. (deceased)._

_Also Available:_
**Volumes 1-4** (1983-1986)                                    $63.50 each

## JAI PRESS INC.

55 Old Post Road - No. 2
P.O. Box 1678
Greenwich, Connecticut 06836-1678
Tel: 203-661-7602